REFERENCE

W9-AEH-849

Title Withdrawn

DETROIT
PUBLIC
LIBRARY

ED-R

Junior Worldmark Encyclopedia of World Cultures

Junior Worldmark Encyclopedia of

World Cultures

Edison Branch Library
18400 Joy Rd.
Detroit, MI 48228
(313) 852-4515

VOLUME 5

Japan to Mali

AN IMPRINT OF GALE

DETROIT · LONDON

JUNIOR WORLDMARK ENCYCLOPEDIA OF WORLD CULTURES

U•X•L Staff

Jane Hoehner, *U•X•L Senior Editor*
Carol DeKane Nagel, *U•X•L Managing Editor*
Thomas L. Romig, *U•X•L Publisher*
Mary Beth Trimper, *Production Director*
Evi Seoud, *Assistant Production Manager*
Shanna Heilveil, *Production Associate*
Cynthia Baldwin, *Product Design Manager*
Barbara J. Yarrow, *Graphic Services Supervisor*
Pamela A. E. Galbreath, *Senior Art Director*
Margaret Chamberlain, *Permissions Specialist (Pictures)*

This publication is a creative work copyrighted by U•X•L and fully protected by all applicable copyright laws, as well as by misappropriation, trade secret, unfair competition, and other applicable laws. The authors and editors of this work have added value to the underlying factual material herein through one or more of the following: unique and original selection, coordination, expression, arrangement, and classification of the information. All rights to this publication will be vigorously defended.

Copyright © 1999
U•X•L
An Imprint of Gale
All rights reserved including the right of reproduction in whole or in part in any form.

Library of Congress Cataloging-in-Publication Data
Junior worldmark encyclopedia of world cultures / Timothy L. Gall and
   Susan Bevan Gall, editors.
    p.   cm.
   Includes bibliographical references and index.
   Summary: Arranges countries around the world alphabetically,
subdivides these countries into 250 culture groups, and provides
information about the ethnology and human geography of each group.
    ISBN 0-7876-1756-X (set : alk. paper)
   1. Ethnology--Encyclopedias, Juvenile. 2. Human geography-
-Encyclopedias, Juvenile. [1. Ethnology--Encyclopedias. 2. Human
geography--Encyclopedias.] I. Gall, Timothy L. II. Gall, Susan B.
GN307.J85 1999
306' .03--dc21   98-13810
                                                 CIP
                                                 AC

ISBN 0-7876-1756-X (set)
ISBN 0-7876-1757-1 (vol. 1)   ISBN 0-7876-1758-X (vol. 2)   ISBN 0-7876-1759-8 (vol. 3)
ISBN 0-7876-1760-1 (vol. 4)   ISBN 0-7876-1761-X (vol. 5)   ISBN 0-7876-1762-8 (vol. 6)
ISBN 0-7876-1763-6 (vol. 7)   ISBN 0-7876-1764-4 (vol. 8)   ISBN 0-7876-2761-5 (vol. 9)

Printed in the United States of America
10 9 8 7 6 5 4 3 2

Contents REFERENCE
Volume 5

Cumulative Contents

Volume 1

Afghanistan **3**
 Afghanis..3
 Hazaras...10
 Pashtun...13
Albania **19**
 Albanians...19
Algeria **27**
 Algerians...27
Andorra **35**
 Andorrans..35
Angola **39**
 Angolans...39
Antigua and Barbuda...........................**49**
 Antiguans and Barbudans 49
Argentina **57**
 Argentines...57
Armenia..**65**
 Armenians...65
Australia **73**
 Australians..73
 Australian Aborigines 80
Austria **87**
 Austrians...87
Azerbaijan **95**
 Azerbaijanis..95
Bahamas..**101**
 Bahamians...101
Bahrain..**107**
 Bahrainis...107
Bangladesh **113**
 Bangladeshis...113
 Bengalis 121
 Chakmas..127
Barbados **133**
 Barbadians...133
Belarus...**139**
 Belarusans...139
Belgium **145**
 Belgians 145
 Flemings...151
 Walloons 155
Belize...**159**
 Belizeans..159
 Garifuna...166
Benin **173**
 Beninese...173
Bhutan...**179**
 Bhutanese..179

Bolivia **185**
 Bolivians...185
 Aymara 193
Bosnia and Herzegovina **201**
 Bosnians 201

Volume 2

Brazil **1**
Brazilians **1**
 Afro-Brazilians 11
 Kayapos 17
 Xavante 22
Bulgaria...**31**
 Bulgarians..31
Burkina Faso **39**
 Burkinabe 39
 Mossi 43
Burundi **51**
 Burundians 51
 Tutsi 57
Cambodia **61**
 Khmer...61
 Hill Tribespeople 70
Cameroon..**77**
 Cameroonians 77
Canada **83**
 Canadians 83
 French Canadians 89
 Inuit 94
Cape Verde...**101**
 Cape Verdeans...101
Central African Republic........................**105**
 Central Africans 105
Chad...**113**
 Chadians 113
Chile...**119**
 Chileans 119
 Araucanians 126
China..**131**
 Chinese 132
 Dong 141
 Han 148
 Man (Manchus) 153
 Miao 157
 Tibetans 163
 Uighurs 168
 Zhuang 173

CUMULATIVE CONTENTS

Volume 5

Volume 6

CUMULATIVE CONTENTS

Volume 7

Volume 8

CUMULATIVE CONTENTS

Volume 9

Contributors

Editors: Timothy L. Gall and Susan Bevan Gall

Senior Editor: Daniel M. Lucas

Contributing Editors: Himanee Gupta, Jim Henry, Kira Silverbird, Elaine Trapp, Rosalie Wieder

Copy Editors: Deborah Baron, Janet Fenn, Jim Henry, Patricia M. Mote, Deborah Ring, Kathy Soltis

Typesetting and Graphics: Cheryl Montagna, Brian Rajewski

Cover Photographs: Cory Langley

Data Input: Janis K. Long, Cheryl Montagna, Melody Penfound

Proofreaders: Deborah Baron, Janet Fenn

Editorial Assistants: Katie Baron, Jennifer A. Spencer, Daniel K. Updegraft

Editorial Advisors

P. Boone, Sixth Grade Teacher, Oak Crest Middle School, San Antonio, Texas

Jean Campbell, Foothill Farms Middle School, Sacramento, California

Kathy Englehart, Librarian, Hathaway Brown School, Shaker Heights, Ohio

Catherine Harris, Librarian, Oak Crest Middle School, San Antonio, Texas

Karen James, Children's Services, Louisville Free Public Library, Louisville, Kentucky

Contributors to the Gale Edition

The articles presented in this encyclopedia are based on entries in the *Worldmark Encyclopedia of Cultures and Daily Life* published in 1997 by Gale. The following authors and reviewers contributed to the Gale edition.

ANDREW J. ABALAHIN. Doctoral candidate, Department of History, Cornell University.

JAMAL ABDULLAH. Doctoral candidate, Department of City and Regional Planning, Cornell University.

SANA ABED-KOTOB. Book Review Editor, Middle East Journal, Middle East Institute.

MAMOUD ABOUD. Charge d'Affaires, a.i., Embassy of the Federal and Islamic Republic of the Comoros.

JUDY ALLEN. Editor, Choctaw Nation of Oklahoma.

HIS EXCELLENCY DENIS G. ANTOINE. Ambassador to the United States, Embassy of Grenada.

LESLEY ANN ASHBAUGH. Instructor, Sociology, Seattle University.

HASHEM ATALLAH. Translator, Editor, Teacher; Fairfax, Virginia.

HECTOR AZEVES. Cultural Attaché, Embassy of Uruguay.

VICTORIA J. BAKER. Associate Professor of Anthropology, Anthropology (Collegium of Comparative Cultures), Eckerd College.

POLINE BALA. Doctoral candidate, Asian Studies, Cornell University.

MARJORIE MANDELSTAM BALZER. Research Professor; Coordinator, Social, Regional, and Ethnic Studies Sociology, and Center for Eurasian, Russian, and East European Studies.

JOSHUA BARKER. Doctoral candidate, Department of Anthropology, Cornell University.

IGOR BARSEGIAN. Department of Sociology, George Washington University.

IRAJ BASHIRI. Professor of Central Asian Studies, Department of Slavic and Central Asian Languages and Literatures, University of Minnesota.

DAN F. BAUER. Department of Anthropology, Lafayette College.

JOYCE BEAR. Historic Preservation Officer, Muscogee Nation of Oklahoma.

SVETLANA BELAIA. Byelorussian-American Cultural Center, Strongsville, Ohio.

HIS EXCELLENCY DR. COURTNEY BLACKMAN. Ambassador to the United States, Embassy of Barbados.

BETTY BLAIR. Executive Editor, Azerbaijan International.

ARVIDS BLODNIEKS. Director, Latvian Institute, American Latvian Association in the USA.

ARASH BORMANSHINOV. University of Maryland, College Park.

HARRIET I. BRADY. Cultural Anthropologist (Pyramid Lake Paiute Tribe), Native Studies Program, Pyramid Lake High School.

MARTIN BROKENLEG. Professor of Sociology, Department of Sociology, Augustana College.

REV. RAYMOND A. BUCKO, S.J. Assistant Professor of Anthropology, LeMoyne College.

JOHN W. BURTON. Department of Anthropology, Connecticut College.

DINEANE BUTTRAM. University of North Carolina-Chapel Hill.

RICARDO CABALLERO. Counselor, Embassy of Paraguay.

CHRISTINA CARPADIS. Researcher/Writer, Cleveland, Ohio.

SALVADOR GARCIA CASTANEDA. Department of Spanish and Portuguese, The Ohio State University.

SUSANA CAVALLO. Graduate Program Director and Professor of Spanish, Department of Modern Languages and Literatures, Loyola University, Chicago.

BRIAN P. CAZA. Doctoral candidate, Political Science, University of Chicago.

VAN CHRISTO. President and Executive Director, Frosina Foundation, Boston.

YURI A. CHUMAKOV. Graduate Student, Department of Sociology, University of Notre Dame.

J. COLARUSSO. Professor of Anthropology, McMaster University.

FRANCESCA COLECCHIA. Modern Language Department, Duquesne University.

DIANNE K. DAEG DE MOTT. Researcher/Writer, Tucson, Arizona.

MICHAEL DE JONGH. Professor, Department of Anthropology, University of South Africa.

GEORGI DERLUGUIAN. Senior Fellow, Ph.D., U. S. Institute of Peace.

CHRISTINE DRAKE. Department of Political Science and Geography, Old Dominion University.

ARTURO DUARTE. Guatemalan Mission to the OAS.

CALEB DUBE. Department of Anthropology, Northwestern University.

BRIAN DU TOIT. Professor, Department of Anthropology, University of Florida.

LEAH ERMARTH. Worldspace Foundation, Washington, DC.

NANCY J. FAIRLEY. Associate Professor of Anthropology, Department of Anthropology/Sociology, Davidson College.

GREGORY A. FINNEGAN, Ph.D. Tozzer Library, Harvard University.

ALLEN J. FRANK, Ph.D.

DAVID P. GAMBLE. Professor Emeritus, Department of Anthropology, San Francisco State University.

FREDERICK GAMST. Professor, Department of Anthropology, University of Massachusetts, Harbor Campus.

PAULA GARB. Associate Director of Global Peace and Conflict Studies and Adjunct Professor of Social Ecology, University of California, Irvine.

HAROLD GASKI. Associate Professor of Sami Literature, School of Languages and Literature, University of Tromsø.

STEPHEN J. GENDZIER.

FLORENCE GERDEL.

ANTHONY P. GLASCOCK. Professor of Anthropology; Department of Anthropology, Psychology, and Sociology; Drexel University.

LUIS GONZALEZ. Researcher/Writer, River Edge, New Jersey.

JENNIFER GRAHAM. Researcher/Writer, Sydney, Australia.

MARIE-CÉCILE GROELSEMA. Doctoral candidate, Comparative Literature, Indiana University.

ROBERT GROELSEMA. MPIA and doctoral candidate, Political Science, Indiana University.

MARIA GROSZ-NGATÉ. Visiting Assistant Professor, Department of Anthropology, Northwestern University.

ELLEN GRUENBAUM. Professor, School of Social Sciences, California State University, Fresno.

N. THOMAS HAKANSSON. University of Kentucky.

ROBERT HALASZ. Researcher/Writer, New York, New York.

MARC HANREZ. Professor, Department of French and Italian, University of Wisconsin-Madison.

ANWAR UL HAQ. Central Asian Studies Department, Indiana University.

LIAM HARTE. Department of Philosophy, Loyola University, Chicago.

FR. VASILE HATEGAN. Author, *Romanian Culture in America*.

BRUCE HEILMAN. Doctoral candidate, Department of Political Science, Indiana University.

JIM HENRY. Researcher/Writer, Cleveland, Ohio.

BARRY HEWLETT. Department of Anthropology, Washington State University.

SUSAN F. HIRSCH. Department of Anthropology, Wesleyan University.

MARIDA HOLLOS. Department of Anthropology, Brown University.

HALYNA HOLUBEC. Researcher/Writer, Cleveland, Ohio.

YVONNE HOOSAVA. Legal Researcher and Cultural Preservation Officer, Hopi Tribal Council.

HUIQIN HUANG, Ph.D. Center for East Asia Studies, University of Montreal.

ASAFA JALATA. Assistant Professor of Sociology and African and African American Studies, Department of Sociology, The University of Tennessee, Knoxville.

STEPHEN F. JONES. Russian Department, Mount Holyoke College.

THOMAS JOVANOVSKI, Ph.D. Lorain County Community College.

A. KEN JULES. Minister Plenipotentiary and Deputy Head of Mission, Embassy of St. Kitts and Nevis.

GENEROSA KAGARUKI-KAKOTI. Economist, Department of Urban and Rural Planning, College of Lands and Architectural Studies, Dar es Salaam, Tanzania.

EZEKIEL KALIPENI. Department of Geography, University of Illinois at Urbana-Champaign.

CONTRIBUTORS

DON KAVANAUGH. Program Director, Lake of the Woods Ojibwa Cultural Centre.

SUSAN M. KENYON. Associate Professor of Anthropology, Department of History and Anthropology, Butler University.

WELILE KHUZWAYO. Department of Anthropology, University of South Africa.

PHILIP L. KILBRIDE. Professor of Anthropology, Mary Hale Chase Chair in the Social Sciences, Department of Anthropology, Bryn Mawr College.

RICHARD O. KISIARA. Doctoral candidate, Department of Anthropology, Washington University in St. Louis.

KAREN KNOWLES. Permanent Mission of Antigua and Barbuda to the United Nations.

IGOR KRUPNIK. Research Anthropologist, Department of Anthropology, Smithsonian Institution.

LEELO LASS. Secretary, Embassy of Estonia.

ROBERT LAUNAY. Professor, Department of Anthropology, Northwestern University.

CHARLES LEBLANC. Professor and Director, Center for East Asia Studies, University of Montreal.

RONALD LEE. Author, *Goddam Gypsy, An Autobiographical Novel.*

PHILIP E. LEIS. Professor and Chair, Department of Anthropology, Brown University.

MARIA JUKIC LESKUR. Croatian Consulate, Cleveland, Ohio.

RICHARD A. LOBBAN, JR. Professor of Anthropology and African Studies, Department of Anthropology, Rhode Island College.

DERYCK O. LODRICK. Visiting Scholar, Center for South Asian Studies, University of California, Berkeley.

NEIL LURSSEN. Intro Communications Inc.

GREGORIO C. MARTIN. Modern Language Department, Duquesne University.

HOWARD J. MARTIN. Independent scholar.

HEITOR MARTINS. Professor, Department of Spanish and Portuguese, Indiana University.

ADELINE MASQUELIER. Assistant Professor, Department of Anthropology, Tulane University.

DOLINA MILLAR.

EDITH MIRANTE. Project Maje, Portland, Oregon.

ROBERT W. MONTGOMERY, Ph.D. Indiana University.

THOMAS D. MORIN. Associate Professor of Hispanic Studies, Department of Modern and Classical Literatures and Languages, University of Rhode Island.

CHARLES MORRILL. Doctoral candidate, Indiana University.

CAROL A. MORTLAND. Crate's Point, The Dalles, Oregon.

FRANCIS A. MOYER. Director, North Carolina Japan Center, North Carolina State University.

MARIE C. MOYER.

NYAGA MWANIKI. Assistant Professor, Department of Anthropology and Sociology, Western Carolina University.

KENNETH NILSON. Celtic Studies Department, Harvard University.

JANE E. ORMROD. Graduate Student, History, University of Chicago.

JUANITA PAHDOPONY. Carl Perkins Program Director, Comanche Tribe of Oklahoma.

TINO PALOTTA. Syracuse University.

ROHAYATI PASENG.

PATRICIA PITCHON. Researcher/Writer, London, England.

STEPHANIE PLATZ. Program Officer, Program on Peace and International Cooperation, The John D. and Catherine T. MacArthur Foundation.

MIHAELA POIATA. Graduate Student, School of Journalism and Mass Communication, University of North Carolina at Chapel Hill.

LEOPOLDINA PRUT-PREGELJ. Author, *Historical Dictionary of Slovenia.*

J. RACKAUSKAS. Director, Lithuanian Research and Studies Center, Chicago.

J. RAKOVICH. Byelorussian-American Cultural Center, Strongsville, Ohio.

HANTA V. RALAY. Promotions, Inc., Montgomery Village, Maryland.

SUSAN J. RASMUSSEN. Associate Professor, Department of Anthropology, University of Houston.

RONALD REMINICK. Department of Anthropology, Cleveland State University.

BRUCE D. ROBERTS. Assistant Professor of Anthropology, Department of Anthropology and Sociology, University of Southern Mississippi.

LAUREL L. ROSE. Philosophy Department, Carnegie-Mellon University.

ROBERT ROTENBERG. Professor of Anthropology, International Studies Program, DePaul University.

CAROLINE SAHLEY, Ph.D. Researcher/Writer, Cleveland, Ohio.

VERONICA SALLES-REESE. Associate Professor, Department of Spanish and Portuguese, Georgetown University.

MAIRA SARYBAEVA. Kazakh-American Studies Center, University of Kentucky.

DEBRA L. SCHINDLER. Institute of Arctic Studies, Dartmouth College.

KYOKO SELDEN, Ph.D. Researcher/Writer, Ithaca, New York.

ENAYATULLAH SHAHRANI. Central Asian Studies Department, Indiana University.

ROBERT SHANAFELT. Adjunct Lecturer, Department of Anthropology, The Florida State University.

TUULIKKI SINKS. Teaching Specialist for Finnish, Department of German, Scandinavian, and Dutch, University of Minnesota.

JAN SJÅVIK. Associate Professor, Scandinavian Studies, University of Washington.

MAGDA SOBALVARRO. Press and Cultural Affairs Director, Embassy of Nicaragua.

MICHAEL STAINTON. Researcher, Joint Center for Asia Pacific Studies, York University.

RIANA STEYN. Department of Anthropology, University of South Africa.

PAUL STOLLER. Professor, Department of Anthropology, West Chester University.

CRAIG STRASHOFER. Researcher/Writer, Cleveland, Ohio.

SANDRA B. STRAUBHAAR. Assistant Professor, Nordic Studies, Department of Germanic and Slavic Languages, Brigham Young University.

VUM SON SUANTAK. Author, *Zo History.*

MURAT TAISHIBAEV. Kazakh-American Studies Center, University of Kentucky.

CHRISTOPHER C. TAYLOR. Associate Professor, Anthropology Department, University of Alabama, Birmingham.

EDDIE TSO. Office of Language and Culture, Navajo Division of Education.

DAVID TYSON. Foreign Broadcast Information Service, Washington, D.C.

NICOLAAS G. W. UNLANDT. Assistant Professor of French, Department of French and Italian, Brigham Young University.

GORDON URQUHART. Professor, Department of Economics and Business, Cornell College.

CHRISTOPHER J. VAN VUUREN. Professor, Department of Anthropology, University of South Africa.

DALIA VENTURA-ALCALAY. Journalist, London, England.

CATHERINE VEREECKE. Assistant Director, Center for African Studies, University of Florida.

GREGORY T. WALKER. Associate Director, Office of International Affairs, Duquesne University.

GERHARD WEISS. Department of German, Scandinavian, and Dutch, University of Minnesota.

PATSY WEST. Director, The Seminole/Miccosukee Photographic Archive.

WALTER WHIPPLE. Associate Professor of Polish, Germanic and Slavic Languages, Brigham Young University.

ROSALIE WIEDER. Researcher/Writer, Cleveland, Ohio.

JEFFREY WILLIAMS. Professor, Department of Anthropology, Cleveland State University.

GUANG-HONG YU. Associate Research Fellow, Institute of Ethnology, Academia Sinica.

RUSSELL ZANCA. Department of Anthropology, College of Liberal Arts and Sciences, University of Illinois at Urbana-Champaign.

Reader's Guide

Junior Worldmark Encyclopedia of World Cultures contains articles exploring the ways of life of over 290 culture groups worldwide. Arranged alphabetically by country in nine volumes, this encyclopedia parallels the organization of its sister set, *Junior Worldmark Encyclopedia of the Nations*. Whereas the primary purpose of *Nations* is to provide information on the world's nations, this encyclopedia focuses on the traditions, living conditions, and personalities of many of the world's culture groups.

Defining groups for inclusion was not an easy task. Cultural identity is shaped by such factors as history, geography, nationality, ethnicity, race, language, and religion. Sometimes the distinctions are subtle, but important. Most chapters in this encyclopedia begin with an article on the people of the country as a nationality group. For example, the chapter on Kenya begins with an article entitled "Kenyans." This article explores the national character shared by all people living in Kenya. However, there are separate articles on the Gikuyu, Kalenjin, Luhya, and Luo—four of the largest ethnic groups living in the country. They are all Kenyans, but each group is distinct. Many profiled groups—like the Kazaks—inhabit lands that cross national boundaries. Although profiled in the chapter on Kazakstan, Kazaks are also important minorities in China, Uzbekistan, and Turkmenistan. In such cases, cross-references direct the student to the chapter where the group is profiled.

The photographs that illustrate the articles show a wonderfully diverse world. From the luxury liners docked in the harbor at Monaco to the dwellings made of grass sheltering the inhabitants of the rain forest, people share the struggles and joys of earning a living, bringing children into the world, teaching them to survive, and initiating them into adulthood. Although language, customs, and dress illustrate our differences, the faces of the people pictured in these volumes reinforce our similarities. Whether on the streets of Tokyo or the mountains of Tibet, a smile on the face of a child transcends the boundaries of nationality and cultural identity to reveal something common in us all. Photographer Cory Langley's images on pages 93 and 147 in Volume 6 serve to illustrate this point.

The picture of the world this encyclopedia paints today will certainly differ from the one painted in future editions. Indigenous people like the Jivaro in Ecuador (Volume 3, page 77) are being assimilated into modern society as forest lands are cleared for development and televisions and VCRs are brought to even the most remote villages. As the global economy expands, traditional diets are supplemented with Coke, Pepsi, and fast food; traditional storytellers are replaced by World Cup soccer matches and American television programs; and cultural heroes are overwhelmed by images of Michael Jordan and Michael Jackson. Photographer Cynthia Bassett was fortunate to be among a small group of travelers to visit a part of China only recently opened to Westerners. Her image of Miao dancers (Volume 2, page 161) shows a people far removed from Western culture . . . until one looks a little closer. Behind the dancers, in the upper corner of the photograph, is a basketball hoop and backboard. It turns out that Miao teenagers love basketball!

ORGANIZATION

Within each volume the chapters are arranged alphabetically by country. A cumulative table of contents for all volumes in the set follows the table of contents to each volume.

Each chapter covers a specific country. The contents of the chapter, listing the culture group articles, follows the chapter title. An overview of the composition of the population of the country appears after the contents list. The individual articles follow, and are organized according to a standard twenty-heading outline explained in more detail below. This structure allows for easy comparison between cultures and enhances the accessibility of the information.

Articles begin with the **pronunciation** of the group's name, a listing of **alternate names** by which the group is known, the group's **location** in the world, its **population**, the **languages** spoken, and the **religions** practiced. Articles are illustrated with maps showing the primary location of the group and photographs of the culture group being profiled. The twenty standard headings by which the articles are organized are presented below.

1 ● INTRODUCTION: A description of the group's historical origins provides a useful background for understanding its contemporary affairs. Information relating to migration helps explain how the group arrived at its present location. Political conditions and governmental structure(s) that affect members of the profiled ethnic group are also discussed.

2 ● LOCATION: The population size of the group is listed. This information may include official census data from various countries and/or estimates. Information on the size of a group's population located outside the traditional homeland may also be included, especially for those groups with large scattered populations. A description of the homeland includes information on location, topography, and climate.

3 ● LANGUAGE: Each article lists the name(s) of the primary language(s) spoken by members. Descriptions of linguistic origins, grammar, and similarities to other languages may also be included. Examples of common words, phrases, and proverbs are listed for many of the profiled groups, and some include examples of common personal names and greetings.

4 ● FOLKLORE: Common themes, settings, and characters in the profiled group's traditional oral and/or literary mythology are highlighted. Many entries include a short excerpt or synopsis of one of the group's noteworthy myths, fables, or legends. Some entries describe the accomplishments of famous heroes and heroines or other prominent historical figures.

5 ● RELIGION: The origins of traditional religious beliefs are profiled. Contemporary religious beliefs, customs, and practices are also discussed. Some groups may be closely associated with one particular faith (especially if religious and ethnic identification are interlinked), while others may have members of diverse faiths.

6 ● MAJOR HOLIDAYS: Celebrations and commemorations typically recognized by the group's members are described. These holidays commonly fall into two categories: secular and religious. Secular holidays often include an independence day and/or other days of observance recognizing important dates in history that affected the group as a whole. Religious holidays are typically the same as those honored by people of the same faith worldwide. Some secular and religious holidays are linked to the lunar cycle or to the change of seasons. Some articles describe customs practiced by members of the group on certain holidays.

7 ● RITES OF PASSAGE: Formal and informal events that mark an individual's procession through the stages of life are profiled. These events typically involve rituals, ceremonies, observances, and procedures associated with birth, childhood, the coming of age, milestones in education or religious training, adulthood, and death.

8 ● RELATIONSHIPS: Information on greetings, body language, gestures, visiting customs, and dating practices is included. The extent of formality to which members of a certain ethnic group treat others is also addressed, as some groups may adhere to customs governing interpersonal relationships more or less strictly than others.

9 ● LIVING CONDITIONS: General health conditions typical of the group's members are cited. Such information includes life expectancy, the prevalence of various diseases, and access to medical care. Information on urbanization, housing, and access to utilities is also included. Transportation methods typically utilized by the group's members are also discussed.

10 ● FAMILY LIFE: The size and composition of the family unit is profiled. Gender roles common to the group are also discussed, including the division of rights and responsibilities relegated to male and female group members. The roles that children, adults, and the elderly have within the group as a whole may also be addressed.

11 ● CLOTHING: Many entries include descriptive information (design, color, fabric, etc.) regarding traditional clothing (or national costume) for men and women, and indicate the frequency of its use in contemporary life. A description of typical clothing worn in modern daily life is also provided, especially if traditional clothing is no longer the usual form of dress. Distinctions between formal and work attire and descriptions of clothing preferences of young people are described for many groups as well.

12 ● FOOD: Descriptions of items commonly consumed by members of the group are listed. The frequency and occasion for meals is also described, as are any unique customs regarding eating and drinking, special utensils and furniture, and the role of food and beverages in ritual ceremonies. Many entries include a recipe for a favorite dish.

13 ● EDUCATION: The structure of formal education in the country or countries of residence is discussed, including information on primary, secondary, and higher education. For some groups, the role of informal education is also highlighted. Some articles include information regarding the relevance and importance of education among the group as a whole, along with parental expectations for children.

14 ● CULTURAL HERITAGE: Since many groups express their sense of identity through art, music, literature, and dance, a description of prominent styles is included. Some articles also cite the contributions of famous individual artists, writers, and musicians.

15 ● EMPLOYMENT: The type of labor that typically engages members of the profiled group is discussed. For some groups, the formal wage economy is the primary source of earnings, but for other groups, informal agriculture or trade may be the usual way to earn a living. Working conditions are also highlighted.

16 ● SPORTS: Popular sports that children and adults play are listed, as are typical spectator sports. Some articles include a description and/or rules to a sport or game.

17 ● RECREATION: Listed activities that people enjoy in their leisure time may include structured pastimes (such as public musical and dance performances) or informal get-togethers (such as meeting for conversation). The role of popular culture, movies, theater, and television in everyday life is also discussed where it applies.

18 ● CRAFTS AND HOBBIES: Entries describe arts and crafts commonly fabricated according to traditional methods, materials, and style. Such objects may often have a functional utility for everyday tasks.

19 ● SOCIAL PROBLEMS: Internal and external issues that confront members of the profiled group are described. Such concerns often deal with fundamental problems like war, famine, disease, and poverty. A lack of human rights, civil rights, and political freedom may also adversely affect a group as a whole. Other problems may include crime, unemployment, substance abuse, and domestic violence.

20 ● BIBLIOGRAPHY: References cited include works used to compile the article, benchmark publications often recognized as authoritative by scholars, and other reference sources accessible to middle school researchers. Website addresses are provided for researchers who wish to access the World Wide Web. The website citation includes the author and title of the website (if applicable). The address begins with characters that follow "http://" in the citation; the address ends with the character preceding the comma and date. For example, the citation for the website of the German embassy appears as follows:

German Embassy, Washington, D.C. [Online]
   Available http://www.germany-info.org/, 1998.

To access this site, researchers type:
   www.germany-info.org

A glossary and an index of groups profiled appears at the end of each volume.

ACKNOWLEDGMENTS

The editors express appreciation to the members of the U•X•L staff who were involved in a number of ways at various stages of development of the *Junior Worldmark Encyclopedia of World Cultures.*

SUGGESTIONS ARE WELCOME: We appreciate any suggestions that will enhance future editions. Please send comments to:

Editors
*Junior Worldmark Encyclopedia
of World Cultures*
U•X•L
27500 Drake Road
Farmington Hills, MI 48331-3535
(800) 877-4253

Japan

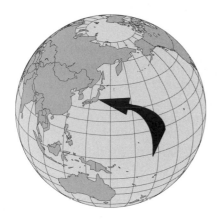

The people of Japan are called Japanese. The one distinct ethnic group in Japan, the Ainu, live on the Japanese island of Hokkaido.

Japanese

PRONUNCIATION: jap-uhn-EEZ
LOCATION: Japan
POPULATION: 125 million
LANGUAGE: Japanese
RELIGION: Shinto; Buddhism; Confucianism; Christianity

1 ● INTRODUCTION

The Japanese islands have been inhabited by humans since Paleolithic times. Archaeologists there have discovered some of the oldest pottery known to exist.

Migration has not been a significant feature of Japan's history. The Japanese are a mixture of northeast Asians with others from the China coast, Southeast Asia, and Polynesia. By the Heian Period (AD 794–1185), the dominant Japanese population extended control over the northern region of the island of Honshu, displacing (pushing aside) the indigenous (native) Ainu people. In the nineteenth century, the Ainu were displaced from the island of Hokkaido when the majority Japanese settled there.

Throughout Japan's history, the government has been dominated by emperors, whose authority has decreased in modern times. During various historical periods, the Japanese government has been in the hands of the military (*bakufu*), with power shifted to warriors (*samurais*).

Japan suffered an economic crisis following World War I (1914–18). Tokyo and Yokohama were devastated by an earthquake in 1923. During World War II (1941–45), Japan attacked the United States and Great Britain (in 1941). Defeat in World War II stripped Japan of its overseas empire and military. Its economy and most of its large cities were devastated. Hiroshima and Nagasaki were destroyed by atomic bombs. Allied military forces (mostly American) occupied Japan (1945–52) and imposed sweeping reforms to promote democracy. After the occupation Japan rebuilt its country.

JAPANESE

Japan grew dramatically as an economic force beginning in the 1960s, and has enjoyed a high standard of living since that time.

Politically, Japan is a parliamentary democracy modeled on the British system. Representatives are elected to the *Diet*, a parliament (government council) with two legislative chambers. The majority party in the lower house, the House of Representatives, elects its Prime Minister, who forms a cabinet. The conservative Liberal Democratic Party is the largest party, but its long-running control of the lower house was broken in 1993. Parties are now going through a period of reorientation.

Mythology says that the ruling line of Japanese emperors descended from the Shinto sun goddess. Since the late Yamato Period (AD 300–710), one family has occupied the throne—the world's oldest dynasty. In 1990, Akihito (1933–) succeeded his father, Hirohito (1901–1989), becoming the 125th ruler in the dynasty. During most history, the emperor exercised no political power but only validated the rule of others who claimed to act in his name. The Meiji government (1868–1912) created a cult around the emperor to rally popular support. This culminated in the excesses of emperor worship in the wartime 1930s and 1940s. Since World War II (1939–45), the emperor has publicly denied his divinity, and mythology has been removed from school history texts.

2 ● LOCATION

Japan's population is about 125 million. Practically all Japanese speakers live in Japan. Small communities have moved to Hawaii and North and South America, but most of their descendants no longer speak Japanese.

Japan is a chain of approximately 3,000 islands off the eastern coast of Asia. Throughout history the main islands of Honshu, Kyushu, and Shikoku have been the homeland of the Japanese. During the seventeenth century political influence was extended southward over the Ryukyu Islands, including Okinawa. These are occupied by a closely related population that speaks a variant of Japanese. The Ryukyus became part of Japan in the nineteenth century. Hokkaido was fully annexed in the nineteenth century.

Approximately two-thirds of the land area is too mountainous for development.

This compresses the population into a few large plains, the Kanto (around Tokyo), the Kansai (around Osaka), and the Nobi (around Nagoya), mountain basins, and coastal strips. The population is overwhelmingly urban, drawn by jobs and city life.

Japan suffers extensive seismic activity. It has many active volcanoes and experiences frequent earthquakes. A huge earthquake on September 1, 1923, destroyed Tokyo and Yokohama and killed approximately 130,000 people. Kobe was devastated by an earthquake on January 17, 1995, which took over five thousand lives. Japan also endures seasonal typhoons. While often destructive, these storms cause little loss of life.

3 ● LANGUAGE

The Japanese language is essentially spoken only in Japan. It is an Altaic language and its nearest relative is Korean. It is not related to Chinese, but writing was learned from China. Chinese characters *(kanji)*, each with a meaning and multiple pronunciations, are part of the writing system.

Japanese words are composed of many syllables, and endings are attached to change tense, form a negative, or otherwise modify meaning. The standard sentence order is subject, object, verb.

STANDARD PHRASES AND WORDS

Japanese	*English*
Ohayoo-gozaimasu	good morning
Kon-nichi wa	good day
Kon-ban wa	good evening
O genki desu-ka	How are you?
O-kagesama de	I'm well, thank you.
Sayoonara	goodbye (formal)
Arigatoo-gozaimasu	thank you
Doo itashimashite	you are welcome

EPD Photos

A newspaper showing an example of the printed Japanese language.

Family names come first and given names second. Hence, Tanaka Junko is a female name for Junko of the Tanaka family. Titles of respect follow a name. *San* is a universal title of respect equal to Mr., Miss, Mrs.; therefore Tanaka-san could mean Mr. Tanaka, Ms. Tanaka, Miss Tanaka, or Mrs. Tanaka.

4 ● FOLKLORE

Japanese folklore combines Shinto religious myths, stories of nature spirits, Buddhist tales, and historical figures to whom mythical deeds are attributed. For example, Minamoto Yoshitsune helped his half brother, Minamoto Yoritomo, win the Gempei War (1180–85). He was a brilliant general who supposedly learned warrior skills as a boy from *tengu*—half-man, half-bird figures who live in mountain forests. Later, Yoshitsune used these skills to defeat a giant Buddhist warrior-monk, Benkei, in a duel on the Go-jo Bridge in Kyoto. Overwhelmed by Yoshitsune's skill, Benkei surrendered and became his loyal follower. Benkei has become a model of loyalty. Yoshitsune and Benkei died in a battle against Yoritomo, who became jealous of his brother and turned against him.

Japanese folklore is rich in strange beings who inhabit nature. In addition to tengu, mentioned above, there are *kappa,* water demons about three feet tall that have bird beaks and turtle shells on their backs. They often lure people into the water to drown. They love cucumbers, and one can protect oneself from kappa by carving one's name on a cucumber and tossing it into the local stream. When out of the water, kappa carry water in a depression on their heads. If encountered, it is advisable to bow to the kappa. It will return the bow, spilling the water and becoming too weak to cause harm.

Japanese myths include Shinto tales collected in the oldest surviving Japanese book, the *Kojiki.* These describe the creation of the world and the Japanese islands by Izanagi and Izanami, a pair of male and female deities (gods). The primary deity is the Sun goddess, Amaterasu. On sending her descendant to rule Japan, she gave him three sacred treasures: a bronze mirror, a sword, and a string of comma-shaped jewels called *magatama.* These items are still associated with the imperial family. Amaterasu is honored at the Ise Grand Shrine, where the original mirror is supposedly housed.

5 ● RELIGION

Traditional Japanese religion includes Shinto, Buddhism, and Confucianism.

Shinto ("The Way of the Gods") is the name given to religious practices that were indigenous to Japan before Buddhism was introduced. It is concerned with humanity's relationship to nature, to agriculture, and to society. Prayers and offerings petition deities *(kami)* for health, a good crop, children, and safety. Harvest festivals are Shinto events. Shinto also concerns itself with community relationships; hence, marriages are usually Shinto ceremonies.

The richness of Buddhism and its ties to Chinese culture helped it gain support at the Japanese court. Buddhism also answered spiritual needs that Shinto neglected, including questions of morals and life after death. By the Nara Period (AD 710–794), Shinto and Buddhism began to exist side by side. Shinto deities (gods) were explained as Japan's local versions of the universal beings represented by the many Buddhas. Shinto dealt with issues of this world (crops, social relations, clan ancestors), while Buddhism concentrated on ethical (moral) and metaphysical (supernatural) issues. This division still works for many Japanese. Weddings may be Shinto ceremonies, but Buddhism deals with morality, funerals, and questions about the future life of the human soul.

Confucianism is imported from China. Confucianism emphasizes the need to find one's place within the greater social order, and to be a responsible member of the social units to which one belongs. Confucianism is hierarchical: in social relations one party is superior, the other inferior. It is the duty of the superior to teach, protect, and nurture the inferior. The inferior should respect and learn from the superior. Ideally, Confucianism leads to a highly ethical, supportive

© Corel Corporation

A busy commercial district.

social order. It also stresses study, a value widely accepted in Japan.

Christianity was introduced to Japan by St. Francis Xavier in 1549. Catholic missionaries had considerable success for nearly one century before the military government expelled them and made the practice of Christianity a crime punishable by death. Christianity was again made legal in the 1870s. At that time Catholic, Protestant, and Orthodox missions were established. They are all active throughout the country today, especially in education and charity work. Only 1 percent of Japanese are Christians. However, Christian teachings have significantly influenced Japanese thinking.

6 ● MAJOR HOLIDAYS

Holidays celebrated by the Japanese include the following:

January 1, New Year's Day: The major holiday of the year with three days off from work. Buddhist temple bells are rung 108 times at midnight. People eat noodles for long life and visit Shinto shrines, as well as friends and relations.

January 15, Coming of Age Day: Honors all who have become legal adults (those who have turned twenty).

February 11, National Foundation Day: Anniversary of the enthronement of the mythical first emperor, Jimmu Tenno.

March 3, Hina Matsuri: Not a legal holiday, but girls display elaborate sets of dolls representing a prince, princess, and their court.

March 21, the Vernal Equinox: Has Buddhist origins; it is a day for visiting and tending family graves.

April 29, Greenery Day: Previously marked the Showa Emperor's birthday; after his death, it became a day to appreciate nature.

May 3, Constitution Day: Commemorates the 1947 Constitution.

May 5, Children's Day: Celebrates Japan's children. Families with children fly carp (fish)-shaped streamers. The concentration of holidays between April 29 and May 5 is called "Golden Week."

July 13–15 (August 13–15 in some areas), Bon Festival: Not a legal holiday, but traditionally considered second only in importance to New Year's Day. This Buddhist festival honors deceased family members. Celebrations include visiting the ancestral home, tending family graves, and prayer services. Publicly, communal dancing (bon-odori) takes place during the three evenings of the festival.

September 15, Respect the Aged Day: Honors Japan's elderly.

September 23, The Autumnal Equinox: Similar to the Vernal Equinox; a day for visiting and tending family graves.

October 10, Sports Day: Commemorates the 1964 Tokyo Olympics and encourages good health through sports.

November 3, Culture Day: Fosters cultural activities.

November 23, Labor Thanksgiving Day: Commemorates those who work and expresses thanks for the fruits of their effort.

December 23, the Emperor's Birthday: Current emperor's birthday.

In this non-Christian country Christmas is celebrated as a gift-giving holiday for children. Except for Christians, it has no religious significance.

7 ● RITES OF PASSAGE

One hundred days after birth, an infant is presented at a local Shinto shrine for blessing.

November 15 is "Shichi-Go-San," or "7, 5, 3." On that day, children of those ages are taken to a Shinto shrine to be blessed. Originally, this ceremony was for girls three or seven years old and boys five years old.

Educational milestones are celebrated. At the beginning of formal schooling, a child is presented with a leather backpack for books and may receive a private study desk. School entrance ceremonies and graduations are attended by parents in formal dress. University entrance examinations are a major turning point in a teenager's life. Admission to a good university can be critical to an individual's future. Much is made of the preparation, the exam, and the results.

January 15 is "Coming of Age Day." All who have turned twenty are recognized as legal adults. Fancy dress—usually a kimono for young women—is worn to ceremonies, which are often followed by parties and the presentation of significant gifts.

Formal company ceremonies mark the hiring of new employees as well as an individual's retirement.

Marriage is usually celebrated at a commercial wedding hall. Shinto ceremonies are conducted in private with the couple, priest, witnesses, and parents. In place of vows, cups of *sake* are exchanged and drunk. Christian church weddings strike many Japanese as romantic; many wedding halls have an imitation church in which a church-style ceremony can be held before guests. The ceremony is followed by an elaborate dinner with multiple speeches and the formal cutting of a Western-style wedding cake.

Death is usually associated with Buddhist rituals. Visitors honor the dead at a wake, in which guests burn incense in front of a photo of the deceased. The body is cremated. Ashes are placed in a family grave, which has space for numerous urns under a single tombstone. A plaque bearing the Buddhist name of the deceased is added to the family Buddhist altar. Memorial ceremonies are held over several years to pray for the person.

8 ●RELATIONSHIPS

Japan is more formal than America, and phrases and forms of polite exchange are more fixed. Manners require that the speaker use language to honor or elevate the other party, while denigrating (lowering in importance) oneself. Japanese society pays great attention to who is superior to whom in any relationship. This is reflected in language and gestures.

Japanese bow to greet each other. The person of lower status bows lower and should initiate the greeting. Shaking hands is rare among Japanese, who usually do not engage in physical contact. Distinctive gestures include pointing to one's nose to indicate oneself. Women cover their mouths with their hands when laughing. Men, when embarrassed, scratch the backs of their heads. If really uncomfortable, Japanese will often suck wind between their teeth.

Because houses are very small, Japanese usually entertain outside the home. Home visits are usually confined to a brief meeting over tea. The guest brings a gift such as flowers, fruit, or pastries. Such gifts are used to reinforce relationships with relatives, friends, teachers, doctors, business contacts, and so forth. Two gift-giving seasons, New Year's and midsummer, are marked by a large-scale buying and giving of gifts.

Dating is usually confined to high school students and young adults. Schools actively discourage it. Group dating is common and takes the form of outings, picnics, karaoke parties, or visits to amusement parks. Student couples who are dating usually limit themselves to a visit to a coffee shop or fast food restaurant. Japanese students rarely work (many schools forbid it) and often have limited extra incomes. This and busy study schedules restrict dating options. Dating among working adults is common. Most marriages today are based on romantic attachments rather than the arranged marriages that were the norm in the past.

9 ●LIVING CONDITIONS

Japanese generally enjoy good health and have the greatest life expectancy (predicted life span) in the world. Medical care is generally good and includes both modern scientific and traditional Chinese-style herbal medicines.

Housing is a major problem in Japan's crowded cities. While Japanese prefer single-family houses, the enormous cost of land prevents them from having a real yard; as many as forty houses may be built on one acre. Small apartments are very common. Traditionally, houses were furnished with wall-to-wall straw mats *(tatami);* recent trends are toward carpet or wooden floors and Western-style furniture.

The Japanese standard of living is very high. Material possessions are comparable to those in the United States, and the general safety of Japanese city streets adds a sense of well-being. The major problems are restricted living space and the limited personal time left by demanding work and study hours.

10 ● FAMILY LIFE

Social values place women secondary to men in status. However, even in traditional families Japanese women enjoy considerable autonomy (independence) and power. Japanese schooling treats boys and girls equally, guaranteeing well-educated women. Traditionally, the wife has charge of the house and oversees the children. This is her full-time job and includes two important responsibilities: money and education. The wife keeps the family budget, manages savings and large purchases, and even gives her husband his weekly allowance. She also monitors the children's education. Most Japanese children have few household chores, but devote regular time to study under their mother's watchful eye.

Family size has declined to an average of 1.8 children per couple. The average age for marriage has risen to about twenty-six years for women and twenty-eight for men. Most marriages are based on romantic attachment; however, the separate lives led by men and women in Japanese society often limits the emotional closeness of married couples. Expectations regarding the personal satisfactions to be gained from married life are not as demanding as in the United States. This, plus stress on the importance of the family unit, help to hold the annual divorce rate to 1.3 per 1,000 people (1990). The practice of the eldest son's family living with his parents in a three-generation household is rapidly declining.

Some Japanese have pet dogs and cats, but many are prevented from having them by limited living space. Goldfish and birds are popular. Some keep crickets for their song.

11 ● CLOTHING

Traditional clothing is the *kimono,* a robe that is wrapped around the body, left side over right, and tied with a sash *(obi)*. Women's kimonos vary from the simple everyday designs preferred by older women to the elaborate painted silk robes worn for ceremonial occasions. Men rarely wear kimonos except for formal occasions and when performing traditional arts. The light summer cotton style *(yukata)* remains very popular for relaxing at home, resorts, and summer festivals.

Traditional footwear is sandals *(zori)* or wooden clogs *(geta)* with a thong that passes between the big toe and the second toe. *Tabi,* a split-toed sock that accommodates the thong, is worn with them.

Most Japanese wear Western-style clothing for daily use. Japanese tend to dress more formally and neatly than Americans. Jeans are popular with the young. Middle-

and high-school students wear dark blue or black uniforms with badges that indicate their school and grade.

12 ● FOOD

Japanese eat a wide range of foods, including imports from China and the West. The staple of their diet is rice, usually eaten plain from a bowl without seasoning or butter. Rice is complemented with other dishes, including fish, meat, vegetables, various pickles, and soup. Japanese people eat much seafood. Some fresh fish is eaten raw with soy sauce as *sashimi,* or combined raw with rice in *sushi.* However, most fish is cooked, often grilled or deep fried in batter *(tempura).*

Buddhism discouraged the eating of meat, but this taboo (prohibition) has largely disappeared. Japanese eat chicken, pork, and beef, but servings are small. Soup is made from fermented soy bean paste *(miso)* or dried bonito shavings *(katsuobushi).* Noodles in various forms are a common main dish.

Most Western foods can be found in Japan. Hamburgers and pizza are popular, and many U.S. restaurant chains are well represented.

Meals do not include desserts. Sweets are served separately with tea or coffee. Japanese sweets are often based on sweet bean paste. Western baked goods are widely available.

The national beverage is green tea. Black tea, coffee, soda, and beer are all popular. Milk and dairy products, a recent addition to the Japanese diet, have become popular in recent years. A recipe for green tea ice

Recipe

Green Tea Ice Cream

Ingredients
1 pint softened vanilla ice cream
1 Tablespoon green tea powder

Directions
Blend together ice cream and green tea powder. Return to freezer until ready to serve.

cream, combining traditional and modern ingredients, follows.

Japanese food is served in numerous small dishes. Pieces are cut to be eaten with chopsticks. Soup is drunk from the bowl. It is inappropriate to stick chopsticks upright in a rice bowl or pass food from one pair of chopsticks to another; these gestures are associated with cremation ceremonies.

13 ● EDUCATION

Japanese people place great value on education and see it as the major path toward self-improvement and a successful career. Japan claims a 100 percent literacy rate (percentage of the population able to read and write).

The academic year begins in April and ends in March. Japanese children begin kindergarten at age four and elementary school at age six. Compulsory (required) education covers only elementary school (six grades) and middle school (which consists of three grades), but 94 percent go on to high school (three grades). Most schools are coeducational. Elementary education stresses basic skills, especially reading and math, and seeks to develop the individual into a socially responsible group member. Elementary school teachers establish strong ties with their students, and children often find early education an enjoyable experience.

Middle- and high-school becomes more challenging as emphasis shifts to intensive study with limited electives (optional classes). For a professional career a university degree is essential, but university entry is by competitive examination. Preparation for these exams, called "examination hell," drives much of Japanese middle- and high-school education. Students often supplement regular classes by attending a *juku* (cram school) after hours. Critics rightly charge that Japanese education stresses memorization for university examinations, but Japanese schools also cultivate problem-solving and group work skills more than is usually recognized.

One-third of high school graduates enter college or university and most of those graduate. Two-year colleges are common for women and for vocational education. Four-year universities are similar to those in the U.S., but many students arrive burned out by "examination hell" and exert minimal effort. Graduate study is not as common as in the U.S.

14 ● CULTURAL HERITAGE

Japanese classical musical instruments include the *koto* (thirteen-string, horizontal harp), the *shakuhachi* (vertical bamboo flute), and the *shamisen* (a three-stringed banjo-like instrument). The shakuhachi is usually played solo or with the koto. The koto is frequently played solo or in group ensembles. The shamisen is a popular folk instrument that is played solo.

Western instruments such as the piano, violin, and guitar are more popular now than traditional instruments. Modern popular music reflects strong Western influences, and Western classical music is well known in Japan.

In dance, stately classical forms continue to be studied, while a dynamic folk tradition preserves lively dances. The annual Bon Festival includes group dancing open to all.

Japan's literary heritage is very rich. The oldest surviving text, *Kojiki (*published in AD 721), blends Shinto myth and history. Poetry anthologies, *Manyoshu,* date back to the Nara Period (AD 710–794). The Heian Period (AD 794–1185) produced a rich outpouring of literature, especially by court women. During the Middle Ages (1185–1335) military tales were popular, the greatest being the *Tale of the Heike*. The Muromachi Period (1336–1568) produced poetic Noh play texts that often reflect Buddhist values. Most poetry was written in the *tanka* form, five lines of 5-7-5-7-7 syllables. The first three lines of the tanka gave rise to the seventeen-syllable haiku. The most famous haiku author was Basho. The Tokugawa Period gave rise to the *bunraku* puppet drama and kabuki theater, for which Chikamatsu wrote tragedies. In the nineteenth century, Western influences inspired many autobiographical novels. Natsume Soseki's *Kokoro* is an early twentieth-century favorite. Japanese writers are read overseas in translation, and Kawabata Yasunari and Oe

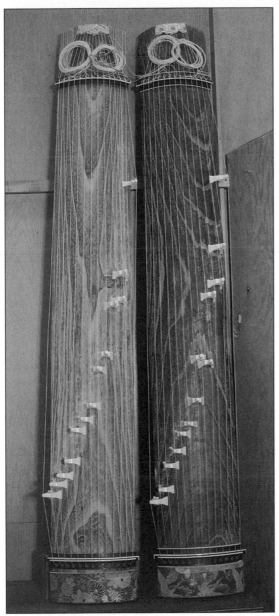

EPD Photos

The koto has thirteen strings, and is held in a horizontal position when played. The performer wears plectra, plastic or ivory plucks, on the thumb and first two fingers. Courtesy of Center for the Study of World Musics, Kent State University.

Kenzaburo have won Nobel Prizes for literature.

15 ● EMPLOYMENT

Most men join a company directly after graduating from high school (for nonprofessional jobs) or college (for professional jobs). The ideal is to remain with the same company until retirement around age sixty. In return for loyalty and long hours of work, the company makes a commitment to preserve the jobs of their employees. This "lifetime employment" ideal extends to only about one-third of Japanese workers. Many younger Japanese question the lack of mobility required by lifetime employment and opt for more risky and potentially rewarding career paths.

Most women work outside of the home in retail, service, or clerical jobs. They are expected to quit work upon marrying or when their first child is due. These women represent an affluent portion of the Japanese public and many enjoy their status prior to marriage. After raising children, many return to work. Until recently, true career options were not open to many women in corporations. Teaching and some government offices provided careers, but corporations only began to recruit women executives seriously in the 1980s. They are still rare in many industries.

The work environment in Japan is group-oriented. Employers expect employees to put company interests before personal concerns. Long hours are typical for office workers.

Wages start very low and rise with longevity (duration with a company). The average per capita income in Japan is higher than in America, but many things, especially housing, are more costly than in the U.S.

16 ● SPORTS

The Japanese are great sports enthusiasts. Physical education classes in high school include an elective (optional class) in one of Japan's traditional martial arts such as judo, karate, or archery. Baseball is extremely popular, and the annual national high school baseball tournament in August is followed throughout Japan. The teams of Japan's universities compete in baseball, rugby, martial arts, and other sports.

The most popular professional sport in Japan is baseball. Games in the two leagues, the Pacific and the Central, draw large crowds, including noisy but well-organized fan clubs. There is some interest in American football and basketball. The new "J-League," a professional soccer league, fostered a soccer craze in the early 1990s.

Sumo wrestling is a native sport centered upon six annual fifteen-day tournaments. Two wrestlers seek to force each other out of a circle or to touch the ground with some part of their bodies (other than the soles of their feet). A striking feature is the huge size of the wrestlers; top-ranked wrestlers usually exceed three hundred pounds and can weigh over five hundred pounds.

Popular participatory sports include golf, tennis, skiing, hiking, swimming, and fishing. Gateball, similar to croquet, is popular with elderly people.

17 ● RECREATION

The Japanese people are fans of television and have more television sets per person than do Americans. Song and variety shows and celebrity quiz shows are popular, and there are extensive sports and news broadcasts. Family dramas are also popular. Historical dramas often feature stories about samurai (warriors).

Movies are a popular entertainment form but depend heavily upon imports, especially from America. Japan's own movie industry is productive but has faded since it achieved international fame for its art and sophistication in the 1950s and 1960s. The director Akira Kurosawa made a lasting international impression with films such as *Rashomon* and *Seven Samurai*.

Traditional live theater forms survive, including Noh drama, Bunraku puppet plays, and live kabuki theater. The Japanese also attend concerts, including those of classical Western music and pop groups.

A popular form of participatory entertainment is karaoke. This form of singing along with recorded orchestral accompaniment to popular songs began as entertainment in bars and has since spread overseas.

Appreciation of seasonal changes and holiday festivals are traditional pastimes that remain popular. Major festivals attract huge crowds, and famous sites for admiring plum and cherry blossoms, irises, azaleas, chrysanthemums, and the bright leaves of fall draw many visitors.

18 ● CRAFTS AND HOBBIES

Japan is a land in which many handicrafts have been raised to the level of art. Japan has many regional variations on pottery. Some fine pottery is delicate and finely detailed; there is also a strong tradition of heavier folk pottery that is more simple and rustic. The aesthetic values of "*wabi cha*" (poverty tea) of the Tea Ceremony encourages this style of pottery.

Handmade paper, produced from mulberry bark, remains a popular art form. Special papers with distinct textures and patterns are prized for letter writing, calligraphy (decorative lettering), and wrapping. A variety of dying, painting, and decorative styles and methods have developed to decorate the panels of silk used for women's kimonos. Tie-dying is also employed.

The Japanese government cherishes these arts, recognizing masters as National Living Treasures to honor and support their work.

19 ● SOCIAL PROBLEMS

Japan's major social problem concerns its population. Japanese enjoy the greatest longevity (longest lives) in the world, but their low birth rate is below the replacement level. As a result, their population is the most rapidly aging in the world and will soon begin to decline in size. This raises serious questions about how, in the twenty-first century, a shrinking work force will support a huge population of retirees.

Civil rights are a problem for some small minority groups. Resident aliens (less than 1 percent of the population), primarily Koreans, may have been born and raised in Japan but are required to register as foreign residents and have been excluded from certain jobs. A campaign to remove these barriers is gradually easing restrictions.

Another minority group (about 2 percent of the population) is the *burakumin* (hamlet people). Physically indistinguishable from the majority Japanese, these are descendants of outcasts who suffered severe discrimination in pre-modern times. Despite attempts to legislate equality, they are subject to widespread discrimination. The tiny population of Ainu on the island of Hokkaido are an indigenous people who were overrun by the majority Japanese population. Most have intermarried with the majority Japanese.

An issue of concern in modern Japan is the status of women. Laws pertaining to women have changed faster than social values. Legally, Japanese women enjoy considerable protection. However, social values tend to emphasize gender-based career paths. While many Japanese women appear content with their status, those who wish to pursue careers previously limited to men find the door only partially open.

Japanese society tolerates and even encourages considerable drinking, and alcoholism is a problem. Relieving stress and renewing personal bonds over a drink after work is common in Japan, and leads to heavy drinking. Japan's island geography has helped to restrict the inflow of hard drugs and firearms to very low levels, but there are signs that these problems may be on the rise.

20 ● BIBLIOGRAPHY

Castle, Coralie, and Margaret Gin. *Peasant Cooking of Many Lands*. San Francisco: 101 Productions, 1972.

Famighetti, Robert, ed. *The World Almanac and Book of Facts 1996*. Mahwah, NJ: World Almanac Books, 1996.

Japan: An Illustrated Encyclopedia. New York: Kodansha International, 1993.

Japan: Profile of a Nation. New York: Kodansha International, 1994.

Reischauer, Edwin O., and Marius B. Jansen. *The Japanese Today: Change and Continuity*. Cambridge, MA: The Belknap Press of Harvard University Press, 1995.

WEBSITES

Embassy of Japan. Washington, D.C. [Online] Available http://www.embjapan.org/, 1998.

Microsoft. Encarta Online. [Online] Available http://encarta.msn.com/introedition, 1998.

Microsoft. Expedia.com. [Online] Available http://www.expedia.msn.com/wg/places/Japan/HSFS.htm, 1998.

Ainu

PRONUNCIATION: EYE-noo
LOCATION: Japan (Hokkaido)
POPULATION: 25,000
LANGUAGE: Japanese; Ainu (few present speakers)
RELIGION: Traditional pantheistic beliefs

1 ● INTRODUCTION

Until 400 years ago, the Ainu controlled Hokkaido, the northernmost of Japan's four main islands. Today they are a small minority group of Japan. They are a hunting and fishing people whose origins remain in dispute. They probably came from Siberia or from the southern Pacific, and originally comprised different groups. For centuries, the Ainu culture developed alongside, but distinctive from, that of the Japanese. However, in recent centuries (particularly with the 1889 Hokkaido Former Aborigines Protection Law) they have been subject to Japanese government policies of modernization and integration. As with indigenous (native) peoples in the United States and many other nations, the Ainu have largely assimilated (adapted to the dominant culture). And like many other such groups, there have been signs of cultural revival recently.

The oldest ruins found in Hokkaido, the Ainu homeland, date from 20,000 to 30,000 years ago in the old Stone Age. Iron was introduced approximately 2,000 years ago from either southern Japan or the Asian continent, probably by ancestors or groups related to the Ainu. Between the eighth and thirteenth centuries, earthenware unique to Hokkaido and the northern mainland appeared. Its producers were the direct ancestors of the Ainu. The subsequent 300 to 400 years saw the development of the culture known today as uniquely Ainu.

2 ● LOCATION

Hokkaido, one of Japan's four main islands, is 32,247 square miles (83,520 square kilometers)—comprising one-fifth of Japan. Hokkaido is twice as large as Switzerland. A small number of Ainu live on southern Sakhalin. Earlier, the Ainu also lived in the southern Kuril Islands, along the lower reaches of the Amur River, and in Kamchatka, as well as the northern part of the Northeast region of Honshu. Their ancestors may have once lived throughout Japan.

Hokkaido is surrounded by beautiful coasts. The island has many mountains, lakes, and rivers. Its land was densely wooded with ancient trees into the twentieth century. Two major mountain ranges, Kitami in the north and Hidaka in the south, divide Hokkaido into the eastern and western regions. The Saru basin area in southeastern Hokkaido is a center of Ainu ancestral culture.

An 1807 survey reported the Hokkaido and Sakhalin Ainu population as 23,797. Mixed marriages between Ainu and mainland Japanese became more common over the last century. In 1986 the total number of people in Hokkaido identifying themselves as Ainu was 24,381.

In the late nineteenth century, the Japanese government created a colonial office for Hokkaido's economic development and encouraged settlers from other parts of Japan. A similar government office now continues to promote Hokkaido's development. With the loss of their land, their livelihood, and their traditional culture, the Ainu had to adapt to a rapidly industrializing society.

3 ● LANGUAGE

Ainu is said to belong either to a Paleo-Asiatic or a Paleo-Siberian group of languages. It has two dialects. The Ainu have no written language. The Japanese phonetic syllabaries (characters representing syllables) or the Roman alphabet is used to transcribe (write) Ainu speech. Few people now speak Ainu as their primary language.

Ainu and Japanese share many single words. God (male or female) is *kamui* in Ainu and *kami* in Japanese. Chopstick(s) is *pasui* in Ainu and *hashi* in Japanese. The word *sirokani* (silver) and *konkani* (gold) in literary Ainu correspond to *shirokane* and *kogane* in literary Japanese (see quotation below). The two languages, however, are unrelated. Two well-known Ainu words still commonly used refer to venerated Ainu individuals: *ekasi* (grandfather or sire) and *huci* (grandmother or grand dame).

The name Ainu comes from a common noun *ainu,* meaning "human(s)." Once the term was felt to be derogatory, but more Ainu now use the name positively, taking pride in their ethnic identity. Their land is called "Ainu Mosir"—peaceful land of humans. The phrase *ainu nenoan ainu* means "human-like human." The following is a famous refrain from a poem about the owl deity:

> *sirokanipe ranran piskan*
> (fall, fall, silver drops, all around)

> *konkanipe ranran piskan*
> (fall, fall, golden drops, all around)

4 ● FOLKLORE

According to mythic poetry, the world was created when oil floating in the ocean rose like a flame and became the sky. What was left turned into land. Vapor gathered over the land and a god was created. From the vapor of the sky, another god was created who descended on five colored clouds. Out of those clouds, the two gods created the sea, soil, minerals, plants, and animals. The two gods married and produced many gods including two shining gods—the Sun god and the Moon god, who rose to Heaven in order to illuminate the fog-covered dark places of the world.

Okikurmi of the Saru region is a semi-divine hero who descended from Heaven to help humans. Humans lived in a beautiful land but did not know how to build fire or make bows and arrows. Okikurmi taught them to build fire, to hunt, to catch salmon, to plant millet, to brew millet wine, and to worship the gods. He married and stayed in the village, but eventually returned to the divine land.

Ainu historical heroes include Kosamainu and Samkusainu. Kosamainu, who lived in eastern Hokkaido, led an Ainu rebellion against the mainland Japanese ruling the southern tip of Hokkaido, called Matsumae. He destroyed ten out of the twelve Japanese bases but was killed in 1457. Samkusainu organized Ainu in the southern half of the island during a 1669 uprising, but after two months they were destroyed by Matsumae forces armed with guns.

5 ● RELIGION

Ainu religion is pantheistic, believing in many gods. Traditional belief held that the god of mountains dwelled in the mountains, and the god of water dwelled in the river. The Ainu hunted, fished, and gathered in modest quantities in order not to disturb these gods. Animals were visitors from the other world temporarily assuming animal shapes. The bear, striped owl, and killer whale received the greatest respect as divine incarnations.

The most important god in the home was the female god of fire. Every house had a firepit where cooking, eating, and rituals took place. The main offerings made to this and to other gods were wine and *inau,* a whittled twig or pole, usually of willow, with shavings still attached and decoratively curled. A fence-like row of taller *inau* stood outside between the main house and the raised storehouse. Outdoor rituals were observed before this sacred altar area.

6 ● MAJOR HOLIDAYS

The spirit-sending festival, called *i-omante,* either for a bear or striped owl, was the most important Ainu festival. I-omante, the bear, was observed once in five or ten years. After three days of reverence to a bear cub, accompanied by prayers, dancing, and singing, it was shot with arrows. The head was decorated and placed at the altar, while the meat was eaten by the members of the village community. The spirit, while visiting this world, had temporarily adopted the form of a bear; the bear ritual released the spirit from the form so it could return to the other realm. Similar festivals are observed by many northern peoples.

7 ● RITES OF PASSAGE

In preparation for adulthood, boys traditionally learned hunting, carving, and making tools such as arrows; girls learned weaving, sewing, and embroidery. In mid-teen years, girls were tattooed around the mouth by a skilled older woman; long ago they were also tattooed on the forearms. The Japanese government banned tattooing in 1871.

The gift of a knife mounted in carved wood from a young man indicated both his skill and his love. The gift of embroidery from a young woman similarly indicated her skill and her willingness to accept his proposal. In some cases, a young man visited the family of a woman he wished to marry, helping her father in hunting, carving, and so forth. When he proved himself an honest, skilled worker, the father approved the marriage.

A death was mourned by relatives and neighbors. All were fully dressed in embroidered costume; men also wore a ceremonial sword and women a necklace of beads. Funerals included prayers to the fire deity and verse laments expressing wishes for a smooth journey to the other world. Items to be buried with the dead were first broken or cracked so that the spirits would be released and travel together to the other world. Sometimes burial was followed by the burning of the dwelling. The funeral for an unnatural death could include a tirade (raging speech) against the gods.

8 ● RELATIONSHIPS

A formal greeting, *irankarapte,* which corresponds to "how are you" in English, literally means "let me softly touch your heart."

It is said that Ainu people always shared food and drink with neighbors, even a cup of wine. The host and the guests seated themselves around the firepit. The host then dipped his ceremonial chopstick in the cup of wine, sprinkled a few drops onto the firepit giving thanks to the fire god (goddess of fire), and then shared the wine with his guests. The first salmon caught each year in early fall was a special item to be shared with neighbors.

Ukocaranke (mutual argumentation) was a custom of settling differences by debating instead of fighting. The disputants sat and argued for hours or even days until one side was defeated and agreed to compensate the other. Representatives with oratorical (public speaking) skills and endurance were chosen to resolve disputes between villages.

9 ● LIVING CONDITONS

Formerly, an Ainu house was made of poles and thatch plant. It was well insulated and had a firepit at the center of the main room. An opening below each end of the ridge allowed smoke to escape. Between three and twenty such houses formed a village community called *kotan*. Houses were built close enough together that a voice would reach in case of emergency, and far enough apart that fire would not spread. A kotan was usually located by waters for convenient fishing but also in the woods to remain safe from floods and close to gathering grounds. If necessary, the kotan moved from place to place in search of a better livelihood.

10 ● FAMILY LIFE

Besides weaving and embroidering, women farmed, gathered wild plants, pounded grains with a pestle, and cared for babies. Men hunted, fished, and carved. Some accounts suggest that married couples lived in separate houses; other accounts suggest that they stayed with the husband's parents. Until recently, men and women traced descent differently. Males traced descent through various animal crests (such as a killer whale insignia) and females through hereditary chastity belts and forearm tattoo designs. The inheritance could include the art of a bard (male or female), a midwife, or a shaman. The midwife and shamaness Aoki Aiko (1914–) inherited her arts as the fifth generation offspring of the female line of the family.

Dogs were favorite animals. In one scene of an epic poem describing the descent of a divine youth to this world, a dog was mentioned as guarding millet grains. Dogs were also used in hunting.

11 ● CLOTHING

The Ainu traditional robe was made of the woven fibers of inner elm bark. It was worn with a woven sash similar in shape to the sash worn with a mainland Japanese kimono. The male robe was calf-length. In winter a short sleeveless jacket of deer or other animal fur was also worn. The female robe was ankle-length and worn over a long undershirt with no front opening. The robes were hand-embroidered or appliqued with rope designs. A pointed edge at the tip of each front flap was characteristic of the Saru region.

The traditional Ainu costume is still worn on special occasions. However, in everyday life the Ainu wear international-style clothing similar to that worn by other Japanese people.

12 ● FOOD

Traditional staple foods of the Ainu were salmon and deer meat, in addition to millet raised at home and herbs and roots gathered in the woods. Millet was largely replaced by rice earlier in this century. Fresh salmon was cut up and boiled in soup. A rice porridge called *ciporosayo* was prepared by adding salmon roe (eggs) to boiled grains.

As in other cold regions, Ainu children used to enjoy making maple ice candy. On a late March or early April evening when a cold night was expected, they made cuts in the bark of a large sugar maple and placed containers of hollow sorrel stalks at the roots of the tree to collect dripping syrup. In the morning, they found the sorrel cylinders heaping with frozen white syrup.

13 ● EDUCATION

Traditionally children were educated at home. Grandparents recited poems and tales while parents taught practical skills and crafts. From the late nineteenth century on, Ainu were educated in Japanese schools. Many concealed their Ainu background.

14 ● CULTURAL HERITAGE

The Ainu have handed down a vast body of oral traditions. The main categories are *yukar* and *oina* (longer and shorter epic poems in literary Ainu), *uwepekere* and *upasikma* (old tales and autobiographical stories, both in prose), lullabies, and dance songs. *Yukar* usually refers to heroic poetry, chanted mainly by men, dealing with demi-gods and humans. It also includes *oina,* or *kamui yukar,* shorter epics chanted principally by women about the gods. The Saru region of south central Hokkaido is particularly known as the homeland of many bards and storytellers.

Yukar was narrated by the fireside for a mixed gathering of men, women, and children. Men sometimes reclined and beat time on their bellies. Depending upon the piece, yukar lasted all night or even for a few nights. There were also festival songs, group dance-songs, and stamping dances.

The best known Ainu musical instrument is the *mukkuri,* a mouth harp made of wood. Other instruments included coiled-bark horns, straw flutes, skin drums, five-string zithers, and a type of lute.

15 ● EMPLOYMENT

Since the mid-nineteenth century, the traditional subsistence activities of hunting, fishing, gathering of wild plants, and millet raising have been replaced by rice and dry-crop cultivation and commercial fishing. Other activities in Hokkaido include dairy farming, forestry, mining, food processing, wood working, pulp, and paper industries. The Ainu contribute to all these activities.

16 ● SPORTS

Traditional sports for children included swimming and canoeing. In the early twentieth century there was a children's game called *seipirakka* (shell clogs). A hole was bored through the shell of a large surf clam and a thick rope passed through it. Children wore two clams each, with the rope between the first two toes, and walked or ran about on them. The shells made a clicking noise like horseshoes. Another indigenous Ainu game was making toy *pattari* in the creek when the snow thawed in spring. The pattari were made from hollow stalks of sorrel filled with creek water. With the accumulation of water, one end of the stalk dropped to the ground under the weight. On the rebound, the other end hit the ground with a thump. Adults used real pattari to pound millet grains.

17 ● RECREATION

See the article on "Japanese" in this chapter.

18 ● CRAFTS AND HOBBIES

Weaving, embroidery, and carving are among the most important forms of folk art. Some types of traditional Ainu weaving were once almost lost, but were revived around the 1970s. Chikap Mieko, a second generation professional embroiderer, builds her original embroidery on the foundation of the traditional art. Carved trays and bears are treasured tourist items.

Among the many traditional items made are the poison arrow, unattended trap arrow, rabbit trap, fish trap, ceremonial sword, mountain knife, canoe, woven bag, and loom. In the early 1960s, Kayano Shigeru began to privately collect many such genuine items in and around his village in the Saru region, when he realized that all that was left of the Ainu cultural heritage was scattered among the communities. His collection developed into the Biratori Township Nibutani Ainu Cultural Museum and the Kayano Shigeru Ainu Memorial Museum. Also famous is the Ainu Museum established in 1984 in Shiraoi in southeastern Hokkaido on the Pacific.

19 ● SOCIAL PROBLEMS

The 1899 Ainu law that classified the Ainu as "former aborigines" remained in effect into the 1990s. As an Ainu representative to the National Diet since 1994, Kayano Shigeru has taken the lead in fighting to eliminate this law. A new Ainu law is now under consideration.

The recent construction of a dam in Kayano's homeland, Nibutani village in Biratori town, exemplifies forceful development of Hokkaido at the cost of the Ainu's civil rights. Despite the resistance led by Kayano Shigeru and others, construction proceeded. In early 1996 the village was buried under water. At a meeting on the use of Hokkaido lands, Kayano stated that he would accept the Nibutani dam construction plan if only the salmon fishing rights be returned to the Nibutani Ainu in exchange for the destruction of their homes and fields. His request was ignored.

20 ● BIBLIOGRAPHY

Encyclopedia of Japan. New York: Kodansha, 1983.

Japan: An Illustrated Encyclopedia. Kodansha, 1993.

Kayano, Shigeru. *Our Land Was a Forest: An Ainu Memoir* (trans. Kyoko Selden and Lili Selden). Boulder, Colo.: Westview Press, 1994.

Munro, Neil Gordon. *Ainu Creed and Cult.* New York: K. Paul International, distributed by Columbia University Press, 1995.

Philippi, Donald L. *Songs of Gods, Songs of Humans: The Epic Tradition of the Ainu.* Princeton, N.J.: Princeton University Press, 1979.

WEBSITES

Embassy of Japan. Washington, D.C. [Online] Available http://www.embjapan.org/, 1998.

Microsoft. Encarta Online. [Online] Available http://encarta.msn.com/introedition, 1998.

Microsoft. Expedia.com. [Online] Available http://www.expedia.msn.com/wg/places/Japan/HSFS.htm, 1998.

Jordan

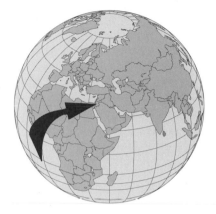

The people of Jordan are called Jordanians. Most of the population trace their heritage to more than one of the many people that lived in Jordan throughout history, including Greeks, Egyptianss, Persians, Europeans, and Africans. The Bedu, or Bedouin, nomads inhabit the desert.

Jordanians

PRONUNCIATION: jawr-DAY-nee-uhns
LOCATION: Jordan
POPULATION: 4 million
LANGUAGE: Arabic; English
RELIGION: Islam (majority Sunni Muslim)

1 ● INTRODUCTION

The land of Jordan lies along an ancient and well-used trade route, making it geographically valuable. Many powers have ruled the land, under many different names. The modern Hashemite Kingdom of Jordan was established on May 25, 1946. The current King Hussein was barely eighteen years old when he took the throne.

2 ● LOCATION

Jordan is located on the East Bank of the Jordan River, with the Palestinians as its neighbors on the West Bank. South of the West Bank, Jordan shares a border with Israel. To the north lies Syria, and to the east and south lies Saudi Arabia. Iraq shares a northeastern border with Jordan.

Jordan has three distinct zones: the Jordan River valley, which is green and fertile; mountainous regions in the north and south, which have a cool, Mediterranean climate; and the majority of the country, an arid desert.

Among the 4 million people who live in Jordan, there is an ancient distinction between the people of the desert and the pople of the valley. The desert people are descended from warlike tribes. The valley people are considered more peaceful and more tolerant of other cultures.

3 ● LANGUAGE

The official and most commonly spoken language of Jordan is Arabic. Many Jordanians also speak English. "Hello" in Arabic is *marhaba* or *ahlan,* to which one replies, *arhabtayn* or *ahlayn.* Other common greetings are *as-salam alaykum* (peace be with you), with the reply of *walaykum as-salam* (and to you peace). The numbers one to ten in Arabic are: *wahad, itnin, talata, arba'a, khamsa, sitta, saba'a, tamania, tisa'a,* and *ashara.*

Common names for boys are *Talal, Muhammad,* and *'Abdullah.* Common names for girls are: *Fadwa, Leila, Fatima,* and *Reem.*

4 ● FOLKLORE

Jordanians are very superstitious people. They are firm believers in fate and omens. When someone is sick or injured, it is believed to be the result of *rire* (jealousy) and *hassad* (envy). "Coffee ladies" read fortunes in the dregs of a cup of coffee. To ward off the "evil eye," incense is burned, a lamb is offered to the poor, and a blue medallion is worn around the neck.

Jordanian folktales, particularly those of the Bedu (Bedouin), often feature themes of honor, generosity, and hospitality, all considered important Arab attributes. One folk story revolves around the legendary Hatim al-Ta'i, whose name means "generosity." Before Hatim's birth, when his mother was newly married, she dreamt that she was offered a choice: she could either bear ten brave sons or she could have one son, Hatim, who would possess superior generosity. She chose to have Hatim, and indeed he proved to be highly generous.

When Hatim was sent to take the family's camels to pasture, Hatim proudly returned to tell his dismayed father that he had given away every one of the camels, and that this no doubt would bring fame to the family name. This story typifies the importance that Jordanians place on generosity.

5 ● RELIGION

More than 90 percent of Jordanians are Sunni Muslim, the majority sect of Islam. The remaining Jordanians belong to a wide range of Muslim and Christian sects. Islam impacts almost every aspect of the lives of Jordanians. There is no such thing as the "separation of church and state" in an Islamic country such as Jordan. Religion plays just as large a part in government as it does in the everyday life of Jordanians.

6 ● MAJOR HOLIDAYS

Friday is the Islamic day of rest, so most businesses and services are closed on Fridays. The main Muslim holidays include: Ramadan, the ninth month of the Muslim year during which everyone fasts from dawn to dusk; *Eid al-Fitr,* a three-day festival at the end of Ramadan; the First of *Muharram,* or the Muslim New Year; *Mawoulid An-Nabawi,* the Prophet Muhammad's birthday; and *Eid al-Isra wa Al-Miraj,* a feast celebrating the nocturnal visit of Muhammad to heaven.

Fixed public holidays in Jordan include the Christian New Year (January 1); Tree Day (January 15); Arab League Day (March 22); Labor Day (May 1); Independence Day (May 25); Arab Renaissance Day (commemorating the Arab Revolt) and Army Day (both on June 10); King Hussein's accession to the throne (August 11); King Hussein's birthday (November 14); and Christmas (December 25).

7 ● RITES OF PASSAGE

Weddings are the most important event in a Jordanian's lifetime. The cost of the celebration is second only to that of buying a home. Guest lists can number anywhere from 200 to 2,000 people. Births are also joyfully celebrated, with the mother's family providing the child's first wardrobe and furniture.

The *aza,* or "condolence period," following a death is a very important ritual in Jordanian society. It is essential to attend the aza of a neighbor or colleague. It is even required of the relative of a neighbor or colleague of a deceased person. During the aza, men and women sit in separate rooms in the house of the deceased and drink black, unsweetened Arabic coffee. For forty days after the death, the aza is reopened every Monday and Thursday at the deceased's home. Jordanians wear black for mourning, contrary to the Islamic custom of wearing white or beige during mourning.

8 ● RELATIONSHIPS

Jordanians are generally introverted and conservative, yet they are extremely hospitable. When invited to a Jordanian home, a guest is expected to bring nothing and eat everything. In personal encounters, Jordanians are formal and polite.

9 ● LIVING CONDITIONS

Before 1979, few houses had piped water. Most houses still simply have home storage tanks and rely on water deliveries by truck. Due to a severe water shortage, rationing is in effect.

About 70 percent of Jordanians live in urban areas, most of them in the capital city of Amman (considered one of the cleanest and most efficient cities of the Arab world). Jordan is among the top ten countries of the world in reducing infant mortality, and life

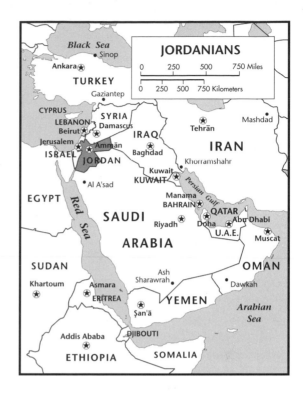

expectancies are fairly high: sixty-seven years for men and seventy-one for women.

Because of the difficulty in finding employment in Jordan, particularly for skilled workers, many Jordanians go abroad in search of work. The majority go to the Persian Gulf oil states (Kuwait, Saudi Arabia, and the United Arab Emirates), whose small populations require them to import laborers from neighboring states. Working in the Gulf allows Jordanians to earn steady incomes, a percentage of which they send to family members in Jordan, thus helping the Jordanian economy.

10 ● FAMILY LIFE

Traditional values are very important to Jordanians. Marriages usually result from family introductions, if not outright matches.

Couples are almost never forced to marry against their will, however. Upper-middle-class couples court each other in the Western style.

One out of five marriages ends in divorce, and divorced women rarely remarry because of the stigma attached to them by society. A married woman's primary role is to produce children, preferably sons. A woman with many sons is considered more powerful than a woman with only daughters. The average Jordanian family has seven children, giving Jordan one of the highest birth rates in the world.

Women are guaranteed equal rights in the Jordanian constitution. Religious laws and social custom often undermine this. However, there are a few women in the Jordanian Parliament, suggesting their improved status.

Homes are built so that floors can be added when sons marry. Sons bring their brides home and they raise their family there. Most Jordanians live in three- or four-story homes containing extended families who eat together. Daughters-in-law are expected to do most of the cooking. Men never cook or do housework.

11 ● CLOTHING

The Islamic tradition of women covering their faces is currently becoming more popular in Jordan. Everyday Jordanian dress is generally conservative, particularly for women. They are not allowed to wear tight clothes, sleeveless blouses, shorts, short skirts, or low-cut backs on shirts or dresses.

There are basically three styles of clothing for women in Jordan. Westernized

Susan D. Rock

This man in Petra, Jordan (a popular tourist destination), is wearing traditional attire including the red and white Jordanian kaffiyyeh, *a scarflike headdress.*

women dress in modern Western clothes. Very religious women wear an outfit called the *libis shar`i* or *jilbab*. This is a floor-length, long-sleeved, button-front dress worn with the hair covered by a scarf. Stores catering to religious women are common in Jordan. Women from other Muslim countries shop in Jordan for libis shar`i clothing.

The third type of attire is the national costume. This is a handmade dress with embroidered and cross-stitched patterns that represent the region of the country that the wearer comes from. For example, in northern Jordan, women wear black cotton dresses embroidered with multicolored tri-

Recipe

Mansaf (Fatiyyeh)

Ingredients

1 cup of orzo, rice-shaped pasta
water
dash of salt
3 pounds lean lamb chunks
1 large onion, finely chopped
¼ teaspoon black pepper
1 teaspoon ground allspice
4 loaves pita bread, or 2 loaves *shraj* bread
3 cups cooked white rice
½ cup sautéed pine nuts

Directions

1. Cook orzo according to package directions; purée it with a little plain yogurt and a dash of salt in a blender or food processor to make a sauce.
2. Place lamb chunks and 4 cups of water into a large kettle, and bring the water to a boil.
3. Add chopped onion, black pepper, and ground allspice, and simmer for about one hour.
4. Add the puréed kishk to the stewed lamb mixture in the kettle. Simmer for another hour.
5. While the stew is simmering, cut rounds of pita bread into quarters. Cover the bottom of a large round pan with 2 layers of pita pieces.
6. When the lamb mixture has finished simmering, ladle about 2 cups of the orzo sauce over the pita bread and allow to soak 10 minutes.
7. Spread rice over the soaked bread. Ladle another cup of sauce over the entire pan, and cover the rice with all of the lamb chunks. Sprinkle pine nuts over the lamb and serve.

angles. In central Jordan, women wear dresses made from over sixteen yards (sixteen meters) of fabric, with sleeves measuring ten feet (three meters) in length. Blue panels are stitched around the sleeves and the hem of the dress.

Jordanian men dress in Western clothing. Some men wear a Jordanian *kaffiyyeh,* or scarflike headdress. (The Jordanian kaffiyyeh is red and white, in contrast to the black and white Palestinian kaffiyyeh.) The kaffiyyeh is folded in a triangle and laid over the head. It is secured to the head with a double-coiled rope called an *i`gal.*

12 ● FOOD

Jordan has one of the world's most elaborate and sophisticated cuisines, mostly taken from its neighbors. Few dishes are unique to Jordan; one unique dish is *mansaf,* chunks of stewed lamb in a yogurt-based sauce served with rice. Mansaf, also called *fatiyyeh,* is the traditional Jordanian meal served for special occasions. *Kishk* is required for the preparation of mansaf. Kishk dough is made of yogurt, salt, and semolina flour. The kishk is shaped into pellets or balls that fit into the palm of the hand, and then allowed to dry and harden. A recipe for mansaf that uses pasta in place of kishk, follows.

Cory Langley

Refugees from the former nation of Palestine are straining the Jordanian economy. A growing number of Jordanians live in poverty.

Jordanians love sweets and eat lots of them. A favorite kind of sweet is layers of a thin pastry called *filo*, filled with nuts or creams, similar to *baklava*.

13 ● EDUCATION

Jordan is a very well-educated country. It has the highest number of university graduates per person in the Arab world. Its main export is skilled labor and professionals to other Arab countries. At 82 percent (with a target of 92 percent by the year 2000), Jordan also has one of the highest literacy rates in the Arab world.

Education is free and required from grades one through ten, and then it continues to be free for another two years. Literacy training is free to all Jordanian residents.

Girls must attend school through the tenth grade and are encouraged to finish secondary and even higher education. More than half of the 20,000 students at the University of Jordan in Amman are women.

14 ● CULTURAL HERITAGE

Islam teaches that it is unholy to depict the human figure. This has significantly shaped Jordanian art. Western-style fine arts became popular in the late twentieth century as more Jordanians traveled to other countries. Recently, however, there has been a revival of more traditional Jordanian art forms. This is especially true of stylized Islamic calligraphy, or artistic writing.

The traditional dance of Jordan is the *dabkeh,* a group dance performed by both men and women. Traditional musical instruments include the *qassaba* and *nay,* woodwinds; the *rababa,* a one-stringed instrument; the *kamanja,* resembling a violin; the *ud* (lute), with five double strings; the *qanun,* a long, guitarlike instrument with twenty-six strings; and the *daff* and *durbakkeh,* percussion instruments.

15 ● EMPLOYMENT

Working conditions are regulated by law, including minimum wages, minimum age for employment, vacation, and sick leave. There is no required retirement age. Unions are legal.

Although women are guaranteed equal rights in Jordan's constitution and are just as well-educated as men, women make up only 13 percent of the labor force. This is due primarily to the traditional belief that a woman's job is to marry well and have many children. Unemployment has become a serious problem since about 300,000 workers returned from Kuwait in 1991 after the Persian Gulf War (1990–91). Many Jordanians now take jobs for which they are overqualified, simply to survive.

16 ● SPORTS

The most popular sports in Jordan are football (called soccer in America) and basketball. Also enjoyed are horse and camel racing. In the 1950s, car racing was begun as a weekend sport attracting a few spectators. It has since developed into one of Jordan's major sporting events. The royal family strongly supports the car races, with King Hussein himself having raced in the rallies. King Hussein's eldest son, Prince 'Abdullah, also competes in the national rallies. Competitions are international, with most racers representing countries of the Middle East, such as Qatar, Kuwait, Oman, and the United Arab Emirates.

17 ● RECREATION

All films in Jordan, both in cinemas and in video form, are censored for kissing and sex scenes. Martial arts and low-grade action movies are popular among Jordanian youth.

Jordan has two domestic television stations. One provides Arabic entertainment and news. The other features foreign-language programming. Jordanians also produce their own television shows. A particular favorite is a soap-opera called a *musalsal,* that is shown in successive episodes every night.

Jordan receives Arabic radio broadcasts from around the Middle East and also has its own domestic stations. A favorite among young people is the English-language Jordanian station. It plays all of the latest music that is enjoyed in the West. "Radio Monte Carlo" also plays Western music.

Jordanians listen more to European music than to American, but American pop star Michael Jackson is a favorite among teenagers.

18 ● CRAFTS AND HOBBIES

There are many traditional folk arts and crafts in Jordan, among them pottery, silver and gold jewelry making, glass blowing, and basket weaving. Textile arts are women's crafts, particularly embroidery and cloth weaving. As young girls learn embroidery stitches from older women, they are initiated into the culture.

19 ● SOCIAL PROBLEMS

Jordan's economy is struggling. This is due to a lack of resources, a large foreign debt, and the problems caused by refugees. These refugees arrived after the 1967 war with Israel (in which Jordan lost the West Bank territory) and the Persian Gulf War in 1990–91. Almost one-third of the population lives below the poverty level, and the percentage is increasing. A severe water shortage also causes difficulties in both the public and private sectors.

Attitudes toward mentally and physically disabled people keep them hidden away, thus they do not receive the help they should.

There is an ongoing conflict between the government's desire to maintain ties with Western powers and popular support for the Palestinians and Iraq. Support for the Palestinians is necessary because more than 60 percent of the population is Palestinian.

The country's relationship with Iraq is similarly important to Jordanians. Iraq has been home to thousands of Jordanians and Palestinians. Its oil economy has provided jobs that have been vital to the Jordanian and Palestinian economies. So, when Iraq invaded Kuwait in 1990, the Jordanian government announced its opposition to the invasion, but it refused to participate in the forces organized to reverse the invasion.

Jordanian friendship with both the Palestinians and the Iraqis has led to problems with the United States.

20 ● BIBLIOGRAPHY

Foster, L. *Jordan*. Chicago, Ill.: Children's Press, 1991.

Jordan in Pictures. Minneapolis, Minn.: Lerner Publications Co., 1988.

Salibi, Kamal S. *The Modern History of Jordan*. New York: I. B. Tauris, 1993.

Stannard, Dorothy, ed. *Insight Guides: Jordan*. Boston: Houghton Mifflin, 1994.

WEBSITES

ArabNet. [Online] Available http://www.arab.net/jordan/jordan_contents.html, 1998.

Embassy of Jordan, Washington, D.C. [Online] Available http://www.jordanembassyus.org/, 1998.

World Travel Guide, Jordan. [Online] Available http://www.wtgonline.com/country/jo/gen.html, 1998.

Kazakstan

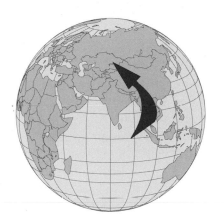

The people of Kazakstan are called Kazaks (or Kazakhs). About 38 percent of the population of Kazakstan is Russian; about 6 percent is German; and about 5 percent is Ukrainian. For more information on the Russians, see the chapter on Russia in Volume 7; on the Germans, the chapter on Germany in Volume 4; on the Ukrainians, the chapter on Ukraine in Volume 9.

Kazaks

PRONUNCIATION: kuh-ZAKS
LOCATION: Kazakstan; China; Uzbekistan; Turkmenistan; Tajikistan.
POPULATION: More than 8 million
LANGUAGES: Kazak; Russian
RELIGION: Islam (Sunni Muslim)

1 ● INTRODUCTION

For centuries the Kazak people were nomads. They have traditionally divided themselves into three territorial *zhüz* (tribal unions, or hordes): Greater, Central, and Lesser. The Greater Horde occupied much of what is now southern Kazakstan. The Central Horde occupied the northern and eastern parts of modern Kazakstan. The Lesser Horde occupied the land between the Ural and Volga Rivers.

Since the Kazaks were nomads, during the 1800s it was possible for large numbers of Slavic settlers to move into and seize the land inhabited by the Kazaks. Many of these were ethnic Russians. Eventually, the modern land of Kazakstan became part of the Soviet Union. Kazakstan became an independent nation in 1991 when the Soviet Union collapsed. It changed its name from Kazakhstan to Kazakstan (dropping the *h*) in 1996.

2 ● LOCATION

The Kazak homeland covers more than 1 million square miles (2.6 million square kilometers). Approximately 80 percent of the area consists of long plains and plateaus. Strong winds often sweep through these flat lands. The only mountains are the Tien Shan and Altai ranges in the southeast and east.

The climate in Kazakstan varies greatly. Some areas become bitterly cold in the winter and intensely hot during the summer. The massive Kara Kum Desert ("black sand") occupies much of central Kazakstan. It is the world's fourth largest desert. Much

EPD Photos

This Kazak newspaper illustrates the written Kazak language.

of it extends into other nations of Central Asia.

There are presently between 8 and 9 million Kazaks. About 80 percent live in Kazakstan, with the others living in China, Uzbekistan, Turkmenistan, and Tajikistan. Kazaks make up only 42 percent of the population in Kazakstan. Ethnic Russians make up about 38 percent of the population. The remainder are Germans, Ukrainians, Uzbeks, and Tatars (ethnic group living in Russia).

3 ● LANGUAGE

Kazak is a central Turkic language. Modern Kazak has many words borrowed from Russian, Arabic, Persian, and other languages. There are three primary dialects that correspond to the three historic Kazak hordes.

Written Kazak, which dates back only to the late nineteenth century, is based on the dialect of the Central Horde.

Examples of the Kazak language include words for traditional occupations, like *balykshi* (fisher) and *eginshi* (grain-grower). Words for animals that played an important part in the traditional way of life include *at* or *jïlqï* (horse), *qazaqi qoy* (fat-tailed sheep), *ayïr tüye* (Bactrian camel), and *yeshki* (goat).

A traditional Kazak greeting that is still sometimes used in rural areas literally translates as: "Are your livestock and your soul still healthy?" A traditional Kazak wish for good fortune is literally translated as: "May God give you one thousand sheep with lambs, eighty camels, and eight married sons."

4 ● FOLKLORE

Oral tradition forms the basis of Kazak folklore. Over the centuries, sagas were passed down by memory from one generation to the next. Most of the stories are heroic epics

Cory Langley

Kazaks living in the major city of Almaty wait for bus in the city center.

where the *batir* (warrior) and his trusty horse save the clan and its livestock from danger. There are also stories about Alash, the legendary first Kazak.

The most famous heroic stories are *Koblandy-Batir*, *Er Sain*, and *Er Targyn*, all of which are from the fifteenth or sixteenth century. The most famous poetic epics are *Kozy Korpesh–Bain Sulu* and *Aiman–Sholpan*. The most famous Kazak love story is *Kiz-Jhibek*, which contains historic information about Kazak betrothal and marriage customs and ceremonies.

The folklore of the "White Swan" explains the creation of the Kazak people. One version tells of an orphan shepherd who dreamed one night of a white swan coming from the sky singing and dancing before him. The next day, his dream came true. Unfortunately, a windstorm appeared from nowhere and scattered all his sheep. The swan rescued him and helped him find his sheep. To the shepherd's surprise, the swan turned into a beautiful lady. The two were married, and together produced a number of children who became the first Kazaks. A similar story tells of a general who was rescued in the desert by a white swan. It turned into a beautiful lady. They married and had a son who grew up, married, and had three sons—the ancestors of the three largest tribes of Kazak.

5 ● RELIGION

Most Kazaks are Sunni Muslim. The Kazaks were introduced to Islam through contact with the Tatars. Tatars traditionally were not as conservative as other Muslim peoples.

Because the Kazaks were wanderers who depended on livestock for their survival, animals were at the core of the ancient Kazak religion. Until the mid-1800s, elements of this ancient animist belief system (including shamanism and ancestor worship) were still widely practiced among many Kazak Muslims.

6 ● MAJOR HOLIDAYS

The Republic of Kazakstan celebrates the following national holidays: New Year's Day (January 1), International Women's Day (March 8), *Nawruz* (the day of the spring equinox around March 21), May Day (May 1), Victory Day (May 9), Independence Day (October 25), and Democracy Day (December 16). To celebrate Nawruz, families will take *kuji,* a meal made of seven ingredients including beef, barley, wheat, and milk products.

The Kazak also celebrate religious holidays. December 10 (Islamic calendar) is the Corban Festival. The word *corban* in Arabic means "sacrificial offering." When the day comes, the Kazak kill oxen or sheep as a sacrifice, entertain guests, and present gifts to their friends or relatives.

The Festival of Fast-Breaking (Lesser Bairam) is the day ending the Muslim holy month of Ramadan. According to Islamic tradition, in September (Islamic calendar) every year, every adult Kazak should abstain from food and drink from daybreak to sunset. The beginning and the end of the month of fast depend on the new moon being visible. When the fast is broken, there are festive activities in a lively atmosphere.

7 ● RITES OF PASSAGE

Kazaks typically have large birthday parties with many relatives and friends. Celebrations are held for a birth, a baby's fortieth day of life, the first day of school, and graduation. Voting and driving privileges are granted at eighteen years of age.

Weddings are very important in Kazak society, not only for honoring the married couple, but also as an event to assemble an extended family or clan. The traditional wedding is called the *toi*. In the past, arranged marriages were common. The payment of *kalym* (a dowry) was expected upon betrothal.

When a person dies, the horse he or she used during his or her lifetime is not allowed to be ridden any longer. The horse tail is cut after the master's death, and the horse is killed one year later as a sacrifice. When nomadic Kazaks migrate to new pasture lands, the hat and clothes of the deceased are put on horseback and moved with the family.

8 ● RELATIONSHIPS

Hospitality is an important part of Kazak culture. A traveler, no matter what his or her nationality, will be put up for the night in any Kazak's home. Proverbs recognize Kazak hospitality. For example, one states: "As long as there are Kazak on the way, you may travel for a year without a cent or a grain in your bag." A host will be offended

Jeannine Davis-Kimball

Kazak women traditionally assemble and disassemble the yurt, sometimes with the help of the men. Here a group of Kazaks are winding cord around the side before the felt is placed over the wooden frame.

if a guest does not accept offers of refreshments. Asking a guest questions is considered bad manners. Guests in a Kazak home are allowed to rest and are given fermented mare's milk to drink. The guests sit cross-legged on a felt rug. They must not straighten their legs. It is considered impolite to take off one's shoes or to point.

Long-separated friends usually embrace when meeting again. They talk about the well-being of their livestock first, then the families greet each other.

Kazak men and women are skilled horseback riders; riding therefore plays an important role in their festivals.

9 ● LIVING CONDITIONS

At one time, the nomadic Kazaks lived in *yurts,* cone-shaped tents of white felt stretched over a framework of wooden poles. Yurts are light and easy to assemble, dismantle, and transport. Today, yurts are only used as temporary shelters by shepherds in remote, seasonal pastures.

The modern Kazak home is typically an apartment in the city or a permanent single dwelling in rural areas. To keep their homes clean, Kazaks always remove their shoes upon entering. Kazak interior design emphasizes the use of stucco walls and artwork as well as ornate carpets.

Jeannine Davis-Kimball

A family of Kazaks and their neighbors stand in front of their winter home made from logs plastered with mud. These Kazaks are nomadic and herd their sheep in the Tien Shan Mountains.

10 ● FAMILY LIFE

The average urban Kazak family has two children. The typical rural family has three or four. By tradition, every Kazak is supposed to know the names of his or her ancestors going back seven generations.

According to custom, a Kazak woman is supposed to compose her own wedding song before getting married. A popular tradition at weddings, anniversaries, and holidays is the *kyz-kuu* (girl chase). A *kyz-kuu* is a lighthearted event in which a man on horseback chases a woman on horseback and tries to catch her in order to steal a kiss. The woman tries to flee. She may even use a small horsewhip to keep the man or his horse away.

Before 1950, wealthy men and nobles were polygynous (had more than one wife). Now they practice monogamy. Men and women share authority in the family. Each spouse performs the tasks required of them to maintain their household. As soon as a young man has grown up and married, he leaves his parents and receives a part of the property from his father. The family property will ultimately be inherited by the youngest son.

In the past, if a husband died, his widow had to marry her brother-in-law or another member of the clan. Although a married

Jeannine Davis-Kimball

Kazak interior design features colorful artwork and ornate carpets.

woman had no right to ask for divorce, a man was allowed to abandon his wife at any time. Nowadays, according to the new laws, Kazak women are free to marry and to divorce.

11 ● CLOTHING

Kazaks like to wear boots with a pair of felt stockings in winter. By the late 1990s, some women in rural areas still wore the traditional dress, but most young women and men wore modern, Western-style clothes.

Young people living in towns dress much like school children everywhere, and carry backpacks to school.

12 ● FOOD

A unique Kazak culinary custom is the *dastarkhan,* a feast for special occasions consisting primarily of meat dishes and dairy products. For a dastarkhan, an entire animal (usually a sheep) is slaughtered. The oldest member of the family gets the honor of carving the head and serving the family. The various parts of the animal symbolize desired traits for those eating them. For example, children are often served the ears as a symbol of being better listeners. Someone who is served the tongue will speak more eloquently. The person who receives the eye should seek wisdom.

Jeannine Davis-Kimball

Two Kazak girls who live in a village join their younger sister when they get home from school.

Most food comes from livestock. There are a variety of milk products, including cheese, butter, and boiled milk. In spring or summer, the herders pour mare's milk into a leather bag, stir it frequently, and wait for it to ferment. The final product is a semitransparent sour milk wine, a favorite beverage in summer. The Kazak eat a lot of mutton, mostly boiled in water and eaten without silverware. Horse meat is also popular. *Kuirdak* is a dish prepared from a freshly slaughtered horse, sheep, or cow and consists of the animal's liver, heart, kidneys, and other organs cut into pieces, boiled in oil, and served with onions and pepper.

13 ● EDUCATION

The Kazak educational system consists of kindergarten (not required), secondary school (eleven years), higher education institute (four to five years), graduate research program (two years), and post-graduate program (three years). There are also three-year colleges for training to become a professional such as a lawyer, pharmacist, or business manager.

In the past, children of Kazaks who practiced nomadism lived in boarding schools in small towns during the school year. Today, most live with their parents in villages and cities during the school year. For those children whose families do not live in a village or town, there are mobile primary schools. The teacher visits the *yurt* (the cone-shaped tent dwelling) and teaches the children on the spot.

Higher education carries much prestige, and parents strongly encourage children to earn their diplomas. Kazakstan has more than sixty institutions of higher learning.

14 ● CULTURAL HERITAGE

The ancient Kazak homeland has produced numerous talented musicians and singers. Music is a part of everyday Kazak life. It is played for military expeditions, weddings, funerals, parties, and games. Almost every Kazak knows how to sing and play a musical instrument by ear.

A traditional form of Kazak music is the *sazgen,* a folk music quintet that includes traditional string and percussion instruments. The most popular folk instrument is the *dombra,* which has two strings and is played by plucking. Other traditional instruments include the *sybyzgy* and *uran* (wind instruments), the *dangyra* and *dabyl* (percussion instruments), and the *sherter* and *kobyz* (stringed instruments).

The fifteenth-century poetry of Asan Kaigy, and the seventeenth-century poems of Zhyrau and Dosmambet are highly revered among the Kazak people. The founder of modern Kazak literature was the humanist and poet Abai Ibragim Kunanbayev (1845–1904). Prominent Kazak writers during the Soviet years (1917–91) included Zhambyl Zhabaev, Saken Seifullin, Mailin, Ilias Dzansugurov, Sabit Mukanov, and Mukhtar Auezov.

15 ● EMPLOYMENT

During the Soviet years (1917–91), many Kazaks worked on large, state-run farms growing cotton. A very high birth rate among the Kazaks during the 1980s has led to higher unemployment today. This has caused bitterness among young Kazaks.

16 ● SPORTS

Playing soccer is popular among Kazaks in the warmer months, and hockey is popular during the winter. The national sport of Kazakstan is Kazak-style wrestling, which is similar to judo.

In the country, horse racing and other horse events are common. Among the Kazaks living in China, "Snatching the Lamb" *(diaoyang)* is a popular game played during festivals. A respected elder puts a headless lamb carcass on the grass. Five to eight horsemen, riding their horses at full gallop, try to bend down and grab the lamb with one hand. The winner is the first horse-

Jeannine Davis-Kimball

A young Kazak woman plays the dombra, *the traditional two-stringed instrument similar to a guitar.*

man who brings the lamb to a designated place.

Although the risk of an avalanche is fairly high, skiing in the Tien Shan Mountains is popular. The slopes have received international attention as a future site for expert and world-class skiing. Skiers are flown by helicopter to the tops of slopes, from which they make their descent.

17 ● RECREATION

City dwellers often spend the weekends with their families in recreational parks, which can be found in almost any Kazak town. Urban Kazaks frequently go to the movies or watch videos.

A popular Kazak pastime is the *itys,* a formal or informal competition of wit between two singers. During the itys, each singer plays the *dombra* (a two-stringed instrument) and cleverly makes up the lyrics as he or she sings. This requires a rich knowledge of the Kazak language. Usually the singer will brag about aspects of his or her hometown or region and make fun of the other person's. The loser is the first person who cannot sing a comeback quickly enough.

18 ● CRAFTS AND HOBBIES

In recent years, there has been a revival in Kazak folk art and crafts, including carpet and jewelry making. Collecting stamps and small pins are also popular hobbies.

19 ● SOCIAL PROBLEMS

Since the 1970s, nationalist attitudes among the Kazaks have grown, leading to violence several times. In 1979, Kazaks rioted because there were rumors that the government was going to set aside land for local Germans who wanted to create their own independent region. Suspicion of ethnic Russians increased during the late 1980s because the Soviet Union often gave them preference in leadership positions.

Testing of nuclear bombs in northern Kazakstan in the 1950s weakened the health of many residents. These people and their descendants are often born with deficient immune systems, a condition similar to acquired immune deficiency syndrome (AIDS). Some researchers have estimated that it will take another fifty years for the condition to reverse through intermarriage with people from unaffected families.

20 ● BIBLIOGRAPHY

Allworth, Edward, ed. *Central Asia: 130 Years of Russian Dominance, A Historical Overview.* Durham, N.C.: Duke University Press, 1994.

Bradley, Catherine. *Kazakstan.* Brookfield, Conn.: Millbrook Press, 1992.

Geography Department. *Kazakstan.* Minneapolis, Minn.: Lerner Publications Co., 1993.

Olcott, Martha Brill. *The Kazaks.* Stanford, Calif.: Hoover Institution Press, 1987.

WEBSITE
World Travel Guide. Kazakstan. [Online] Available http://www.wtgonline.com/country/kz/gen.html, 1998.

Kenya

The people of Kenya are called Kenyans. The estimated proportions of the main tribal groups are Gikuyu (Kikuyu), 21 percent; Luhya, 14 percent; Luo, 13 percent; Kalenjin, 11 percent; and Gusii (Kisii), 6 percent. Another important group living in Kenya are the Maasai. To learn more about the Maasai see the chapter on Tanzania in Volume 9.

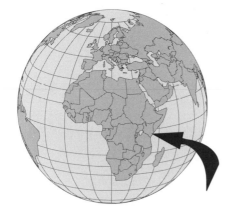

Kenyans

PRONUNCIATION: KEN-yuhns
LOCATION: Kenya
POPULATION: 28 million
LANGUAGE: KiSwahili; English; regional ethnic languages
RELIGION: Christianity; Islam; traditional indigenous beliefs; independent Christian churches; small numbers of Hindus, Sikhs, Parsis, Bahais, Jews

1 ● INTRODUCTION

Kenya is a multiracial society of about 28 million people. The overwhelming majority are indigenous (native) ethnic groups; the rest are Asian, Arab, and European. Europeans in Kenya are mostly of British heritage.

Their ancestors came to Kenya during the late nineteenth and early twentieth centuries in search of commercial and agricultural opportunities. The original British colonizers created the White Highlands, areas with large, commercial farms. The indigenous Africans were displaced from their own extremely fertile land.

Kenya's Land and Freedom Movement (called Mau Mau) won independence from Britain in 1963. The following year, Kenya became a republic under the leadership of President Jomo Kenyatta (1894–1978). Currently, Kenya is a multi-party democracy. Its government consists of a president and a legislative assembly of twelve members nominated by the president, 188 elected members, an attorney general, and a

KENYANS

manent snow of Mounts Kenya and Kilimanjaro to tropical shores with palm trees. Some areas are desert, but most of the country is forests or rolling grasslands. The major geological feature, the Rift Valley, stretches from Zimbabwe (to the south) to the Red Sea (to the north). It is 50 miles (80 kilometers) wide and 9,000 (2,745 meters) feet above sea level in some places. Numerous lakes are found along its base. Kenya's Lake Victoria is the second largest fresh water lake in the world.

Kenya's climate has two rainy seasons. Evenings can be quite chilly in the Central Highlands, and the coastal areas are typically hot and humid. Kenya's capital, Nairobi, although close to the Equator, is 5,449 feet (1,661 meters) above sea level, making it comfortable most of the year.

3 ●LANGUAGE

The official national languages of Kenya are KiSwahili and English. English is spoken in government, courts, universities, and secondary schools. Newspapers, magazines, radio, and television are predominantly in English. Nevertheless, KiSwahili is widely spoken in everyday life as a lingua franca (common language), especially in commerce and by those who do not know English. KiSwahili is the dominant language along the coast, particularly in the major port city of Mombasa. Nowadays, KiSwahili is usually taught along with English in schools throughout Kenya. Regional ethnic languages spoken at home are typically used for elementary school teaching along with English and KiSwahili. Major ethnic languages in Kenya include Kikuyu, Luo, Kiluyia, Kikamba, Samburu,

speaker. Kenya is divided into eight provinces (including the Nairobi area, which has a special status), all of which are under the authority of the president. Several villages form what is known as a sublocation, which is part of a unit called a location. Several locations form a division, divisions form districts, and districts are included in provinces.

2 ●LOCATION

The Republic of Kenya is located in East Africa on the Equator. It borders the Indian Ocean to the east, Ethiopia and Sudan to the north, Somalia to the northeast, Tanzania to the south, and Uganda to the west. Kenya measures 225,000 square miles (583,000 square kilometers). There is considerable variation in landform, ranging from the per-

Maasai, and others. Major Asian languages are Hindi and Gujarati. Kenyans are typically multilingual (speaking several languages).

4 ● FOLKLORE

Folklore historically told of a group's history and offered wisdom about everyday mysteries and dilemmas. Riddles, proverbs, and sayings that describe proper behavior for both young and old Kenyans are still common. Questions such as, Why do cats like to stay by the fireplace?, Why do hyenas limp?, How did circumcision come to be practiced?, and What is the origin of death?" are answered in folktales. Examples of proverbs include: The eye you have treated will look at you contemptuously; A cowardly hyena lives for many years; The swimmer who races alone praises the winner. Riddles are also commonly heard. For example: "A lake with reeds all around? The eye." Another is: "A snake that breathes out smoke? A train."

5 ● RELIGION

The majority religion in Kenya is Christianity; about 37 percent are Protestant (including Quaker) and 25 percent are Roman Catholic. About 4 percent of Kenyans are Muslim (followers of Islam). The remainder practice traditional native beliefs or are members of other Christian churches. Small numbers of Kenyans are Hindus, Sikhs, Parsis, Bahais, and Jews.

Traditional religions generally believed in a High God, spiritual forces such as respected ancestors, and evil forces such as witches. The Creator God was known by different names, but was always thought to be kind and forgiving. For example, the Abaluyia people believed that the god *Were* created Heaven first and then Earth. He created humans so that the Sun could have someone on whom to shine. Were created plants and animals as food for humans.

6 ● MAJOR HOLIDAYS

Kenya celebrates the religious holidays of Good Friday and Easter Monday (in March or April), Christmas Day (December 25), and the Muslim festival *Eid Al-Fitr* (which depends on the sighting of the new moon after the Muslim holy month of *Ramadan).* Secular (nonreligious) holidays include New Year's Day and Labor Day (May 1).

The most significant secular holidays unique to Kenya are related to their struggle for independence from colonial rule. *Madaraka* (June 1) celebrates internal self-government day, and Independence Day is celebrated on December 12. Kenyatta Day (October 20) is celebrated annually in honor of Jomo Kenyatta, Kenya's first president and an important leader in Kenya's struggle for independence.

During all holidays in Kenya, schools and businesses are closed. Many Kenyans who live in cities travel to rural areas to visit and celebrate with family members. Celebrations include eating, drinking, and dancing in homes, bars, and nightclubs. On such occasions, *Nyama Choma* (roasted meat) is a common treat. Goat or beef is consumed. On secular holidays, the Kenyan military is on parade and politicians give speeches in public and on radio and television. Newspapers typically honor past and present political leaders.

David Johnson

In rural areas, women in Kenya wear multicolored cotton dresses with large shawl-like pieces of cloth wrapped around their shoulders to provide protection from rain, sun, and cold. They usually wear flat shoes or go barefoot.

7 ● RITES OF PASSAGE

Most births take place in hospitals or small rural clinics under the care of a midwife. Infants are commonly breast-fed and carried in a sling of cloth. An older sibling often helps the mother care for infants or toddlers. For this reason, a special bond prevails between a caretaker and her "follower" in the birth order. If no girl is available, a boy can also be a caretaker. Parents value the birth of both boys and girls. Boys are valued because most groups in Kenya trace descent (family line) through males (patrilineal), who then inherit land. Girls are valued because upon marriage, future in-laws give gifts—known as bride wealth—to the girl's family. Although women may now own land, bride wealth is still common and is a sign of prestige for highly educated women.

Many groups in Kenya mark adolescence with initiation rites such as male circumcision or female clitoridectomy. Young men who undergo circumcision at the same time become part of a social group that lasts for a lifetime. There are, however, many societies in Kenya that do not circumcise, including the Luo, Kenya's second largest ethnic group.

Most ethnic groups do not practice clitoridectomy (female circumcision), although it is found among the Gusii, Pokot, Gikuyu, and a few other societies. Unlike circumcision, this practice is very controversial and the subject of considerable national and international debate, even when undertaken with modern medical precautions. It is often referred to by outsiders as "female genital mutilation" and is considered a human rights issue. Many folk explanations for this practice, such as the control of female sexuality or the enhancement of female solidarity, are discounted in modern Kenya.

Land is a strong symbol of family bonds; consequently, regardless of where a person lives in Kenya, there is a strong pull to return home whenever possible. A high priority is placed on being buried in one's homeland so that both body and soul will be at peace.

8 ● RELATIONSHIPS

Ethnic groups each have elaborate greeting patterns. The simplest and most common Kiswahili greeting is *Jambo* (hello), to which a person replies likewise. *Jambo* or *Hujambo, Bwana* is said to a man (You have nothing the matter, Sir?) while a woman is addressed *Jambo, mama.* If addressing more than one person, the greeting would become *Hamjambo.* The reply to this is *Sijambo,* or *Hatujambo* if with others. These greetings are usually followed by additional exchanges depending on social context, time of day, weather, and so forth.

Politicians frequently try to mobilize Kenyans for development projects by encouraging a national slogan meant to appeal to group bonds. The late President Kenyatta initiated *Harambee* (Let's pull together) as a national symbol. Individuals "pulled together" to raise money for construction of schools, hospitals, and other public works. Today, political leaders and other prominent people attend harambee functions and donate large sums of money. Some Kenyans do not approve of the custom, although it is difficult to trace how widely it is practiced since harambee requests are not made in public.

Young people have many opportunities for social interaction, especially in the cities. In rural areas, dating is supervised by family members. Funerals, where several days of ceremonies end in feasting and dancing, are popular occasions for courtship. Secondary schools and churches, both in towns and in the country, also sponsor social events where teenagers may interact. Dating in the city of Nairobi may involve outings to nightclubs, restaurants, movie theaters, malls, and drive-in movie theaters.

9 ● LIVING CONDITIONS

The majority of Kenyans live in rural areas where electricity and running water are often not available, and roads are not paved. Homes are constructed of waddle and daub (woven sticks and mud) with thatched roofs. Wealthier people generally live closer to towns and have access to electricity and running water. Their homes are usually constructed of stone or brick. A growing number of Kenyans (about 25 percent) live in cities.

Nairobi is by far Kenya's largest city; other large cities include Naivasha, Nakuru, Mombasa, and Kisumu. A significant portion of Kenyans are middle class or richer and live in comfortable homes or even mansions in suburban areas. Nevertheless, Nairobi has many shantytowns where homes are little more than shacks built out of discarded items. Many who reside in these shantytowns are squatters with no ownership rights, so they can be forcibly evicted at a moment's notice.

Health problems are generally more severe in shanty towns. These include gastrointestinal problems and diarrhea afflicting children, and respiratory infections, cholera, typhoid, and typhus afflicting adults. Human immunodeficiency virus (HIV) is a growing problem. In addition, most Kenyans experience periodic bouts with malaria.

10 ● FAMILY LIFE

Families tend to be quite large. For all ethnic groups in Kenya, an extended family (including aunts, uncles, cousins, and grandparents) is common. Several generations may live in the same compound or neighborhood.

Marriage laws vary for the different cultural groups. The European heritage is recognized in one legal code, which allows only monogamous marriages (one man wed to one woman). Under customary law, which recognizes indigenous (native) customs, plural marriages such as polygyny (multiple wives) and wife inheritance (where a widow automatically marries her deceased husband's brother) are allowed. Religiously contracted marriages are recognized for Muslim and Hindu unions under separate legal codes.

11 ● CLOTHING

European and Arabic clothing are now commonplace throughout the country. In rural areas, women wear multicolored cotton dresses or skirts and blouses. Large shawl-like cloths are commonly worn as protection from rain, sun, and cold. Babies are carried in a sling on the back or side. Scarves are worn on the head. Flat shoes or bare feet are standard. Men generally wear Western-style trousers and shirts with jackets and ties for special occasions. Styles of clothing in cities reflect social class differences. The most stylish and expensive clothes are available for those who can afford them. Long pieces of colorful cloth are often worn as skirts, wrapped around shorter dresses, or by themselves along with matching headpieces. Arabic influences are strong, especially along the coast where the fez (a type of hat) and turban are commonplace. Asian dress is the sari for women, and white cotton shirts and pants for men. Secondary school children usually wear uniforms to school, but dress similarly to American and European young people at home and at play. Nevertheless, ethnic and religious variations also exist.

12 ● FOOD

Indigenous (native) African crops include sorghum and finger millet. Some 2,000 years ago, crops such as bananas, yams, rice, and coconuts reached east Africa from southeast Asia. About 400 years ago, crops from the Americas such as maize (corn) and cassava spread to east Africa from west Africa. Many crops grown in Kenya were imported from Europe during the colonial era. These include white potatoes, cucumbers, tomatoes, and many others. Native

Recipe

Ugali

Ingredients

1 cup milk
1¼ cups cornmeal
1 cup water

Directions

1. Measure 1 cup of milk into a bowl. Slowly add ¾ cup or cornmeal, beating constantly, until the mixture is like paste.

2. Heat 1 cup of water in a medium saucepan until it boils. Using a wooden spoon, stir cornmeal and milk paste mixture into the boiling water. Reduce heat.

3. Slowly add remaining ½ cup of cornmeal, stirring constantly. The mixture should be smooth, with no lumps.

4. Cook for about 3 minutes. When the mixture begins to stick together and pull away from the sides of the pan, remove from heat.

5. Pour mixture into a greased bowl and allow to cool.

Serve at room temperature. The traditional way to eat ugali is to pinch off a piece of the dough with the right hand. An indentation pressed into the wad of dough is used as a scoop for sauce or stew.

Adapted from Lois Sinaiko Webb, *Holidays of the World Cookbook for Students*, Phoenix, Ariz.: Oryx, 1995 p. 2.

---

fruits such as papaya and mangoes are especially popular throughout the country.

Pastoralism, or cattle herding, has a long history in Kenya. Cattle provide meat, milk, butter, and blood. Other livestock includes poultry, sheep, and goats. Many societies in Kenya combine agriculture with raising livestock.

Today, the major staple throughout Kenya is maize (corn), which is an important cash crop as well. Maize is made into a thick porridge called *ugali* and is eaten with meat, stews, or indigenous greens (*sukuma wiki*). Many Kenyans eat this combination on a daily basis. It takes much practice to cook the mixture of maize meal and boiling water to the right consistency without burning it. *Sukuma wiki* is a combination of chopped spinach or kale that is fried with onions, tomatoes, perhaps a green pepper, and any available leftover meat. This is seasoned with salt and pepper. A recipe for ugali follows.

Modern Kenyans enjoy eating in a variety of international restaurants and fast food chains. Asian restaurants are very popular. In rural areas, children snack on roasted maize and sugarcane. Manufactured candy and bottled drinks such as orange soda and colas are very popular at birthday parties and other festive occasions. Bottled beer brewed in Kenya has largely replaced traditional beers made from millet or maize; however, coconut wine is popular on the coast. Modern eating utensils are common;

nevertheless, most Kenyans prefer eating their *ugali* with their hands.

13 ● EDUCATION

Schools throughout Kenya educate young people from nursery school through university and professional training. Primary and secondary schools vary in size and quality, and education can be costly. Both secular (nonreligious) and religious schools operate on a daily or boarding basis. Harambee schools, which are maintained through an informal network of prominent political and civic leaders, often do not have the same resources as those with international connections through church or the state. Scholarships are available on a competitive basis for both boys and girls. Competitive sports such as football (soccer), swimming, and track and field are common.

The literacy rate (percentage of the population able to read and write) in Kenya is about 69 percent.

A system similar to that in the United States (eight years of elementary school, four years of secondary school, and four years of university) recently replaced a British system of Ordinary and Advanced levels of secondary and advanced education following the primary years. The American system includes more attention to practical subjects and local culture than did the British system, which included more European history and literature.

Graduates of secondary schools in Kenya who do not go on to university or teacher training colleges seek technical or secretarial schooling. Training in computer technology is of growing importance.

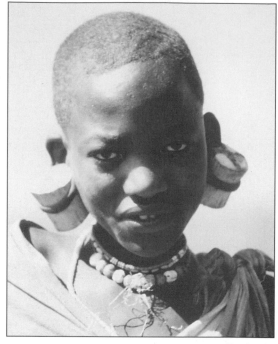

Cory Langley

Various ethnic groups in Kenya have their own traditional dress.

Post-secondary education includes a wide variety of vocational and technical schools and a growing number of national universities and teacher training institutions. Post-graduate education includes academic subjects, law school, and medical school. There is much competition in Kenya for limited places in educational institutions; consequently, many students go abroad to the United States, Europe, and Asia for their education.

14 ● CULTURAL HERITAGE

Kenya's rich cultural heritage is a mixture of ethnic and cultural traditions. The Muslim tradition is embodied in archaeological and written sources from the coastal region.

The historical monument at Gedi, located between Malindi and Mombasa, was founded in the late thirteenth century. Its tombs, monuments, and other remains indicate that an urban Muslim civilization, combining native African practices with those from Arabia and India, existed for many centuries at Gedi and elsewhere along the coast. This civilization produced music, dance, and literature.

The European (primarily British) heritage in Kenya is noticeable in Nairobi and some of its suburban areas such as Karen. The Norfolk Hotel in Nairobi opened in 1904 and was featured in the movie *Out of Africa,* an account of the life of Isak Dinesen, who lived on a coffee estate in Kenya during the colonial period. Elspeth Huxley's writings (including *Flame Trees of Thika*) give another account of Kenya's social life and customs from a European perspective.

Kenya's greatest contemporary writers are world-renowned for their short stories and novels. Ngugi wa Thiong'o is the author of such books as *Petals of Blood* and *Devil on the Cross.* He writes in his traditional Gikuyu language rather than English, stressing the importance of communicating with members of his society in their own language, which the colonists had suppressed. His novels criticize the social inequality in Kenya today. Grace Ogot, in books such as *The Other Woman,* has developed the short story to a high standard.

Music and dance competitions are held frequently in the schools. These are heavily influenced by native styles. The National Theatre regularly hosts competitions among students who come from all over Kenya to display their skills in indigenous dance and song. Radio and television shows commonly feature programs of ethnic music and songs as a popular form of entertainment. Music from the United States is popular today, especially among teenagers.

15 ● EMPLOYMENT

Kenya's industries include processed foods, textiles, glass, and chemicals. However, agriculture is the mainstay of the economy, employing about three-fourths of the population and generating a significant amount of export earnings. Coffee and tea are the main exports; both men and women work on coffee and tea estates. Women work as subsistence farmers (producing enough food to live on but with little or no extra to sell). Typically, men clear the land and help in harvesting. Women also collect wood for charcoal and go to the markets. Young people experience difficulty in finding jobs because Kenya has limited work outside of agriculture.

Tourism is the principal source of foreign money and provides jobs for men and women in the hotel and game park industries. Men work as bus drivers, taxi drivers, and factory workers and play important roles in agriculture, primarily with cash crops (crops raised for export).

In the urban shantytowns, small-scale commercial activities such as vegetable stalls, food stores, carpentry, and tailoring abound. Illegal activities such as brewing of beer, prostitution, and petty theft are common.

16 ● SPORTS

Kenyans in urban areas often become members of clubs where sports such as billiards, squash, swimming, and tennis are played. Golf is available at some clubs and hotels. Cricket is another popular sport. Automobile races are common. Over the Easter weekend, the Malboro/Epson Safari Rally attracts an international audience. On many Sunday afternoons, horse racing is held with legalized gambling at the Ngong Road Race Course.

Football (soccer) is a national pastime; teams of various ethnic groups compete against teams from industries, armed forces, and the police. Boxing is another popular spectator sport. Schools sponsor competitive sports for boys and girls, including soccer and track and field.

17 ● RECREATION

Sports, theater, television, reading, and cultural activities such as dancing and music are popular forms of entertainment and recreation. Modern movies, television, and radio cover global subjects and are popular among young Kenyans. Radio and television also regularly feature traditional folklore as part of their programming.

On weekends and in the evenings, walking, window shopping, and shopping in malls are frequent pastimes for all Kenyans. The most popular form of entertainment, however, is visiting with friends and relatives. Food, drink, and news are exchanged, mixing people of all ages. Visits between rural and urban relatives are occasions for the exchange of food from rural areas for money and material goods from urban areas.

In rural areas, a game of strategy known in KiSwahili as *Bao* is popular. This game involves a wooden board with a varying number of holes and seeds. A player attempts to capture the seeds of an opponent through a series of complex plays whereby the opponent's seeds end up on his side of the board. National *Bao* competitions are held, and children play a simplified version of this game.

18 ● CRAFTS AND HOBBIES

Carvings, batiks, basketry, jewelry, ceramics, and other indigenous crafts are made largely for sale to tourists. Local cooperatives manufacture baskets, women's purses, and mats for sale.

19 ● SOCIAL PROBLEMS

Wildlife management and conservation are major concerns of the Kenyan government and tourist industry. As a result, commercial artifacts made from wild animals that are endangered or are living on game reserves have been banned. Tourists are now limited to photographic rather than hunting safaris. In spite of these limitations, poaching (illegal hunting) continues to be a problem. Some conservationists have expressed concerns that the elephant population (the source of valuable ivory) has grown too large in certain regions, where farmers have been killed by elephants rummaging for food in their gardens. Finding a balance between animal and human needs continues to be a challenge.

Street children can be seen in cities and large towns of Kenya. These children come from poor, often alcoholic, families in rural areas. They earn money by begging, collecting waste products for sale to wholesalers, who resell them to recyclers. Street girls

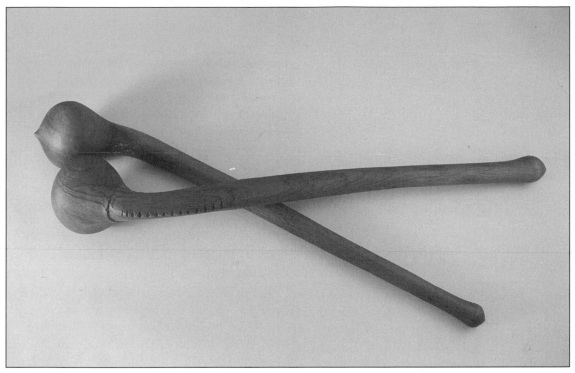

EPD Photos

This traditional wooden rhythm instrument is typical of the type of handcrafted item that collectors and tourists like to acquire from Kenya.

often earn money through prostitution or begging. Glue-sniffing is a widespread addiction among the younger street children.

Due to the large volume of tourists and the relatively poor quality of Kenya's highways, death by motor vehicle accidents has become a major problem in the country. Crashes with wild and domesticated animals are common in rural areas.

From its independence until the early 1990s, Kenya had a one-party democratic system. It is now experiencing a transition to multi-party democracy, but members of opposition parties believe that their political rights are not respected. Members of the ruling party, however, claim that multi-party democracy promotes tribalism. Young people commonly complain that all political parties are led primarily by very old men, leaving little visible leadership by younger adults or by women.

20 ● BIBLIOGRPAHY

Arnold, Gay. *Modern Kenya.* New York: Longman, 1981.

Dinesen, Isak. *Out of Africa.* New York: Random House, 1972.

Kenya in Pictures. Minneapolis, Minn.: Lerner Publications Co., 1988.

Stein, R. *Kenya*. Chicago: Children's Press, 1985.

Themes in Kenyan History. Athens: Ohio University Press, 1990.

Webb, Lois Sinaiko. *Holidays of the World Cookbook for Students*. Phoenix, Ariz.: Oryx, 1995.

WEBSITES

Embassy of Kenya, Washington, D.C. [Online] Available http://www.embassyofkenya.com/, 1998.

Interknowledge Corp. Kenya. [Online] Available http://www.geographia.com/kenya/, 1998.

World Travel Guide. [Online] Available http://www.wtgonline.com/country/ke/gen.html, 1998.

Gikuyu

PRONUNCIATION: kee-KOO-yoo
ALTERNATE NAMES: Kikuyu
LOCATION: Kenya
POPULATION: 5 million
LANGUAGE: Gikuyu; English; KiSwahili
RELIGION: Christianity (Roman Catholicism, Anglicanism, fundamentalist groups, African Separatist Churches); traditional beliefs

1 ● INTRODUCTION

The Gikuyu, like the white settlers in the early twentieth century, were attracted to the Kenya highlands because of cool temperatures, fertile soils, and abundant rainfall. Prior to the arrival of the Gikuyu, the area was occupied by hunters and gatherers known as the Dorobo. It is not known exactly when the Gikuyu first occupied the central highlands, but their oral history indicates that the Gikuyu occupied the area for hundreds of years prior to the arrival of the Europeans in Kenya.

The Gikuyu have figured significantly in the development of contemporary Kenyan political, cultural, and social life. The Land and Freedom Movement (referred to pejoratively as the "Mau Mau" Movement) during the 1950s was primarily a Gikuyu guerrilla war (a war fought without organized government troops) in response to British domination. The British had taken farming lands from the Gikuyu and given these lands to white settlers. Gikuyu were forced to work on these farms and to provide labor for cash crops such as coffee and tea. The Gikuyu nationalist Jomo Kenyatta (1894–1978) became the first president of Kenya at its independence in 1963. He is respected among the Gikuyu for his leadership against colonialism (outside rule) and for his status as is regarded as the father of his country.

Today, the Gikuyu, like other Kenyans, participate in a democratic political system. Gikuyu are organized into two major political parties that are considered to be part of the opposition (to the ruling government) in Kenya. These parties are the Democratic and the Ford-Asili Parties. Political participation is primarily through election to a parliamentary (similar to a congressional) seat (of which there are 188 in Kenya) or through direct election to the national presidency.

2 ● LOCATION

The Gikuyu are the largest ethnic group in Kenya. They number about 5 million among Kenya's total population of about 28 million. The Gikuyu live throughout Kenya but primarily reside in Nairobi Province and Central Province, located in the central region of the country. As Kenya's largest group, the Gikuyu occupy a central position in Kenyan social life.

The capital city of Nairobi lies just at the southern boundary of the area traditionally occupied by the Gikuyu people. Thus, many Gikuyu now are counted among the city's inhabitants of about 1.5 million people.

Gikuyuland is a plateau of about 100 miles (160 kilometers) from north to south and 30 miles (48 kilometers) from east to west. Its elevation ranges from about 3,000 feet (900 meters) to over 7,500 feet (2,300 meters) above sea level. The plateau features deep gorges and parallel ridges. Rainfall is plentiful. However, on the eastern side of the plateau, the terrain is comparatively dry and is dominated by a grassland zone. The elevation increases to the west, giving rise to more rainfall and woodlands with good potential for agriculture. The largest ecological area is characterized by high altitude and rainfall where plant life is abundant and most of the population is concentrated. This is the area where significant cash crops are grown, including pyrethrum (a flower that produces a natural insecticide), coffee and tea. Rich soils aid the growth of traditional crops such as sweet potatoes, bananas, millet, sorghum, cowpeas, and maize (corn), which is the staple throughout Gikuyuland.

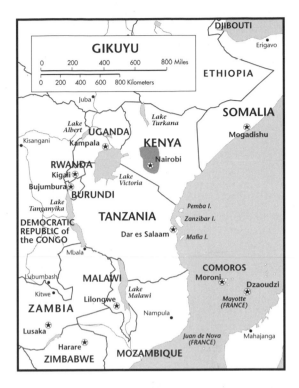

3 ● LANGUAGE

The Gikuyu are generally fluent in three languages. The primary national language in Kenya is English. All children receive instruction in English beginning in primary school and continuing through university. KiSwahili is a second national language, although it is not the language of government, it is widely used as a language of trade and commerce, especially by those without formal education. KiSwahili is also taught in the schools from primary through secondary school. The Gikuyu use either English or KiSwahili when traveling outside the central highlands. Radio, television, and mass media publications are available in both languages throughout Kenya.

The Gikuyu language is the preferred language at home and in the community. Gikuyu is taught in primary schools throughout Gikuyuland.

4 ● FOLKLORE

The Gikuyu people explain their origins as farmers and herders in the following way. The first tribal parents, Gikuyu and Mumbi, had their own children, who then had children who dispersed around Mount Kenya. One day a grandchild's knee started swelling. When he opened his knee, three little boys emerged, who became his sons. In time, one of them became a hunter; one enjoyed collecting fruits and plants; and the third made fire for cooking. The hunter domesticated some animals, and the collector grew crops such as bananas, cassava, and sweet potatoes. The third son applied fire to stones and metals and became a blacksmith. In this way, the Gikuyu culture originated.

The Gikuyu attribute their ultimate origins to sacred intervention by their god Ngai who sometimes resides on Mount Kenya which, for the Gikuyu, is a sacred place. According to legend, Ngai carried the first man, Gikuyu, to the top of Mount Kenya. Ngai showed him the rich land spread out below the mountain. Gikuyu was told that his sons and daughters would inherit the land and multiply. Gikuyu was given a wife named Mumbi, meaning "Creator" or "Molder," and together they had nine daughters. Ngai said that whenever problems arose, the people should make a sacrifice and gaze at Mount Kenya in order to be assisted. One day, Gikuyu was unhappy at not having a male heir. He pleaded with Ngai to provide a son for him. After appropriate rituals, Gikuyu went to a sacred tree where he found nine men waiting to greet him. He arranged for these men to marry his daughters provided they agreed to live under his roof and abide by a matrilineal system of inheritance (tracing descent through the female line). In time, many grandchildren and great-grandchildren were born. Still later, each daughter came to head her own clan, thus giving rise to the clans of the Gikuyu people.

The legend continues that in time the kinship system changed from a matrilineal to a patrilineal one (tracing descent through the male line). It is believed this happened because the women became excessive in their domination over men. The men ganged up on the women when they were all pregnant at the same time. They overthrew female rule and became heads of their families. From then on, polygyny (one man with several wives) replaced polyandry (one woman with several husbands) as a marital practice. Nevertheless, the women were able to maintain their names for the main clans. To this day, most women carry one of these names. The names are Wanjiru, Wambui, Wanjiku, Wangari, Waceera, Wairimu, Wangui, Wangechi, Wambura and Wamuyu.

A number of other important legends provide cultural heroes. Among these are Karuri, who was a past ruler of legendary proportion. Another is Wamugumo, a noted giant believed to have been able to eat an entire goat by himself. He could clear land that took many men a long time to clear, and he was able to kill lions, buffalo, and leopards with ease. A famous woman called Wangu wa Makeri ruled during the period of the matriarchy (when women held the majority of power). At that time, women were allowed to have many husbands, especially young men, and the old men did all of the work.

Traditionally, folktales and riddles combined with myths to provide young people with a strong sense of Gikuyu values. Grandmothers were excellent story tellers. Some common riddles are: A man who never sleeps hungry? Fire (since it is fed throughout the night); My son lives between spears? The tongue; My child travels without rest? The river (always flowing). Proverbs are numerous in modern-day culture and change constantly to reflect the times. For example, one proverb teaches that "A good mortar does not correspond to a good pestle," to explain that successfully matching a husband and a wife may be difficult. Another proverb widely heard is "When the hyenas come, nobody will give shelter," which means that in times of panic, it is every man for himself. Many proverbs teach common sense, such as "When one goes on a journey, he does not leave his bananas cooking in the fire."

One tongue twister refers to a child who saw a tadpole and ran away; when the tadpole saw the child, it also ran away. In Gikuyu, one says *Kaanaka Nikora kona kora kora, nako kora kona kaanaka Nikora kora.*

5 ● RELIGION

The Gikuyu today are prominently represented in a variety of Christian churches. These include the Roman Catholic, the Anglican, fundamentalist, and African Separatist churches. The significance of belief in a high god, Ngai, is maintained or was transferred to the Christian-centered belief in monotheism (the belief in one god). Ngai created everything. He lives in the sky and is invisible. Sometimes he lives on Mount Kenya. He should only be approached for serious problems such as those involving life-and-death questions. During periods of famine or epidemic diseases, Ngai is approached by the elders on behalf of the entire community.

Other traditional beliefs have also persisted into contemporary life. Important among these is the belief in ancestral spirits. These departed relatives are involved in all matters, especially those not considered important enough to seek Ngai's attention. Matters of everyday health, for example, involve the ancestor spirits, who cause sickness when their interests are not taken into consideration. "Traditional doctors" were popular resources for determining which ancestor was responsible for a particular disease and for advice on how to please the ancestor.

In the past, religious values emphasized community solidarity and discouraged individualism. Authority was vested in elders and prophets, who were believed to know what was best for all people. Expressions of individuality and solitary life were not encouraged. Someone perceived to be outside the group might be accused of being a witch and could be killed by the elders. At the same time, considerable security was provided by the emphasis on the group.

6 ● MAJOR HOLIDAYS

The Gikuyu typically celebrate the same holidays as other Kenyans (*see* Kenyans).

7 ● RITES OF PASSAGE

The Gikuyu are well known for their traditional rituals of adolescence. Prior to the arrival of Europeans, there was a custom known as Ngweko. Periodically, elders supervised gatherings of young people who would spend private time with each other for the purpose of getting to know members of the opposite sex. Young people paired off according to mutual attraction. Should a young girl become pregnant, the boy responsible was held accountable and was expected to marry the girl he had impregnated. The Gikuyu considered Ngweko to be a form of sex education. And since Ngweko was associated with reproduction, the Gikuyu considered it a sacred act of carrying out the orders of their high god Ngai to reproduce. Many elder Gikuyu believe that the missionaries made a mistake when they labeled Ngweko as sinful. The schools that were established after the arrival of the Europeans did not include sex education. Since the beginning of co-educational boarding schools, teenage pregnancies have become a major social problem in Kenya, including among the Gikuyu.

Prior to participating in Ngweko, both boys and girls undergo numerous rituals, including surgery on their genital organs. The purpose of these rituals is to enable young people to bond with others with whom they have undergone painful experiences. Clitoridectomy (female circumcision) was, and to some extent still is, practiced by the Gikuyu. It is the topic of much debate by Africans and others, and is often referred to by outsiders as female genital mutilation. A middle-ground position appears to be emerging that grants the social significance of adolescent ritual while working to eliminate clitoridectomy, even under hospital conditions where it now occurs. (The procedure was formerly done in unsterile conditions with crude instruments. Many life-threatening injuries and deaths resulted.) Gikuyu boys continue to be circumcised, a practice widespread in Africa and many other parts of the world as well.

Many dances and songs, called *mambura* (rituals or divine services), take place during initiation ceremonies. Gikuyu history is publicly enacted so as to provide a sense of community solidarity. Each *irua* group is given its own special name. Initiation ceremonies involve special foods and the selection of a sponsor to impart knowledge and to supervise the young person. After several days of instruction, boys and girls are taken together to a compound for their circumcision. Numerous friends and relatives gather for singing and dancing throughout the night. A special feast is made for the parents of the children. The day before the operation, there is a ceremonial dance known as *matuuro*. The next day the physical operations occur. Both boys and girls are expected to endure circumcision without crying or showing signs of weakness.

Many elder Gikuyu people still maintain strong relationships with others with whom they were initiated. While mandatory painful initiation ceremonies are increasingly becoming a thing of the past, many Kenyans are troubled by what they perceive to be a rising tide of individualism and lack of peer group solidarity among the young. Young people today in Kenya must work out for themselves how to combine old customs with modern ones. This issue is a prominent theme and is the subject of stories, plays, and other programs on Kenya radio and television.

8 ● RELATIONSHIPS

The local community, school, and church are central to Gikuyu social relations. Dating, courtship, friendship, and family life are significant concerns around which people construct their social lives. In the past, social life was dominated by rules about age hierarchies and gender distinction. There is evidence that Gikuyus have more individual choice in these matters today. However, some Gikuyu have lost their sense of community responsibility so cherished in the past.

In the past, boys were organized into groups of local boys who had been initiated at the same time. These were grouped into larger groupings, called regiments. Boys in a common group or regiment proceeded through life together and exercised authority over groups and regiments coming after them. Detailed rules governed the roles of various age or generational groupings in the realms of dating and procreation, defense, and social structure.

9 ● LIVING CONDITIONS

The Gikuyu enjoy the abundant natural resources provided by the central highlands of Kenya. Due to the altitude, much of the region is free of malarial mosquitoes and the tsetse and other flies that spread human and animal diseases. The Gikuyu have had success in commercial farming and in many other businesses. Some Gikuyu now own large estates and live an affluent lifestyle. However, many other Gikuyu live in slums, which have grown rapidly in urban areas, especially Nairobi. Thousands of homeless street children have come to Nairobi from Gikuyu towns where they suffered from family dislocation and poverty.

In the past, traditional Gikuyu houses were round with wooden walls and grass thatched roofs. Neighbors generally helped in the construction of a home in exchange

for beer and meat. Building supplies were collected from local materials. A husband and wife typically lived in separate houses. The woman's house had space for her children and her sheep and goats. Well-built homes sometimes lasted for ten years or more, although rethatching the roof was an annual event.

10 ● FAMILY LIFE

Traditionally, the Gikuyu preferred large families living in big compounds. It was considered a religious obligation to have children. Four children—two boys and two girls—was the ideal. Boys were desirable because they carried on the family name, which was passed on through the male line. Girls were desired so the family could collect bride wealth (gifts to her family from her husband-to-be's family), which could in turn be used to obtain wives for their brothers. A married woman became more powerful as she bore more children. Her children stayed with her in her home, separate from their father. Polygyny (one man having multiple wives) was valued as a means to provide large families. Women, too, often preferred polygyny to monogamy (one man and one woman); they often helped their husbands find younger wives. Elder wives had clear authority over younger wives and supervised them in affairs of the compound.

Events leading to marriage began with an initial meeting of the aspiring son-in-law with his perspective parents-in-law. The young woman's agreement was required at this meeting before events could proceed. Later stages included parental visits, exchanges of goods as bride wealth, and finally the young woman moving into the home of her husband. The marriage itself was finalized when, prior to moving in with her husband's family, the young man and his relatives visited the young woman's house bearing special gifts.

Today, marriage no longer involves these traditional rituals and exchanges. Nevertheless, there is still bride wealth, significant involvement of parents in the choice of their children's spouses, and the high value placed on having children. Marriage ceremonies no longer involve Gikuyu religious rituals, which have given way to Christian and Islamic marriage practices.

11 ● CLOTHING

In the past, Gikuyu adults dressed in animal skins, especially sheep and goat skins. Skin tanning was a vital industry for which many men were renowned as specialists. Women's clothing includes three pieces—an upper garment, a skirt, and an apron. Men wore a single garment covering the entire body. Young men preferred bare legs made possible by wearing short skirts, especially those made from kidskin (lambskin or goatskin) because of its smooth hairs. Elders wore more elaborate costumes—often made of fur.

European clothing is now commonplace throughout Gikuyuland. In rural areas, women wear multicolored cotton dresses or skirts and blouses. Men generally wear Western-style trousers and shirts with jackets and ties for formal occasions. Women who prefer to dress in African fashion wear long pieces of colorful cloth as skirts and wrapped around a dress.

12 ● FOOD

Farm produce and meat are abundant and provide excellent nutrition. Maize (corn) made into a thick porridge, called *ugali*, is the national dish of Kenya. (See recipe in article on Kenyans.) Ugali is eaten with meat, stews, or traditional greens known as *sukuma wiki*. *Irio*, a Gikuyu dish, is a mixture of the kernels from cooked green corn boiled with beans, potatoes, and chopped greens.

In the past, beer brewing was a cooperative activity between men and women. Beer was made from sugarcane, maize, and millet. Gourds were used to contain the strained juices for fermenting. Today, bottled beverages generally have replaced traditional beer for daily and social consumption. Distilleries in Kenya provide an assortment of beer and soft drinks.

Eating meat is standard for all ceremonial occasions. A popular meal, especially on Sundays, is *nyama choma* (roasted meat). Goat meat is the most popular choice, although it is more expensive than beef. Chicken is also a regular treat. In the past, the Gikuyu had a ceremonial calendar that involved feasting. Boiled and roasted meat were eaten on these occasions, and beer was the beverage of choice. Although the traditional ceremonial calendar is largely a thing of the past, Gikuyu maintain an intensely social existence involving regular attendance at funerals and weddings. These events are always accompanied by an abundant supply of meat and bottled beverages.

13 ● EDUCATION

Traditionally, children were taught through an educational process that began very early in the life cycle. Infants were sung lullabies emphasizing tribal values. As a child grew, he or she listened intently to tales, riddles, and proverbs having moral messages. Even after the advent of formal schools during the colonial era, a special time was set aside for the telling of folktales. In the past, boys played games emphasizing leadership roles that involved bows and arrows, spears, and slings to teach marksmanship skills. Girls cooked imaginary dishes and played at making pots and grinding grains. Dolls, made with local clay and grass, were also standard play items for girls. As children matured, boys were trained by their adult male relatives, and girls by their mothers, grandmothers, and older sisters. For example, boys were taught to differentiate large herds of cattle or goats by their color, size, and horn texture. Fathers and grandfathers also taught youngsters the boundaries of their land, techniques for preparing land for farming, and family genealogy. Mothers taught girls about crops, soils, weather and other significant details of food production.

Today, the traditional informal educational system has been mostly replaced by formal education. In Kenya, including Gikuyuland, there has been an attempt in recent years to make formal education more sensitive to traditional values and knowledge. A hazard of teaching only modern subject matter is that traditional wisdom—such as, for example, knowledge about wild plants potentially edible during famine—becomes lost to future generations. Reaching a reasonable balance between the old and the new in the school curriculum is a constant challenge faced by Gikuyu educators. *Harambee* (which means "let's pull together") primary and secondary schools are being built throughout Gikuyuland and elsewhere in Kenya. The literacy rate (percentage of people able to read or write) in Kenya is about 50 percent, but it is lower in Gikuyuland.

14 ● CULTURAL HERITAGE

Music and dance, along with storytelling, were all emphasized in the past. Dancing by men and women was mandatory at initiation ceremonies, weddings, and other public events. People of all ages enjoyed dancing. There were three kinds of musical instruments in the past: drums, flutes, and rattles. The last were used for private pleasure, while drums and flutes were played publicly at dances. Song was woven into the fabric of everyday life. There were songs for babies; songs sung by girls while threshing millet; songs sung by boys while practicing archery; songs sung by families and community members during weddings and funerals; songs sung by community members and initiates during ceremonies; songs about everyday problems of life and love that were sung around the campfire; songs for drinking; songs about cultural heroes both past and present; and songs sung in praise of ancestors and the High God, Ngai.

Written literature includes children's literature, which recount tribal stories and tales. One such book, titled *Nyumba ya Mumbi,* graphically illustrates the Gikuyu creation myth. Perhaps the most famous twentieth-century writer is Ngugi wa Thiong'o, whose many stories, plays, and novels have chronicled the Gikuyu struggle for national identity.

15 ● EMPLOYMENT

In the past, there was a very strong division of labor by gender. Nevertheless, men and women worked together as well as separately in tasks that complemented each other. Each woman had her own plots of land where she cultivated crops such as sweet potatoes, millet, maize (corn), and beans. Men were responsible for heavy labor, such as clearing the land and cutting down trees. Household tasks for women involved maintaining granaries and supervising the feeding of sheep, goats, and cows. A polygynous husband (one with multiple wives) had his own hut apart from his wives where he ate with friends or his children and was served food by his wives. On a daily basis, women, together with their children, collected firewood, water, and produce from the garden.

There was also a division of labor by gender concerning industries. Some men were ironsmiths, manufacturing knives, arrowheads, bracelets, axes, hammers, spears, and other utilitarian tools. Only women were potters. Pottery provided for household needs. Women also excelled in making baskets. Men tended to specialize in skin tanning.

The informal educational system of the Gikuyu involved children and young people learning economic tasks from adults and specialists through direct observation and often apprenticeship.

Today, the Gikuyu remain intensely agricultural and devoted to their land. Cash crops are now significant, but the traditional division of agricultural labor is still very much in place. Through formal education and accumulation of private assets, many Gikuyu are now wealthy and enjoy affluent lifestyles. Professional occupations, as well as employment in factories and other working-class jobs, now differentiate the Gikuyu into social categories based on income. Nevertheless, among most Gikuyu, there is still a strong sense of ethnic solidarity and shared cultural heritage.

16 ● SPORTS

Throughout Gikuyuland, schools sponsor competitive sports for boys and girls. Spectators enjoy soccer (football) and track and field. In the past, Gikuyu boys enjoyed games such as wrestling, weightlifting, and club throwing. There were district mock fights pitting young boys from each area against their counterparts from elsewhere. Wrestling produced stars who were widely praised throughout the country. Girls played hide-and-seek and jumping games while still young, but became increasingly more involved with household responsibilities and marriage as they approached their mid-teen years.

17 ● RECREATION

Like other Kenyans, the Gikuyu enjoy watching television, listening to the radio, and going to movie theaters. Radio and television regularly feature tradtional Gikuyu material.

People of all ages play a board game known as *bao* in which players attempt to capture the seeds of their opponents. The game involves a wooden board containing holes in which seeds are placed. A player seeks to capture his opponent's seeds using a complex strategy whereby his opponent's seeds end up on his side of the board. This indigenous (native) African game of strategy is widespread in Africa and is now played elsewhere in the world.

18 ● CRAFTS AND HOBBIES

Traditional industries and crafts have been largely replaced by tourist and commercial markets. The most notable traditional activity still in existence is basket making, which is done by women. The Gikuyu *kiondo* (basket) is now popular in Europe and America, where it is widely used by students as a handbag or bookbag. The kiondo is a knitted basket made in various shapes, colors, and sizes. These baskets are knitted from strings gathered from shrubs. They are sometimes decorated with Gikuyu geometric designs. Another traditional folk art is the manufacture of figurines made from local materials such as clay, discarded wire, and grass. They depict scenes from solitary or communal daily life such as children playing, elders in various kinds of clothing, people dancing, bicycling, and singing.

19 ● SOCIAL PROBLEMS

Perhaps the primary social problem of the Gikuyu is how best to manage their comparative success in Kenyan commerce and politics. The Gikuyu are often opposed by groups trying to lessen the political power they hold by virtue of their large population and their relative wealth among Kenya's ethnic groups. The Gikuyu have expanded into regions outside of their central highlands homeland. Many Gikuyu, therefore, are now wealthy "immigrants," seen by groups elsewhere in Kenya as intruders and landgrabbers.

Problems in Kenya as a whole include alcoholism and the spread of human immunodeficiency virus (HIV). Consumption of alcoholic beverages is common. This combines with poorly maintained roads to produce one of the highest rates of accidental death due to driving anywhere in the world.

20 ● BIBLIOGRPAHY

Arnold, Gay. *Modern Kenya.* New York: Longman, 1981.

Dinesen, Isak. *Out of Africa.* New York: Random House, 1972.

Kenya in Pictures. Minneapolis, Minn.: Lerner Publications Co., 1988.

Presley, Cora Ann. *Kikuyu Women, the Mau Mau Rebellion, and Social Change in Kenya.* Boulder, Colo.: Westview Press, 1992.

Stein, R. *Kenya.* Chicago: Children's Press, 1985.

Themes in Kenyan History. Athens: Ohio University Press, 1990.

Webb, Lois Sinaiko. *Holidays of the World Cookbook for Students.* Phoenix, Ariz.: Oryx, 1995.

WEBSITES

Embassy of Kenya, Washington, D.C. [Online] Available http://www.embassyofkenya.com/, 1998.

Interknowledge Corp. Kenya. [Online] Available http://www.geographia.com/kenya/, 1998.

World Travel Guide. [Online] Available http://www.wtgonline.com/country/ke/gen.html, 1998.

Gusii

PRONUNCIATION: goo-SEE
LOCATION: Western Kenya
POPULATION: 1.3 million
LANGUAGE: Ekegusii
RELIGION: Christianity mixed with traditional beliefs

1 ● INTRODUCTION

At the end of the 1700s, Bantu-speaking peoples were scattered in small pockets at the northern, southern, and eastern margins of the Kisii highlands and in the Lake Victoria basin. Around 1800, the highlands above 4,970 feet (1,515 meters) were probably uninhabited from the northern part of the Manga escarpment south to the river Kuja. At that time, the lowland savannas (grasslands) were settled by large numbers of farmer-herders who were ancestors to present-day Luo and Kipsigis. These farmer-herders displaced the smaller Bantu groups from their territories on the savanna. The Gusii settled in the Kisii highlands; other related groups remained along the Lake Victoria Basin or, as the Kuria, settled in the lower savanna region at the Kenya-Tanzania border.

The British invaded these lands and established a colonial government in 1907, declaring themselves rulers. Native peoples initially responded with armed resistance, which ceased after World War I (1914–18). Unlike the situation in other highland areas of Kenya, the Gusii were not moved from their lands. The seven subdivisions of Gusiiland were converted into administrative units under government-appointed chiefs.

Missions were established to attempt to convert Gusii from their indigenous (native) beliefs to Christianity. This mission activity was not initially very successful, and several missions were looted.

After Kenyan independence in 1963, schools were built throughout Gusii lands, roads were improved, and electricity, piped water, and telephones were extended to many areas. By the 1970s, a land shortage had begun to make farming unprofitable. Since that time, education of children to prepare them for off-farm employment has become a priority.

2 ● LOCATION

Gusiiland is located in western Kenya, about 30 miles (50 kilometers) east of Lake Victoria. Abundant rainfall and very fertile soils have made Gusiiland one of the most productive agricultural areas in Kenya. Between 70 and 80 percent of the land can be cultivated. Since 1989, the Gusii as a single ethnic group have occupied the Kisii and Nyamira districts of southwestern Kenya. The area is a rolling, hilly landscape on a plain reaching altitudes of 3,900 feet (1,190 meters) in the far northwestern corner of the territory, and 6,990 feet (2,130 meters) in the central highlands. Average maximum temperatures range from 83°F (28.4°C) at the lowest altitudes to 73°F (22.8°C) at the highest elevations. The average minimum temperatures are 61.5°F (16.4°C) and 50°F (9.8°C) respectively. Rain falls throughout the year with an annual average of 60 to 80 inches (150 to 200 centimeters). In the nineteenth century, much of present-day Gusiiland was covered by moist upland forest. Today, all forest has been

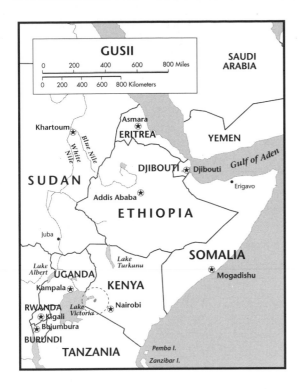

Children may also be named for a recent event, such as the weather at the time of the child's birth. Some common names refer to the time of migrations. For example, the woman's name *Kwamboka* means "crossing a river."

Talking about personal feelings is prohibited. Hence, questions about a person's mental state are answered with statements about physical health or economic situation.

4 ● FOLKLORE

Gusii oral tradition contains a number of prominent figures linked with historical events, especially migrations into the current homeland and the arrival of the British. These prominent folk figures are usually men, but a few are women. Nyakanethi and her stepson Nyakundi are two historical figures linked to the establishment of a densely populated area, the Kitutu. Nyakanethi and Nyakundi fortified themselves in the highlands to the north and gave shelter to families who fled attacks by neighboring peoples. These families were given a home in Kitutu with Nyakundi as their chief.

Other heroes are related to the establishment of the colonial administration. The prophet Sakawa, who was born in the 1840s and died around 1902, is reported to have predicted the arrival of the British in 1907 and the building of the district capital, Kisii Town.

In 1907–08, a prophetess called Muraa tried to start a rebellion against the British. In 1908 she gave her stepson, Otenyo, medicines that she believed could protect him from bullets, and she sent him to kill British Officer G.A.S. Northcote. Although Otenyo

cleared, very little indigenous (native) plants remain, and no large mammals are found.

In 1989, the number of Gusii was 1.3 million. The Gusii are one of the most rapidly growing populations in the world, increasing by 3 to 4 percent each year. The average woman bears close to nine children, and infant mortality (the proportion of infants who die) is low for sub-Saharan Africa (about 80 deaths per 1,000 live births).

3 ● LANGUAGE

The Gusii language, Ekegusii, is a Western Bantu language. It is common to name a child after a deceased person from the father's clan for the first name, and one from the mother's clan for the second name.

wounded Northcote with his spear, he survived and later became the governor of Hong Kong.

5 ● RELIGION

Before Christianity was introduced to the Gusii, they believed in one supreme god who created the world but did not interfere directly in human affairs. Instead, interference was caused by ancestor spirits (ebirecha), witches, and impersonal forces. The Gusii believed that displeased ancestor spirits were responsible for disease, the death of people and livestock, and the destruction of crops.

Today, most Gusii claim to be followers of some form of Christianity. A Roman Catholic mission was first established in 1911 and a Seventh Day Adventist mission in 1913. There are four major denominations in Gusiiland: Roman Catholic, Seventh-Day Adventist, Swedish Lutheran, and the Pentecostal Assemblies of God.

Although churches are very active, some non-Christian beliefs continue to influence the lives of most Gusii. If afflicted by misfortune, many Gusii visit a diviner (abaragori) who may point to displeased spirits of the dead and prescribe sacrifice. In addition to abaragori, who are usually women, various healers also exist. Abanyamoriogi (herbalists) use a variety of plant mixtures for medicines. Indigenous surgeons (ababari) set fractures and treat backaches and headaches through trepanation (needles). Professional sorcerers (abanyamosira) protect against witchcraft and retaliate against witches. Omoriori, the witch smeller, finds witchcraft articles hidden in a house. Witches (omorogi) can be men or women,

but are usually women. They are believed to dig up recently buried corpses to eat the inner organs and use body parts for magic. Among the Gusii, witchcraft is believed to be a learned art handed down from parent to child.

6 ● MAJOR HOLIDAYS

Only the national holidays of Kenya are celebrated (see article on "Kenyans" in this chapter).

7 ● RITES OF PASSAGE

The most important Gusii ceremonies are associated with initiation and marriage. Initiation involves genital surgery for both sexes: clitoridectomy for girls and circumcision for boys. The ceremony is supposed to train children as social beings who know rules of shame (chinsoni) and respect (ogosika). Girls are initiated at the age of seven or eight, and boys a few years later. Initiations are gender-segregated, and the operations are performed by female and male specialists. Afterward, there is a period of seclusion for both genders.

Funerals take place at the dead person's homestead, and a large gathering is a sign of prestige. Christian elements, such as catechism-reading and hymn-singing, are combined with the traditional practices of wailing, head-shaving, and animal sacrifices. Before burial, the corpse is dissected in order to determine whether death was caused by witchcraft. The Gusii tend to fear the spirit of a dead person. They believe the dead person may be angry for having died and may punish survivors. Therefore, sacrifices must be made to the spirit of the dead person to appease it.

8 ● RELATIONSHIPS

Daily interactions follow strict rules of politeness. There are rules for avoiding sexual shame *(chinsoni)* and rules governing respect *(ogosika)*. These rules are many and complicated. They regulate proper behavior between women and men, between generations, and between different kinds of relatives. For example, although anyone within the same generation may joke with each other and talk about sexual matters, this is prohibited between different generations. A father may not set foot in his son's house; a son-in-law has to avoid his mother-in-law; a daughter-in-law must not come too close to her father-in-law (she cannot even cook a meal for him). In everyday interaction, the expected behavior is one of respect and deference by young people toward older people as well as by women toward men. The Gusii are very careful about personal appearance and avoid showing themselves even partially naked. Similarly, bodily functions must not be mentioned or implied between different generations or between women and men. It is important to avoid being seen on the way to the lavatory.

A Gusii person distinguishes her or his own father and mother by specific terms: *tata* (own father) and *baba* (own mother). Likewise, parents distinguish their children as *momura one* (own son) and *mosubati one* (own daughter). However, all women and men of the same generation are considered "brothers" and "sisters." All women and men in one's parents' generation are called *tatamoke* (small father) and *makomoke* (small mother). All members of the next generation are *omwana one* (my child), grandchildrens' generation are *omochokoro* (my grandchild), and grandparents' generation are *sokoro* (grandfather) and *magokoro* (grandmother).

Hospitality and respect toward strangers is common. At the same time, the Gusii are very reserved, polite, and in many ways suspicious about others' intentions. Although interpersonal conflicts are common, people are not supposed to show outwards signs of anger. The strong emphasis on peaceful conduct and emotional control can result in explosions of violent behavior under the influence of alcohol.

One always greets strangers as well as acquaintances of one's own generation with a simple phrase similar to our "Hi, how are you?" *(Naki ogendererete)*. However, when visiting a homestead or meeting a relative, a more complete greeting ritual is necessary. This includes asking about each other's homes, children, and spouses. Unannounced visiting is not considered polite; a message should be delivered before a visit.

Body language is reserved and gesturing is kept to a minimum. Between people of unequal status, such as young and old or woman and man, the person of lower status is not supposed to look directly into the other's eyes.

Interactions between unmarried young people were once strictly regulated. Today, young men and women meet and socialize in many places outside the home. Premarital sex is common, and many girls end up as single mothers. Young people write love letters to each other, and in general subscribe to Western ideas of love.

9 ● LIVING CONDITIONS

Before British colonization, the Gusii lived in two separate groups: the homestead (*omochie*)—where a married man, his wives, and their unmarried daughters and uncircumcised sons lived, and the cattle camps (*ebisarate*) in the grazing areas—where most of the cattle were watched by resident male warriors. A homestead consisted of wives' houses, houses for circumcised boys, and possibly a small day hut for the husband. Married men did not have their own house for sleeping, but alternated between their wives' houses. A compound had several elevated granaries for millet. The traditional Gusii house (*enyomba*) was a round, windowless structure made of a framework of thin branches with dried mud walls and a conical thatched roof. Today, the Gusii continue to live in dispersed homesteads in the middle of farm holdings. Modern houses are rectangular, with thatched or corrugated iron roofs. Cooking is done in a separate building.

10 ● FAMILY LIFE

Mothers are ultimately responsible for the care and raising of children. However, they delegate many childrearing tasks to other children in the family. Fathers take very little part in child rearing. Grandparents play a supportive role and are supposed to teach grandchildren about proper behavior and about sexual matters. Mothers seldom show physical or verbal affection to children. Children stop sleeping in their mother's house when they are still very young.

Marriage is established through the payment of bride wealth (in the form of livestock and money), paid by the husband to the wife's family. This act establishes a socially approved marriage. Residence is at the husband's family's home. Divorce is rare and requires the return of the bride wealth. Upon the death of a husband, a widow chooses a husband from among the dead man's brothers.

Until the 1960s, everyone got married as soon as possible after puberty. However, at the end of the 1960s, elopements started to increase. Since then, the period between the beginning of cohabitation (living together) and payment of bride wealth has become increasingly long. In 1985, at least 75 percent of all new unions between women and men were established without the payment of bride wealth. The lack of bride wealth payment means that a union has no social or legal foundation; this has resulted in a large class of poor single mothers with no access to land.

Households are based on nuclear (husband, wife, and children) or polygynous (multiple-wife) families. In polygynous families, each wife has her own household and there is little cooperation between co-wives. With the decline in polygyny, a domestic unit typically consists of a wife and husband and their unmarried children. It may also include the husband's mother, and for brief periods of time, younger siblings of the wife. Until the birth of the first or second child, a wife and her mother-in-law may cook together and cooperate in farming. Married sons and their wives and children usually maintain their own households and resources.

11 ● CLOTHING

Western-style clothing is always worn.

12 ● FOOD

Before British colonization, the main crop grown in Gusiiland was finger millet, which the Gusii considered very nourishing (they also believed it strengthened a person's physical and mental power and increased a man's sexual prowess). Sorghum, beans, and sweet potatoes were also cultivated. These foods were complemented by meat and milk from livestock as well as wild vegetables.

The staple is now corn, which is ground into flour. Corn flour is mixed into boiling water to form a thick doughlike paste (*obokima*) that is eaten at all meals. A meal usually includes fried cabbage, tomatoes, and some potatoes. Depending on how well-off the family is, chicken or goat may be served. The *obokima* is formed into a spoon with one's fingers, and then used to scoop up the meat. Other popular foods are sour milk, goat intestines, and millet porridge. Finger millet was the traditional staple before the introduction of corn; it is

13 ● EDUCATION

Education is in high demand. There are about 200 high schools, the majority of which are community-supported. There are also a number of private schools. Unfortunately, high school is too expensive for many families. Although primary schools are free, there are other costs, such as books, building fees, and so forth. By the 1980s, fewer than 50 percent of all Gusii children attended secondary school, but all Gusii children attended primary school.

14 ● CULTURAL HERITAGE

Older people know many traditional songs. The favorite instrument is the *obokhano* (lyre).

15 ● EMPLOYMENT

A high population density has forced the Gusii to utilize all available space for agriculture, and families today are unable to produce enough to feed themselves. In part because of this, many Gusii are engaged in non-agricultural employment, either locally or in the large urban centers. Farmers use iron hoes and ox-drawn plows. Farmers still keep cattle (both local zebu and European types), goats, sheep, and chickens. Maize (corn), cassava, pigeon peas, onions, bananas, potatoes, and tomatoes are important commercial crops. By the 1950s Gusiiland had become established as a producer of coffee and tea.

In the late nineteenth century, women were primarily responsible for cultivation, food preparation, and housecleaning. Men were concerned with warfare, house- and fence-building, clearing new fields, and herding. Although women performed most of the cultivation, men participated much more than they do today. As men have withdrawn from cultivation, women must perform most of their traditional tasks in addition to many of the men's former tasks. Women do most of the work to feed their families, and many husbands drink and visit friends while their wives work in the fields and take care of the households.

16 ● SPORTS

Wrestling used to be a popular sport for men, but it has declined in recent years. Various Western athletic activities have been introduced. The most popular sport among boys is soccer, and most schools have a soccer field. Other sports include table tennis, netball (similar to basketball), and cycling.

17 ● RECREATION

Traditional dancing and music were once popular, but today few outlets exist in the countryside for such entertainment. Among men, a main form of recreation consists of drinking beer.

18 ● CRAFTS AND HOBBIES

In pre-colonial Gusiiland, a variety of goods were manufactured: iron tools, weapons, decorations, wooden implements, small baskets for porridge, and poisons. Pottery-making was limited, and most pottery was made by the Luo people and imported. The most technically complex and valuable items manufactured were iron implements, made from smelting locally obtained ore. Smithing was reserved for men, and blacksmiths became wealthy and influential.

Gusii soapstone carvings have become internationally recognized. The stone is mined and carved in Tabaka, South Mugirango, where several families specialize in this art. The craft is bringing a sizable income to the area through the tourist trade.

19 ● SOCIAL PROBLEMS

Alcoholism and violence toward women are the most severe social problems. Traditionally, only older people were allowed to drink large amounts of locally brewed beer (amarua). Today, social control over drinking has broken down, and traditional beer and home-distilled spirits are served in huts all over the district. Probably close to 50 percent of young and middle-aged Gusii are regular drinkers, with a larger proportion of men than women. This heavy drinking leads to violence, neglect of children, and poverty. The Gusii also have high murder rates compared to the rest of Kenya. Although violence toward women (such as rape and beatings) has been part of Gusii culture since earlier in this century, alcohol is probably a factor in its increase.

The exploitation of women in Gusii society is a serious human rights problem. According to customary law, which is usually followed in the countryside, women cannot inherit or own land, cattle, or other resources. This makes them completely dependent on men for survival and attainment of any future security. Until a woman has adult sons, she is under the authority of her husband and has to ask permission from him to leave the homestead. In addition, the Gusii practice female genital mutilation, which is practiced regularly even though it is prohibited by law. Sometimes called female circumcision, this surgery robs girls of the possibility for sexual satisfaction. The practice is intended to keep girls and women "in line," and it has attracted the attention of human rights advocates around the world.

20 ● BIBLIOGRPAHY

Arnold, Gay. *Modern Kenya.* New York: Longman, 1981.

Dinesen, Isak. *Out of Africa.* New York: Random House, 1972.

Kenya in Pictures. Minneapolis, Minn.: Lerner Publications Co., 1988.

LeVine, Sarah. *Mothers and Wives: Gusii Women of East Africa.* Chicago: University of Chicago Press, 1979.

Liyong, Taban lo. *Popular Culture of East Africa.* Nairobi: Longman Kenya, 1972.

Stein, R. *Kenya.* Chicago: Children's Press, 1985.

Themes in Kenyan History. Athens: Ohio University Press, 1990.

Webb, Lois Sinaiko. *Holidays of the World Cookbook for Students.* Phoenix, Ariz.: Oryx, 1995.

WEBSITES

Embassy of Kenya, Washington, D.C. [Online] Available http://www.embassyofkenya.com/, 1998.

Interknowledge Corp. Kenya. [Online] Available http://www.geographia.com/kenya/, 1998.

World Travel Guide. [Online] Available http://www.wtgonline.com/country/ke/gen.html, 1998.

Kalenjin

PRONUNCIATION: KAH-len-jeen
LOCATION: Kenya
POPULATION: About 2.7 million
LANGUAGE: Kalenjin; Swahili; English
RELIGION: Christianity (Africa Inland Church [AIC], the Church of the Province of Kenya [CPK], Roman Catholic Church); Islam

1 ● INTRODUCTION

The Kalenjin live primarily in Kenya. They are an ethnic grouping of eight culturally and linguistically related groups or "tribes": the Kipsigis, Nandi, Tugen, Keiyo, Marakwet, Pokot (sometimes called the Suk), Sabaot (who live in the Mount Elgon region, overlapping the Kenya/Uganda border), and the Terik. Their present-day homeland is Kenya's western highlands and the Rift Valley.

Kalenjin translates roughly as "I tell you." The name has played a crucial role in the construction of this relatively new ethnic identity among formerly independent, but culturally and linguistically similar tribes. The origin of the name Kalenjin and the Kalenjin ethnic identity can be traced to the 1940s. It represents a clear desire to draw political strength from greater numbers.

Beginning in the 1940s, individuals from these groups who were going off to fight in World War II (1939–45) used the term *kale* or *kole* (the process of scarring the breast or the arm of a warrior who had killed an enemy in battle) to refer to themselves. During wartime radio broadcasts, an announcer, John Chemallan, used the phrase *kalenjok* ("I tell you," plural). Later, individuals from these groups who were attending Alliance High School formed a "Kalenjin" club. Fourteen in number, they constituted a distinct minority in this prestigious school in an area dominated by another tribe, the Gikuyu. The Kalenjin wanted an outward manifestation of identity and solidarity to distinguish them from the Gikuyu. These young high school students formed what would become the future Kalenjin elite. Kalenjin identity was consolidated with the founding of a Kalenjin Union in Eldoret in 1948, and the publication of a monthly magazine called *Kalenjin* in the 1950s.

The Kalenjin movement was not simply the development of a people's identity. The British colonial government supported the Kalenjin movement and sponsored the *Kalenjin* monthly magazine out of a desire to foster anti-Gikuyu sentiments during the Mau Mau emergency. The Mau Mau movement was a mostly Gikuyu-led revolt against British colonialism that provoked an official state of emergency lasting from

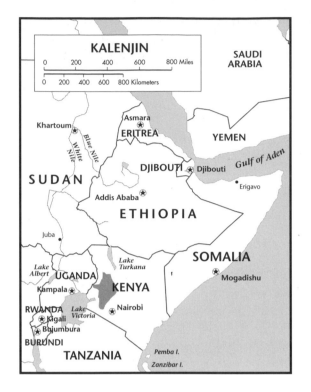

KALENJIN

| 0 | 200 | 400 | 600 | 800 Miles |

| 0 | 200 | 400 | 600 | 800 Kilometers |

elders were given the opportunity to state their opinions. Rather than making decisions himself, the *poiyot ap kokwet* expressed the group's opinion, always phrased in terms of a group decision.

Today, this system has been replaced with a system imposed by the British colonial government. Several villages form a sublocation, which is part of a location. Several locations form a division, divisions form districts, and districts are included in provinces. Each village has a village elder who settles minor disputes and handles routine affairs. Assistant chiefs, chiefs, district officers, district commissioners, and provincial commissioners rule each of the other levels of administration, the latter directly under the president's authority.

2 ● LOCATION

Accurate population estimates for Kenya are difficult to acquire. Recent estimates put Kenya's total population at 27.5 million people in 1993, with the Kalenjin totalling 2.7 million people. In the late 1980s, there were about 1.2 million Kalenjin, while Kenya's total population was some 22 to 24 million people. Together, the Kalenjin comprise Kenya's fourth-largest ethnic group. The Kipsigis are the largest Kalenjin population, with approximately 470,000 people. The rest of the Kalenjin and their estimated populations are as follows: Nandi (260,000); Tugen (130,000); Keiyo (110,000); Pokot (90,000); Marakwet (80,000); Sabaot (40,000); and Terik (20,000).

October 1952 to January 1960. Gikuyu conflicts both with the British and with non-Gikuyu tribes (including the Kalenjin) factored in the creation of Kalenjin solidarity and unity.

Traditionally, the basic unit of political organization among the Kalenjin was the *koret* or parish. This was a collection of twenty to one hundred scattered homesteads. It was administered by a council of adult males known collectively as the *kokwet* and was led by a spokesman called *poiyot ap kokwet*. This spokesman was someone recognized for his speaking abilities, knowledge of tribal laws, forceful personality, wealth, and social position. At public proceedings, although the *poiyot ap kokwet* was the first to speak, all of the

3 ● LANGUAGE

The first language of the Kalenjin peoples is Kalenjin, part of the Chari-Nile language group of Africa. Three Kalenjin dialect groups have been identified. Although the various dialects are all supposedly understood by all Kalenjin, speakers of one dialect often have difficulty understanding speakers of another. Most Kalenjin people also speak KiSwahili and English, since both are official national languages in Kenya and are taught in school.

4 ● FOLKLORE

Oral tradition was and still is very important among the Kalenjin. Prior to the introduction of writing, folktales served to convey a sense of cultural history. The Kalenjin have four oral traditions: stories, songs, proverbs, and riddles. Stories are usually about both people and animals, and certain animals are thought to have particular character traits. For example, the hare is a trickster figure whose cleverness can get him in trouble, the lion is courageous and wise, and the hyena is greedy and destructive.

Songs accompany both work and play, as well as ceremonial occasions such as births, initiations, and weddings. Proverbs convey important messages and are often used when elders settle disputes or advise youths. Riddles involve word play and are especially popular with children.

5 ● RELIGION

Traditional Kalenjin religion is based upon the belief in a supreme god, *Asis* or *Cheptalel,* who is represented in the form of the sun, although this is not God himself. Beneath *Asis* is *Elat,* who controls thunder and lightning. Spirits of the dead, *oyik,* are believed to intervene in the affairs of humans, and can be placated with sacrifices of meat and/or beer, called *koros.* Diviners, called *orkoik,* have magical powers and assist in appeals for rain or to end floods.

Today, nearly everyone claims membership in an organized religion—either Christianity or Islam. Major Christian sects include the Africa Inland Church (AIC), the Church of the Province of Kenya (CPK), and the Roman Catholic Church. Muslims are relatively few in number among the Kalenjin. For the most part, only older people can recall details of traditional religious beliefs.

6 ● MAJOR HOLIDAYS

Today, the major holidays observed by the Kalenjin are mostly those associated with Christianity (Christmas and Easter), and national holidays such as Jamhuri (Republic) Day, Madaraka (Responsibility) Day, Moi (the current president) Day, and Kenyatta (the first president) Day. At Christmas, it is common for people still living in traditional mud-walled houses to give the outer walls a new coat of clay whitewash and paint them with holiday greetings (such as "Merry Christmas" and "Happy New Year").

There are three month-long school holidays in April, August, and December. The first two coincide with peak periods in the agricultural cycle and allow children of various ages to assist their families during these busy times. The December holiday corresponds with both Christmas and the traditional initiation ceremonies, *tumdo.*

7 • RITES OF PASSAGE

For both males and females, becoming an adult in Kalenjin society is a matter of undergoing an initiation ceremony. Traditionally, these were held about every seven years. Everyone undergoing initiation, or *tumdo*, thereby becomes a member of a named age-set, or *ipinda*.

After male youths were circumcised, they were secluded for lengthy periods during which they were instructed in the skills necessary for adulthood. Afterward, they would begin a phase of warriorhood during which they acted as the military force of the tribe. Elders provided guidance and wisdom. Today, age-sets have lost their military function, but still provide bonds between men of the same set. Female age-sets have lost much of their importance.

In the past, only people who had borne children would be buried after death; the others would be taken out to the bush and left to be eaten by hyenas. Today all Kalenjin are buried, but not in a cemetery. People are returned to their farm, or *shamba,* for burial. There is usually no grave marker, but family members, friends, and neighbors know where people are laid to rest.

8 • RELATIONSHIPS

Chamge or *chamuge* is the standard greeting among the Kalenjin. If people meet face-to-face, the spoken greeting is almost always accompanied by a hearty handshake, and people often clasp their own right elbow with their left hand. The response is the same—*chamge*, sometimes repeated several times. It may be emphasized with *mising,* which can mean either "very much" or "close friend," depending upon the context. As a sign of respect, a younger person greets someone of their grandparents' generation by saying, *chamge kogo* (grandmother) or *chamge kugo* (grandfather).

Holding hands after greeting is very common for people of the same sex. Even when walking, these people may hold hands or lock little fingers. There is no sexual connotation to this behavior. People of opposite sexes are strongly discouraged from these and other public displays of affection. In their conversations Kalenjin do not point out objects or people with their fingers. Instead, they point by turning their head in the proper direction and puckering their lips briefly.

Taking leave of someone is accompanied by the farewell, *sait sere* (meaning literally, "blessing time"), and hearty handshakes. Often people walk with their visitor(s) a distance in order to continue the conversation and to give their friend(s) "a push." Once again, these people often hold hands.

In the past, dating and courtship were almost entirely matters of family concern. Today, young men and women have more freedom to exercise their own choice, especially those living at boarding schools. Young people meet and socialize at dances in town discos and in cafes called *hoteli* in KiSwahili. Still, when a young man decides on a wife, he and his father's family must gather together a suitable bride price payment to be given to the bride's family. In the past, this consisted almost entirely of livestock, but today it is becoming more common to use money in place of or in addition to livestock.

9 ● LIVING CONDITIONS

Traditionally, Kalenjin houses were round. Walls were constructed of bent saplings anchored to larger posts and covered with a mixture of mud and cow dung; roofs were thatched with local grasses. While these kinds of houses are still common, there is a growing trend toward the construction of square or rectangular houses built with timber walls and roofs of corrugated sheet metal.

Most Kalenjin are rural dwellers who do not have electricity or indoor plumbing. Radio/cassette players; kerosene lamps and stoves; charcoal stoves; aluminum cooking pots; plastic dishes, plates, and cups; and bicycles are the most common consumer items. Those few people who do not have electricity but who do have televisions use car batteries for power.

10 ● FAMILY LIFE

Typically, after marriage a man brought his wife to live with him in, or very near to, his father's homestead. Marriage of one man to multiple wives (polygyny) was and is permitted, although most men cannot afford the expense of such unions because of the burden of paying the bride price. Regardless of the type of marriage, children were traditionally seen as a blessing from God. As a result of this, until very recently Kenya had the highest population growth rate in the world.

Monogamous marriages (one husband and one wife) now prevail and nuclear families (a man, a woman, and their children) are becoming more common. Moreover, younger people are now expressing a desire to have fewer children when they get married. This is due to the increasing expense of having many children who not only must be fed but also educated. To some degree, young women are also changing their aspirations, wanting careers in addition to being mothers.

11 ● CLOTHING

Traditional Kalenjin clothing consisted of skins of either domesticated or wild animals. Earrings were common for both sexes in the past, including heavy brass coils that made the earlobe stretch down almost to the shoulder. Today, the Western-style dress of most Kalenjin, even in rural areas, is hardly different from that of people in nearby towns. Men wear trousers and shirts, usually with a suit jacket or sport coat. Women wear skirts and blouses, dresses, and/or *khangas*—locally made commercial textiles that are used as wraps (one for the top and one for the bottom). Young people of both sexes like T-shirts with logos, especially those of American sports teams or ones bearing the likeness of famous entertainers such as Michael Jackson or Madonna.

12 ● FOOD

The staple Kalenjin food is *ugali*. This is a cake-like, starchy food that is made from white cornmeal mixed with boiling water and stirred vigorously while cooking. It is eaten with the hands and is often served with cooked green vegetables such as kale. Less frequently it is served with roasted goat meat, beef, or chicken. Before the introduction and widespread diffusion of corn in recent times, millet and sorghum (native African grains) were staple cereals. All of these grains were, and still are, used to make a very thick beer that has a relatively low alcohol content. Another popular beverage is *mursik*. This consists of fermented whole milk that has been stored in a special gourd, cleaned by using a burning stick. The result is that the milk is infused with tiny bits of charcoal.

Lunch and dinner are the main meals of the day. Breakfast usually consists of tea (with milk and sugar) and leftovers from the previous night's meal, or perhaps some store-bought bread. Meal times, as well as the habit of tea-drinking, were adopted from the British colonial period. Lunch and dinner are both eaten late by American standards. In addition to bread, people routinely buy foodstuffs such as sugar, tea leaves, cooking fat, sodas (most often Orange Fanta and Coca-Cola), and other items that they do not produce themselves.

13 ● EDUCATION

Traditionally, education among the Kalenjin was provided during a period of seclusion following circumcision. Young men and women were taught how to be a functioning and productive adult member of society. Nowadays, young men and women are still secluded after initiation, but for shorter periods (one month as compared with three months in the past). The timing of the December school holiday coincides with the practice of initiation and seclusion.

Primary school education in Kenya is free, since no tuition is charged. However, parents must provide their children with uniforms, books, pens, pencils, and paper, as well as contribute to frequent school fundraising activities. These expenses constitute a tremendous financial burden for families in a country where the average adult earns less than $300 per year. Post-primary school education is relatively expensive, even at the cheaper secondary schools, and entry is competitive. Tuition at the more prestigious high schools, which are all boarding schools, is very expensive. Most parents must rely on contributions from a wide circle of family, neighbors, and friends to meet the high tuition costs. Tuition at Kenya's universities is not high, but the selection process is grueling and relatively few students who want to attend are admitted.

14 ● CULTURAL HERITAGE

Traditionally, music and dance served many functions. Songs accompanied many work-related activities, including, for men, herding livestock and digging the fields, and, for women, grinding corn, washing clothes, and putting babies to sleep (with lullabies). Music was also an integral part of ceremonial occasions such as births, initiations, and weddings. Dances for these occasions were performed while wearing ankle bells and were accompanied by traditional instruments such as flutes, horns, and drums.

15 ● EMPLOYMENT

Most Kalenjin make a living by cultivating grains such as sorghum and millet (and more recently corn), and raising cattle, goats, and sheep. Farming and raising animals tend to be separate activities since grazing land is usually located a distance from the fields and homesteads.

In Kalenjin societies, much of the work, is traditionally divided along gender lines. Men are expected to do the heavy work of initially clearing the fields that are to be used for planting, as well as turning over the soil. Women take over the bulk of the farming work, including planting, weeding, harvesting (although men tend to pitch in), and processing crops. Women are also expected to perform nearly all of the domestic work involved in running a household. Men are supposedly more involved with herding livestock than with other pursuits. However, when men are engaged in wage labor away from home, women, children (especially boys), and the elderly care for animals just as often as men.

16 ● SPORTS

Soccer is of major interest to the Kalenjin, especially the youth, as it is with many other Kenyans. Nonetheless, running (especially middle and longer distances) is the sport that has made the Kalenjin people famous in world athletic circles. St. Patrick's High School in Iten has trained many world-class runners.

17 ● RECREATION

In rural areas, the radio is still the main form of entertainment. KBC (Kenya Broadcasting Corporation) programs are popular, as are shortwave radio transmissions by the BBC (British Broadcasting Corporation) and the VOA (Voice of America). A relatively small number of people have televisions, and the only programming available is from KBC. In towns and trading centers, video parlors are becoming common, and action films (starring Chuck Norris, Sylvester Stallone, Bruce and Brandon Lee, and others) are especially popular.

18 ● CRAFTS AND HOBBIES

In other parts of Kenya, the famous sisal bags (called *kiondo* in KiSwahili) are manufactured and marketed worldwide. Although the Kalenjin are not well known for their handicrafts, women do make and locally sell decorated calabashes *(sotet)* from gourds. These are rubbed with oil and adorned with small colored beads.

19 ● SOCIAL PROBLEMS

Cigarette smoking is common among Kalenjin men but not among women. The same is true for alcohol consumption. Commercially bottled beer is expensive, as are distilled spirits. The Kenyan government has banned the brewing and distillation of traditional homemade alcoholic beverages, including *busaa,* a beer made from fried, fermented corn and millet, and *chang'aa,* a liquor distilled from *busaa.* Nevertheless, these beverages continue to be popular, especially with men, and they provide some individuals, mostly women, with supplementary income. *Chang'aa* can be lethal since there is no way to control the high alcohol content (unlike that of *busaa,* which tends to have a very low alcohol content), and there are many opportunities for contamination. It is very common to open the Kenyan daily newspapers and read stories of men dying after attending drinking parties.

Livestock rustling has always been part of Kalenjin culture, and this continues to be true. The difference is that now, instead of spears and bows and arrows, cattle rustlers use semiautomatic weapons such as AK 47 assault rifles.

20 ● BIBLIOGRPAHY

Arnold, Gay. *Modern Kenya.* New York: Longman, 1981.

Chesaina, C. *Oral Literature of the Kalenjin.* Nairobi: Heinemann Kenya, 1991.

Dinesen, Isak. *Out of Africa.* New York: Random House, 1972.

Edgerton, Robert. *Mau Mau: An African Crucible.* New York: Free Press, 1989.

Kenya in Pictures. Minneapolis, Minn.: Lerner Publications Co., 1988.

Miller, Norman, and Rodger Yeager. *Kenya: The Quest for Prosperity.* 2nd ed. Boulder, Colo.: Westview Press, 1994.

Stein, R. *Kenya.* Chicago: Children's Press, 1985.

Themes in Kenyan History. Athens: Ohio University Press, 1990.

Throup, David. *Economic and Social Origins of Mau Mau, 1945–53.* Athens: Ohio University Press, 1989.

Webb, Lois Sinaiko. *Holidays of the World Cookbook for Students.* Phoenix, Ariz.: Oryx, 1995.

WEBSITES

Embassy of Kenya, Washington, D.C. [Online] Available http://www.embassyofkenya.com/, 1998.

Interknowledge Corp. Kenya. [Online] Available http://www.geographia.com/kenya/, 1998.

World Travel Guide. [Online] Available http://www.wtgonline.com/country/ke/gen.html, 1998.

Luhya

PRONUNCIATION: LOO-ee-ah
ALTERNATE NAMES: Luyia, Abaluhya
LOCATION: Western Kenya
POPULATION: 3 million
LANGUAGE: Several Bantu dialects
RELIGION: Christianity (Catholicism, Protestantism); Islam; some indigenous beliefs

1 ● INTRODUCTION

The Luhya, Luyia, or Abaluhya, as they are interchangeably called, are the second-largest ethnic group in Kenya, after the Kikuyu. The Luhya belong to the larger linguistic stock known as the Bantu. The Luhya comprise several subgroups with different but mutually understood linguistic dialects. Some of these subgroups are Ababukusu, Abanyala, Abatachoni, Avalogoli, Abamarama, Abaidakho, Abaisukha, Abatiriki, Abakisa, Abamarachi, and Abasamia.

Migration to their present western Kenya location dates back to as early as the second half of the fifteenth century. Immigrants into present-day Luhyaland came mainly from eastern and western Uganda and trace their ancestry mainly to several Bantu groups, and to other non-Bantu groups such as the Kalenjin, Luo, and Maasai. Early migration was probably motivated by a search for more and better land, and to escape local conflicts, tsetse flies, and mosquitoes. By about 1850, migration into Luhyaland was largely complete, and only minor internal movements took place after that due to food shortages, disease, and domestic conflicts. Despite their diverse ethnic ancestry, the Luhya have a history of intermarriage, local trade, and shared social and cultural practices. Variations in dialects and customs reflect their diverse ancestry.

Colonization of Kenya by the British from the 1890s to 1963 forced many communities, including the Luhya, into migrant labor on settler plantations and in urban centers. Because of their large population, the Luhya are considered a powerful political force and have always been active in politics in Kenya.

2 ● LOCATION

The Luhya people make their home mainly in the western part of Kenya. Administratively, they occupy mostly Western province, and the west-central part of Rift Valley province. Luhya migration into the Rift Valley is relatively recent, only dating back to the first few years after independence in 1963, when farms formerly occupied by colonial white settlers were bought by, or given back to, indigenous (native) Africans.

According to the last national population census conducted in 1989, the Luhya people number just over 3 million, making up over 10 percent of Kenya's total population. The Luhya are the second-largest ethnic group in Kenya, after the Kikuyu. Although most Luhya live in western Kenya, especially in the rural areas, an increasingly large number of Luhya have migrated to major urban centers such as Nairobi in search of employment and educational opportunities. About 900,000 Luhya people live outside of Western province. This is about 30 percent of the total Luhya population.

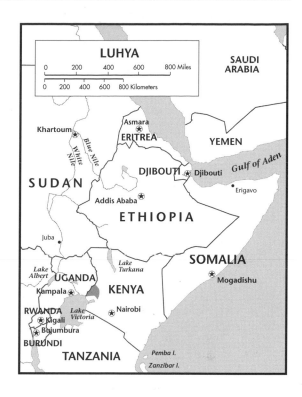

3 ● LANGUAGE

There is no single Luhya language. Rather, there are several mutually understood dialects that are principally Bantu. Perhaps the most identifying linguistic feature of the various Luhya dialects is the use of the prefix *aba-* or *ava-*, meaning "of" or "belonging to." Thus, for example, *Abalogoli* or *Avalogoli* means "people of *logoli*."

Luhya names have specific meanings. Children are named after climatic seasons, and also after their ancestors, often their deceased grandparents or great-grandparents. Among the Ababukusu, the name Wafula (for a boy) and Nafula (for a girl) would mean "born during heavy rains," while Wekesa (for a boy) and Nekesa (for a girl) would mean "born in the harvest season." With European contact and the introduction of Christianity at the turn of the twentieth century, Christian and Western European names began to be given as first names, followed by traditional Luhya names. Thus, for example, a boy might be named Joseph Wafula, and a girl, Grace Nekesa.

4 ● FOLKLORE

One of the most common myths among the Luhya group relates to the origin of the Earth and human beings. According to this myth, *Were* (God) first created Heaven, then Earth. The Earth created by *Were* had three types of soil: top soil, which was black; intermediate soil, which was red; and bottom soil, which was white. From the black soil, *Were* created a black man; from the red soil, he created a brown man; and from the white soil, he created a white man.

5 ● RELIGION

The Luhya people traditionally believed in and worshiped only one god, *Were* (also known as *Nyasaye*). *Were* was worshiped through intermediaries (go-betweens), usually the spirits of dead relatives. The spirits had considerable benevolent (positive) as well as malevolent (destructive) power and thus had to be appeased through animal sacrifices, such as goats, chickens, and cattle.

At the turn of the twentieth century, Christianity was introduced to Luhyaland and to the rest of Kenya. Christianity spread widely during the colonial period. The overwhelming majority of Luhya people now consider themselves Christians. Both Catholicism and Protestantism are prac-

ticed. Among the Abawanga, Islam is also practiced.

Despite conversion to Christianity, belief in spirits and witchcraft is still common. It is not unusual to find people offering prayers in church and at the same time consulting witch doctors or medicine men for assistance with problems.

6 ● MAJOR HOLIDAYS

There are no holidays that are uniquely Luhya. Rather, the Luhya people celebrate the national holidays of Kenya along with the rest of the nation. Among the Abalogoli and Abanyole, an annual cultural festival has recently been initiated, but it is not yet widely adopted. The festival is held on December 31.

7 ● RITES OF PASSAGE

Having many children is considered a virtue, and childlessness is seen as a great misfortune. Many births take place in the home, but increasingly women are urged to give birth in hospitals or other health facilities. The placenta *(engori)* and the umbilical cord *(olulera)* are buried behind the hut at a secret spot so they will not be found and tampered with by a witch *(omulogi)*. For births that take place in hospitals or other places outside of home, these rituals are not observed.

Until about fifteen years ago, elaborate initiation ceremonies to mark the transition from childhood to adulthood were performed for both boys and girls. Among other things, these rites included circumcision for boys. Uncircumcised boys *(avasinde)* were not allowed to marry or join in many other adult activities. Nowadays circumcision still takes place, but the ceremonies are still elaborate and public only among the Ababukusu and Abatiriki peoples.

Death and funeral rites involve not only the bereaved family, but also other relatives and the community. While it is known that many deaths occur through illnesses like malaria and tuberculosis, as well as road accidents, quite a few deaths are still believed to occur from witchcraft. Burial often takes place in the homestead of the deceased. Among the Luhya, funerals and burials are public and open events. Animals are slaughtered, and food and drinks are brought to feed the mourners. Because many people today are Christians, burial ceremonies often involve prayers in church and at the dead person's home, even when traditional rituals are also practiced. Music and dance, both traditional Luhya and Western-style, take place, mostly at night.

8 ● RELATIONSHIPS

Greetings among the Luhya salute a person, and also involve inquiries about their well-being and that of their families. People take a keen interest in one another's affairs. Shaking hands is a very common form of greeting, and for people who are meeting for the first time in a long while, the handshake will involve not just the clasping of hands, but also a vigorous jerking of the arm. Shaking hands between a man and his mother-in-law is not allowed among some Luhya communities. Hugging is not common. Women may hug each other, but cross-gender hugging is rare.

Women are expected to defer to men, especially to their husbands, fathers-in-law,

and the older brothers of their husband. Thus, in a conversation with any of these men, women will tend (or are expected) to lower their heads, fold their hands, and look down.

Visits are very common among the Luhya people. Most visits are casual and unannounced. Families strive to provide food for their visitors, especially tea.

Dating among the Luhya is informal and is often not publicly displayed, especially among teenagers. Unless a marriage is seriously intended and planned, a man or a woman may not formally invite their date to their parents' home and introduce him or her.

9 ● LIVING CONDITIONS

Major health concerns among the Luhya include the prevalence of diseases such as scabies, diarrhea, malaria, malnutrition, and, lately, human immunodeficiency virus (HIV).

In rural areas, the Luhya live in homesteads with extended families. Houses are mostly made of grass-thatched roofs and mud walls, but an increasing number are made with corrugated iron roofs, and in some cases, walls made of concrete blocks. Houses tend to be round or square. Because of the poverty in rural areas, people own very few material goods, and items such as transistor radios and bicycles are highly valued. Cars and televisions are lacking for the most part among the Luhya.

People rely on public transportation (buses and vans), but travel on foot and on bicycles is also very common. Roads in the rural hinterland are not paved and tend to be impassable during heavy rains.

10 ● FAMILY LIFE

In the rural areas among the Luhya, people live in homesteads or compounds, with each homestead comprising several houses. In one homestead may live an old man (the patriarch, or family head), his married sons and their wives and children, his unmarried sons and daughters, and sometimes other relatives. Even though each household may run its own affairs, there is a lot of obligatory sharing within the homestead. Families tend to be large, with the average number of children per woman reaching eight.

Women are expected to yield to the wishes of men. Acts of defiance or insubordination by women toward their husbands, fathers-in-law, or other senior male relatives can result in beatings from male relatives, especially one's husband.

Marriage partners must be chosen from outside one's parents' clans or lineages. Polygyny (a man marrying more than one wife) is not widely practiced these days among the Luhya, but it is still fairly common among the Ababukusu subgroup. Traditionally, a request for marriage is made between the parents of the man and the woman. If the marriage is agreed upon, bride wealth of cattle and cash, called *uvukwi* among the Avalogoli subgroup, is paid. Nowadays, however, young people increasingly get married on their own with little input from their parents. Civil and church (Christian) marriages are also becoming common. Bride wealth is still being paid, but amounts differ widely and payment schedules are not strictly honored.

The Luhya keep dogs for security, and cats are kept to manage the mouse population.

11 ● CLOTHING

Ordinarily, the Luhya dress just like their fellow Kenyans, wearing locally manufactured and imported dresses, pants, shirts, shoes, and so forth. Elementary and high school students wear uniforms to school. Women almost never wear pants. Those who dare to do so are considered abnormal and may even be verbally assaulted by men. It is particularly inappropriate for a married woman to wear pants or a short skirt or dress in the presence of her father-in-law. Earrings, necklaces, and bangle bracelets are commonly worn by women. Men generally do not wear earrings.

Traditional clothing is worn mostly during specific occasions and only by certain people. In cultural dances, performers may put on feathered hats and skirts made of sisal strands. For the Luhya groups that still maintain the traditional circumcision rites (especially the Ababukusu), the initiates will often put on clothing made of skins and paint themselves with red ochre (a pigment) or ash.

12 ● FOOD

Breakfast among the Luhya consists mainly of tea. The preferred tea is made with plenty of milk and sugar. For those who can afford it, wheat bread bought from the stores is eaten with tea. Tea and bread, however, are too expensive for many families to eat on a regular basis; consequently, porridge made of maize (corn), millet, or finger millet flour is consumed instead. Lunch and supper often consist of *ovukima*—maize flour added to boiling water and cooked into a thick paste similar to American grits. *Ovukima* is eaten with various vegetables such as kale and collard greens, and for those who can afford it, beef or chicken. Chicken is a delicacy and is prepared for important guests or for special occasions.

The main cooking utensils are pots made of steel or other metals. They are mass-manufactured in the country as well as imported. Clay pots are also still used by many families for preparing and storing traditional beer, and also for cooking traditional vegetables. Plates and cups are made of either metal, plastic, or china, and are bought from stores, as are spoons, knives, and forks.

13 ● EDUCATION

The literacy rate (percentage of the population able to read and write) among the Luhya is close to that of the country as a whole. The literacy level for the total population of Western province (where the majority of Luhya live) is 67 percent. This is slightly lower than the national average of 69 percent. Literacy among women is slightly lower than among men. Typically, most people (about 75 percent of the population) drop out of school after primary school education, which (since the mid-1980s) lasts eight years. The main reasons for high drop-out rates are the difficult qualifying examinations to enter high school and expensive school fees.

Parents spend a large portion of their income on their children's education in boarding, uniforms, school supplies, transportation to and from school, and pocket money. Often the family will deny itself many of life's necessities and comforts, such as improved housing, food, and clothing, in order to put children through school. Consequently, students are expected to finish school and help with the education of younger siblings, as well as to care for their parents in old age. Because very few students are able to attend a university, parents and the community are very proud of those who manage to attain this level of education.

14 ● CULTURAL HERITAGE

Music and dance are an important part of the life of the Luhya. Children sing songs and dance for play and (especially boys) when herding livestock. Occasions such as weddings, funerals, and circumcision ceremonies all call for singing and dancing. Musical instruments include drums, jingles, flutes, and accordions. The Luhya are nationally renowned for their energetic and vibrant *isukuti* dance, a celebratory performance involving rapid squatting and rising accompanied by thunderous, rhythmic drumbeats.

15 ● EMPLOYMENT

The majority of Luhya families are farmers. Because of the high population density (about 2,450 people per square mile, or 900 people per square kilometer) in Luhyaland, most families own only very small pieces of land of less than 1 acre (0.4 hectares), which are very intensively cultivated. Crops include various vegetables such as kale, collard greens, carrots, maize (corn), beans, potatoes, bananas, and cassava. Beverage crops such as tea, coffee, and sugarcane are grown in some parts of Luhyaland. Livestock, especially cattle and sheep, are also kept. Tending the farm is often a family affair. Because the family farm rarely yields enough food to feed a family and pay for school fees and supplies, clothing, and medical care, family members often seek employment in urban centers and send money back to their rural homes. Women do most of the domestic chores, such as fetching firewood, cooking, taking care of children, and also the farm work.

16 ● SPORTS

Numerous games and sports are played by Luhya children. Jumping rope is very popular among girls. The jumping is counted and sometimes accompanied by rhythmic songs. Hide-and-seek games are common among both boys and girls. Soccer is the most popular game among boys. Any open ground can serve as a playing field.

Adult sports include soccer for men, and to a lesser extent, netball for women. Netball is somewhat like basketball, only the ball is not dribbled. School-based sports also include track-and-field events. The most popular spectator sport is soccer, and some of the best soccer players in Kenya are Luhya.

17 ● RECREATION

Battery-operated radios and cassette players provide musical entertainment for many people. Local bars and shops also have radios, cassette players, juke boxes, and other music systems. Men often gather in these places to drink, play games, and listen and dance to music. Music is mainly of local, Swahili, and Lingala (Congolese) ori-

gin, but Western European and American music are also common.

18 ● CRAFTS AND HOBBIES

Pottery and basket-weaving are quite common among the Luhya, especially in the rural areas. Baskets are made from the leaves of date palms (called *kamakhendu* among the Ababukusu) that grow on river banks. Increasingly, sisal is used. Body ornaments such as bangle bracelets, necklaces, and earrings are mass-produced commercially in Kenya or are imported, and are not in any way uniquely Luhya in form.

19 ● SOCIAL PROBLEMS

Violations of human rights and civil liberties that the Kenya government has been accused of generally apply to most ethnic groups. Problems of alcoholism exist among the Luhya. However, the problems of greatest concern are the high population density and high rate of population growth. Health problems arising from endemic (native) diseases are also of concern.

20 ● BIBLIOGRPAHY

Arnold, Gay. *Modern Kenya.* New York: Longman, 1981.

Dinesen, Isak. *Out of Africa.* New York: Random House, 1972.

Kenya in Pictures. Minneapolis, Minn.: Lerner Publications Co., 1988.

Stein, R. *Kenya.* Chicago: Children's Press, 1985.

Themes in Kenyan History. Athens: Ohio University Press, 1990.

Webb, Lois Sinaiko. *Holidays of the World Cookbook for Students.* Phoenix, Ariz.: Oryx, 1995.

WEBSITES

Embassy of Kenya, Washington, D.C. [Online] Available   http://www.embassyofkenya.com/, 1998.

Interknowledge Corp. Kenya. [Online] Available http://www.geographia.com/kenya/, 1998.

World Travel Guide. [Online] Available http://www.wtgonline.com/country/ke/gen.html, 1998.

Luo

PRONUNCIATION: luh-WO
LOCATION: Kenya; Tanzania
POPULATION: Over 3 million
LANGUAGE: Dholuo; English (official); KiSwahili
RELIGION: Christianity combined with indigenous practices (Anglican church [CPK], Roman Catholicism, and independent Christian churches)

1 ● INTRODUCTION

Throughout the nineteenth century AD, the Luo migrated into the area they now occupy in Kenya. They left lower savanna grasslands for higher and cooler regions with reliable rainfall. As a result of this migration, their traditional emphasis on cattle was supplemented by farming and an increasing importance of crops in their economy. Bantu agriculturalists, with whom the Luo increasingly interacted, exchanged many customs with them.

2 ● LOCATION

According to the last national population census conducted in 1989, the Luo number over 3 million people, or about 13 percent of Kenya's total population. Along with the Luhya, the Luo are the second largest ethnic group in the country, behind the Gikuyu. Most Luo live in western Kenya in Western province or in the adjacent Nyanza province, two of the eight provinces in Kenya. Some Luo live to the south of Kenya in Tanzania. Many Luo also live in Nairobi. Most Luo maintain strong economic, cultural, and social links to western Kenya, which they consider home. Over the past 500 years, the Luo have migrated slowly from the Sudan to their present location around the eastern shore of Lake Victoria. This area changes from low, dry landscape around the lake to more lush, hilly areas to the east. The provincial capital of Kisumu is the third-largest city in Kenya and is a major cultural center for the Luo.

3 ● LANGUAGE

The Luo, like other Kenyans, are typically conversant in at least three languages. The two national languages of Kenya are English and KiSwahili. English, derived from the British colonial era before Kenya's independence in 1963, is the official language of government, international business, university instruction, banks, and commerce. It is taught throughout Kenya in primary and secondary schools. KiSwahili is the primary language of many coastal populations in Kenya and has spread from there throughout East Africa, including Luoland. Today, the KiSwahili language serves as a language of trade and commerce in urban markets and rural towns. Nowadays, KiSwahili is also taught in Kenyan primary and secondary schools. In addition, radio, television, and newspaper materials are available in these two languages.

Nevertheless, the indigenous language of the Luo, referred to as Dholuo, is for most people the language of preference in the home and in daily conversation. Dholuo is taught in primary schools throughout Luoland. Most Luo young people are fluent in English, KiSwahili, and Dholuo. This is particularly impressive because these languages are from three very distinct language families with drastically different grammatical principles and vocabulary.

Children enjoy playing language games in Dholuo. Among these is a tongue-twister game. For example, children try to say without difficulty, *Atud tond atonga, tond atonga chodi,* which means, "I tie the rope of the basket, the rope of the basket breaks." *Acham tap chotna malando chotna cham tapa malando* means, "I eat from the red dish of my lover and my lover eats from my red dish." Most Luo, irrespective of educational attainment and occupation, prefer to speak Dholuo at home and continue to teach this language to their children. Even young Luo teenagers, who nowadays live in Nairobi and rarely visit Luoland, nevertheless have learned to speak Dholuo fluently.

Children are given names that correspond to where they were born, the time of day, or the day of the week. Even the kind of weather that prevailed at the time of a child's birth is noted. For example, one born during a rain storm is called *Akoth* (male) or *Okoth* (female). Just about every Luo also has a pet name used among close friends.

4 ● FOLKLORE

Stories, legends, riddles, and proverbs are an important part of Luo culture. They are traditionally recited in the *siwindhe,* which is the home of a (widowed) grandmother. Luo boys and girls gather there in the evenings to be taught the traditions of their culture. In the evenings, after people have returned from their gardens, they gather to tell and listen to stories. In the siwindhe, however, grandmothers preside over storytelling and verbal games. Riddles take the form of competitive exchanges where winners are rewarded by "marrying" girls in a kind of mock (pretend) marriage situation. Friendly arguments often erupt over interpretations of riddles. One riddle, for example, asks the question, "My house has no door," which is answered by "an egg." Another riddle is, "What is a lake with reeds all around?" The answer is, "an eye." Clever answers are frequently given as alternatives to these standard answers. Proverbs are another part of the siwindhe discussions and are common in everyday use as well. Some examples are, "The eye you have treated will look at you contemptuously," "A hare is small but gives birth to twins," and "A cowardly hyena lives for many years."

Morality tales teach all listeners the proper way to cope with life's circumstances. Such questions as, Why do people die?, What is the value of a deformed child?, What qualities make an appropriate spouse?, What is friendship?, Who is responsible for a bad child?, Why do some people suffer?, and many others are the subject of folklore. For example, the story known as "Opondo's Children" is about a man called Opondo whose wife continuously gave birth to monitor lizards instead of human babies. These lizard babies were thrown away to die because they were hideous. Once, however, the parents decided to keep such a child and he grew to adolescence. As a teenager, this child loved to bathe alone in a river. Before swimming he would take off his monitor skin, and while swimming he mysteriously became a normal human being. His skin was, in fact, only a superficial covering. One day a passerby saw him swimming and told his parents that he was a normal human being. Secretly, his parents went to watch him swim and discovered that he was in fact normal. They destroyed his skin and thereafter, the boy became accepted and loved by all in his community. For this reason, Opondo and his wife deeply regretted that they had thrown away all of their many monitor children. This tale teaches that compassion should be displayed toward children with physical defects.

In an origin tale concerning death, it is told that humans and chameleons are responsible for this calamity. *Were* (God) wanted to put an end to death, which strikes "young and old, boys and girls, men and women, strangers and kinsmen, and the wise and the foolish." He requested that an offering be made to him of white fat from a goat. A chameleon was assigned to carry the offering up to the sky where *Were* lives. Along the way, the fat became dirty and was angrily rejected by *Were*. He declared that death would continue because of this insult. The chameleon became cursed by the Luo, and ever since it must always walk on all fours and take slow steps.

5 ● RELIGION

Christianity has had a major impact on Luo religious beliefs and practices. Today, religious communities draw on beliefs both from indigenous practices and from Christianity. The Anglican Church, known as the CPK, and the Roman Catholic Church are very significant among the Luo. Many people, however, do not draw sharp distinctions between religious practices with European origins and those with African origins. Mainstream churches draw on a rich Luo musical and dance tradition. For many Christians, the ancestors continue to play a significant role in their lives. In traditional belief, the ancestors reside in the sky or underground, from where they may be reincarnated in human or animal form. Ceremonies are sometimes performed when naming a baby to determine if a particular spirit has been reincarnated. The spirits of ancestors are believed to communicate with the living in their dreams.

In the Luo religion, troublesome spirits may cause misfortunes if they are not remembered or respected. Luo refer to spirits by the term *juok,* or "shadow." The Luo refer to God by many names that indicate his power. For example, *Were* means "one certain to grant requests"; *Nyasaye,* "he who is begged"; *Ruoth,* "the king"; *Jachwech,* "the molder"; *Wuon koth,* "the rain-giver"; and *Nyakalaga,* "the one who flows everywhere." Prayers and requests are addressed to God by those in need of his assistance.

Christianity has fused most notably with traditional religious beliefs and customs in "independent Christian churches," which have attracted large followings. For example, the Nomiya Luo Church, which started in 1912, was the first independent church in Kenya. The founder of this church, Johanwa Owalo, is believed to be a prophet similar to Jesus Christ and Muhammad. Owalo later teamed up with a Catholic priest and began teaching a new theology that rejected both the Pope and the doctrine of the trinity.

6 ● MAJOR HOLIDAYS

The Luo recognize the national holidays of Kenza and Tanzania, depending on the country where they reside. In addition, Luo celebrate the Christian religious holidays.

7 ● RITES OF PASSAGE

People are discouraged from noting when someone is pregnant for fear that problems might result from jealous ancestors or neighbors. Older women and midwives assist the woman throughout her pregnancy and in childbirth. The birth of twins, which is believed to be the result of evil spirits, is treated with special attention and requires taboos (prohibitions) on the part of the parents. Only if neighbors engage in obscene dancing and use foul language will the burden of giving birth to twins be lifted. The Luo, however, did not adopt circumcision for men, as practiced in some neighboring Bantu groups.

Adolescence is a time of preparation for marriage and family life. Traditionally, girls obtained tattoos on their backs and had their ears pierced. Girls spent time in peer groups where conversation centered on boys and their personal attributes. Sex education was in the hands of older women who gave advice in a communal sleeping hut used by teenage girls. Lovers sometimes made secret arrangements to meet near these huts, although premarital pregnancy was strictly forbidden. Nowadays, neighborhood and boarding schools have replaced communal sleeping huts and elders, although sex education is not taught in these schools.

Since there are no initiation ceremonies in earlier stages of the life cycle, the funeral serves as the most important symbol for family and community identity. Burials must take place in Luoland, regardless of where a person may have lived during his or her adult years.

8 ● RELATIONSHIPS

Social relations among the Luo are governed by rules of kinship, gender, and age. Descent is patrilineal (traced through the male line) to determine kinship. Kin align themselves for purposes of exchange of goods, marriage, and political alliance. Names are received through the male line, and after marriage women reside in the homesteads of their husbands. A married woman builds up alliances for her husband's family by maintaining strong relationships with her brothers and sisters who live at her birthplace or elsewhere. It is expected that after marriage a woman will bear children for her husband's lineage. Bride wealth, given by her husband and his family, contributes to the woman's ability to maintain ties with her own family throughout her life.

By having children, a woman greatly enhances her power and influence within the lineage of her husband. As the children grow, they take special care of her interests. Perhaps as many as 30 percent of Luo homesteads are polygynous (in which a man has more than one wife). This contributes to solidarity between a mother and her children, and between children born of the same mother. Polygyny is commonly accepted by both men and women, provided traditional ideas and regulations are maintained. These include, for example, a special recognition for the first wife or "great wife," whose house and granary are located prominently at the back of the homestead opposite the main gate. Subsequent wives have homes alternatively to her right and left in the order of their marriage. Sons are provided with homes adjacent to the main gate of the compound in the order of their birth. The husband maintains a homestead for himself near the center of the compound. His own brothers, if they have not yet formed their own homesteads, reside on the edge of the compound near its center. As Luo become wealthy in Luoland or elsewhere, it is common for them to build a large house for their mother. This is especially necessary if she is a "great wife," as it is considered improper for younger wives to have larger homes than wives more senior to themselves.

Visiting and being visited is the major source of pleasure for the Luo. The social principles regarding age, kinship, and gender impose a heavy schedule of ritual obligations on Luo, regardless of their place of residence. Attendance at funerals is a significant obligation for all Luo. At funerals, Luo consume large amounts of meat, beer, and soft drinks and socialize with friends and relatives. Funerals last for four days for a male and three days for a female. After the burial and expression of grief through speeches and viewing of the body, there is a period of feasting and celebration. After the funeral of a man, a rooster (which symbolizes masculinity to the Luo) is taken from his house and eaten by his relatives. This signifies the end of his homestead. (When a new homestead is founded, a man is given a rooster from his father's home.)

Visitors for funerals gather from far and wide and are housed around the compound of the dead person, which is where he or she will be buried. This location and the duration of the ritual is an excellent opportunity for young people to meet and observe members of the opposite sex, or for elders to discuss marriage alliances that they might wish to promote. Dating may well follow initial meetings or deliberations at the funeral.

9 ●LIVING CONDITIONS

There are several types of rural houses. A common house is made of mud and wattle (woven twigs) walls with a thatched roof. Another style includes mud and wattle walls, with a roof made of corrugated metal. A more elaborate, permanent house has brick walls and a roof covered with iron sheets or tiles. Bricks, iron sheets, and tiles are all items of prestige, and their ownership symbolizes success in farming, animal husbandry, or some modern occupation such as teaching, the ministry, or shopkeeping. Homes vary in shape as well as size. Some homes of the old variety made of wattle and mud are circular. Those with more permanent materials tend to be rectangular. A prosperous man who is the head of a large extended family may have several wives whose homes are situated by their rank within a large circular homestead.

Luo living in Kisumu, the regional capital, or in Nairobi have homes that vary according to their social status. Some Luo are numbered among the elite Kenyans whose homes are elaborate, with facilities for automobiles, sleeping accommodations for visiting relatives, and servants' quarters. Other less fortunate Luo live in Nairobi's crowded slums where homes are quite temporary, made of wattle and mud and short-lived materials such as tin, paper, and plastic.

Malaria is a major killer in Luoland. Children's diseases, such as *kwashiorkor* (a form of protein malnutrition), are a threat in those families without access to a balanced diet or knowledge about nutrition and health standards. In villages, there is an emphasis on preventive medicine; most rural communities have clinics with medical workers who emphasize sanitation, prenatal care, nutrition, and other practices known to reduce the risk of disease.

10 ● FAMILY LIFE

Marriage was traditionally considered to be the most significant event in the lives of both men and women. It was thought inappropriate for anyone to remain unmarried. Large families ensured adequate numbers of workers. The system of polygyny (multiple wives) guaranteed that all people married.

The significance of bride wealth is increasing, even among educated Luo. Members of the groom's family initiate a process of negotiation with the bride's family that may unfold over many years. Negotiations can be intense, and for this reason a "go-between," who is neutral to the interests of each family, is used. Luo believe that divorce cannot occur after bride wealth has been exchanged and children are born. Even if separation happens, the couple is still ideally considered to be married. Failure to have children, however, is thought to be the fault of the bride and, for this, she will be divorced or replaced by another wife. Cattle are the primary item given in bride wealth. In determining the value of a prospective bride, her family takes into account her health, appearance, and, nowadays, her level of formal education. Failure of men to raise a high bride wealth prompts many of them to propose elopement, a practice that is on the rise today.

Young people in Kenya still tend to marry within their own ethnic groups. Tribal elders frequently caution against "intertribal marriages." The more distant the ethnic group in space and customs from the Luo, the greater the cautionary warnings. For this reason, Luo intertribal marriage is most likely to occur with members from neighboring Baluya societies, which are Bantu. However, most Luo marry within their own ethnic group.

11 ● CLOTHING

Traditionally, the Luo wore minimal clothing. Animal hides were used to cover private parts, but there was no stigma (shame) associated with nudity. Nowadays, clothing styles are largely Western in origin. They vary according to a person's social class and lifestyle preferences. It is not uncommon to see people in remote rural areas fashionably dressed according to some of the latest tastes. Luo living in Nairobi tend to wear clothing that is cosmopolitan by rural standards and similar to the clothing worn in New York or Paris.

In rural areas, most people dress according to their work routines. For example, women wear loose-fitting dresses made of solid or printed cotton fabric while farming or attending market. Wearing sandals or going barefoot are typical while working. Men wear jeans as work pants while farming. During the rainy season, the roads can become very muddy; consequently, boots and umbrellas are especially prized by both men and women. These days, there is a strong market in second-hand clothing, making slacks, dresses, coats, undergarments, sweaters, shoes, handbags, belts, and other items available to even poorer families. Luo enjoy dressing up for funerals and weddings and are considered throughout Kenya to be very fashionable.

12 ● FOOD

The primary crops are maize (corn), millet, and sorghum. Coffee, tobacco, cotton, and sugarcane are important cash crops. Important animals include sheep, goats, chickens, and cattle, which are used for bride wealth. Fish from Lake Victoria and its streams are important, especially talapia. Many foods are purchased, including sugar, bread, and butter, which are consumed with tea on a daily basis, a custom known as "tea time" and derived from the British colonial era, which ended in 1963.

The staple food eaten several times a day is *ugali*. This is made from maize meal stirred in boiling water until it becomes a thick and smooth porridge. Ugali is always eaten with an accompaniment such as meat or stew. Greens *(sukumawiki)* are also frequently eaten with ugali. Maize, popular throughout Kenya, is frequently sold for money. This has led many families to sell their maize when financially pressed for money. For this reason, there is a periodic famine throughout Luoland that occurs every year during the long, dry season prior to harvest.

13 ● EDUCATION

Kenya introduced a new system of education in the 1980s known as the "8-4-4 system," modeled after the American system. Luo now go to primary school for eight years, to secondary school for four years, and to college for four years. The previous system was modeled on the British educational system.

After completing high school, Luo attend technical, secretarial, nursing, computer, teacher training, and business schools as alternatives to the university. There is a new university at Maseno near Kisumu, which provides easy access for those Luo who want to attend a university. Education is highly valued among the Luo, and they are well represented in the professions. Nevertheless, there still remains a high level of illiteracy (inability to read and write), especially among females. In polygynous marriages there is a strong tendency for younger wives to be more educated than their older counterparts. More Luo are now recognizing the importance of sending girls to school.

The Luo success in academic pursuits may well be related to the value given to "wisdom" in their culture. Modern philosophers have applied the term "sage philosophy" to describe individuals among the Luo who, in the past and present, excel in teachings and reflections on the human condition. The Luo society is an open one. All individuals are encouraged to express themselves publicly. Truth *(adier)* is expressed through songs and folklore by respected elder men and women who are acknowledged as wise. Most respected, however, is the *japaro,* a term that translates into

English as "thinker," who is consulted on all matters of interest to community welfare. The most famous sage until his death in the mid-1990s was Oginga Odinga, a widely respected elder and former vice-president of Kenya. He spoke out publicly during colonialism and in post-colonial politics against what he considered to be injustices. In his writings, he emphasized communal welfare and concern for preservation of traditional values.

14 ● CULTURAL HERITAGE

The Luo consider their entire traditional way of life to be an important community resource. There is a great deal of disagreement over what should be preserved and what should change. Customs centering on marriage and gender relations are hotly debated.

Songs are popular today as in the past. Musicians praise and lament political, generational, economic, and cultural contradictions in contemporary life. Luo devote much time to listening to music, and regularly purchase records, tapes, and CDs. Christian church music is also a form of entertainment.

It is said that the short story was a well-developed art among the Luo in traditional times. Such stories were often accompanied by music. The most important short-story writer in Kenya today is a Luo woman, Grace Ogot. In her stories she includes traditional themes as well as modern dilemmas, such as an educated woman living in a polygynous arrangement. Some of her best-known stories are "The Other Woman," "The Fisherman," and "The Honorable Minister."

15 ● EMPLOYMENT

The most notable fact about the Luo economy is that women play the primary role in farming. Before the introduction of the modern money economy, the garden was the centerpiece of the women's world of work. Industrious women could earn considerable wealth by exchanging their garden produce for animals, handicrafts, pots, and baskets.

A young girl is expected to help her mother and her mother's co-wives in farming land owned by her father, brothers, and paternal uncles. Even though a girl may go to school and rise to a prominent position in society, there is often still a strong association with the land and digging.

Men are preoccupied with livestock and spend a great deal of time in "social labor" concerned with placing their cattle in good contexts, such as bride wealth exchanges, trading partnerships, and commercial sales. In the modern economy, cattle and goats have a monetary value as well. Men have control over animals and cash crops.

16 ● SPORTS

The Luo participate in all of the major national sports currently played in Kenya. Soccer is a particularly popular sport. Secondary schools provide an assortment of sports for young people, giving them an opportunity to engage in competitive games such as track and field and soccer. Children enjoy games in the village, such as racing, wrestling, and soccer. Some boys enjoy swimming.

17 ● RECREATION

Childhood play activities for girls include grinding soil on a flattened stone in imitation of adults who grind grains. Girls play with dolls made from clay or maize (corn) cobs. Boys and girls play hide-and-seek and house. Girls play a game called *kora* using pieces of broken pottery or stones. In this game, stones are collected and then thrown into the air. The main purpose is to catch more than one stone on the back of the hand. Boys and girls between six and ten years of age play separately. Girls spend more time at home caring for younger siblings and helping with household duties and gardening. Boys have more freedom and combine play activities with herding and care of animals.

Children and adults both play a game called *bao,* a board game played widely throughout Africa. This game of strategy involves trying to place seeds on the opponent's side of the board and capture their seeds.

Radio and television are both available to most Luo. Radio programs are in KiSwahili, English, and Dholuo. Virtually all homes have radios, which are a significant source of both entertainment and education. Books and printed media have now largely replaced public speaking as a form of entertainment. Nevertheless, visiting family and friends continues to be a valued aspect of Luo culture. Visits are typically very lively with lots of animated discussion. The verbally skillful person is still widely admired.

Birthday parties are now much more important than they were in the past, when individuals did not reckon their age in years. Parents try to make their children's birthdays special with a cake, cards, and gifts. Weddings and funerals, as in the past, are still major forms of entertainment for old and young alike. Church groups, clubs, women's organizations, and schools are important organizations for their members' social calendars.

18 ● CRAFTS AND HOBBIES

See the article on "Kenyans" in this chapter for information about crafts and hobbies.

19 ● SOCIAL PROBLEMS

During the colonial era and since independence, the Luo have been isolated from national leadership even though they are the second-largest ethnic group in the country. Specific social problems follow from this isolation. Economic development in western Kenya is poor, Luo roads are badly in need of repair, rates of human immunodeficiency virus (HIV) infection are comparatively high, food shortages are frequent, and infant mortality is among the highest in the country. The municipal water supply is so badly treated that residents suffer from waterborne diseases such as typhoid fever, amoebic dysentery, common dysentery, and diarrhea. Tourism has bypassed Luoland and Lake Victoria, even though Lake Victoria has hippopotami, freshwater fish, and cultural attractions.

Teenage pregnancies are a major social problem in contemporary Luoland. Social responsibility for teenage pregnancy falls entirely on girls, who generally leave school if they become pregnant.

20 ● BIBLIOGRPAHY

Arnold, Gay. *Modern Kenya.* New York: Longman, 1981.

Dinesen, Isak. *Out of Africa.* New York: Random House, 1972.

Kenya in Pictures. Minneapolis, Minn.: Lerner Publications Co., 1988.

Liyong, Taban lo. *Popular Culture of East Africa.* Nairobi: Longman Kenya, 1972.

Stein, R. *Kenya.* Chicago: Children's Press, 1985.

Themes in Kenyan History. Athens: Ohio University Press, 1990.

Webb, Lois Sinaiko. *Holidays of the World Cookbook for Students.* Phoenix, Ariz.: Oryx, 1995.

WEBSITES

Embassy of Kenya, Washington, D.C. [Online] Available http://www.embassyofkenya.com/, 1998.

Interknowledge Corp. Kenya. [Online] Available http://www.geographia.com/kenya/, 1998.

World Travel Guide. [Online] Available http://www.wtgonline.com/country/ke/gen.html, 1998.

Korea,
Republic of

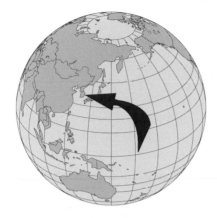

The Koreans are believed to be descended from Mongoloid people from the cold northern regions of Central Asia. However, there are two Koreas, North and South. This chapter profiles the people living in the south, the Republic of Korea. The Republic of Korea has no significant ethnic minorities.

South Koreans

PRONUNCIATION: sowth kaw-REE-uns
LOCATION: Republic of Korea (South Korea)
POPULATION: 40 million
LANGUAGE: Korean
RELIGION: Mahayana Buddhism; Christianity (Protestantism and Roman Catholicism); Ch'ondogyo (combination of Christianity and native pre-Christian beliefs)

1 ● INTRODUCTION

The Korean peninsula is located between China, Japan, and Russia. It has been subject to foreign invasions throughout recorded history. Korea was ruled by the Chinese for several hundred years in the early centuries AD. During this time, China established a lasting influence on Korean culture, especially through its language.

In 1876 the Kanghwa Treaty opened Korea to Japan and to the West. After many wars, Korea was taken over by Japan, which brutally ruled it from 1910 to 1945. During this period, Koreans were treated terribly by the Japanese. Women were kidnapped and used as sex slaves, and many innocent people were horribly murdered. Many Koreans still mistrust the Japanese because of this.

After World War II (1939–45), the peninsula was divided by the Soviets and the Americans. The thirty-eighth parallel became the line separating the zones. Eventually, the line separated two distinct countries: North Korea and South Korea. They have fought one war (1950–53) and have been preparing for another ever since. The border is one of the most heavily armed borders in the world. The United States has maintained troops in South Korea for about fifty years in case of an attack by North Korea. The two countries are still technically at war with each other. South Korea's government has an elected legislature and a strong executive branch.

EPD Photos

A newspaper showing the Korean script.

a Korean alphabet, called Han'gul, was developed. It has been used ever since.

Some common Korean words and expressions are:

EXPRESSIONS

English	Korean
how are you?	anahasiyo?
hello	yoboseyo
goodbye	aniyong ikeseyo
yes	ye
no	anio
thank you	kamsa kamnida

NUMBERS

English	Korean
one	il
two	ee
three	sam
four	sa
five	o
six	yuk
seven	chill
eight	pal
nine	ku
ten	sip
one hundred	paek
one thousand	chon

2 ● LOCATION

South Korea is one of the most densely populated countries both in Asia and in the world. The population is over forty million people, roughly twice that of North Korea. Over ten million people—nearly a quarter of the total population—live in Seoul, the capital and South Korea's largest city.

The Korean people are one of the world's most ethnically homogeneous nationalities. This means that almost all the people in the country are of the same ethnicity. They are almost exclusively descendents of the Han, a people believed to be related to the Mongols of Central Asia. There are no numerically significant ethnic minorities in South Korea.

3 ● LANGUAGE

Korean is generally thought to belong to the Altaic language family, along with Turkish, Mongolian, Japanese, and other languages. Until the fifteenth century, Korean was written using Chinese characters. Then, in 1446,

4 ● FOLKLORE

Korean folklore celebrates human longevity and the survival of the Korean people. A number of folktales involve either animals or heavenly beings who either become human or want to do so. Others celebrate the figure of the wise hermit living a simple, secluded existence on a mountaintop. One tale tells how the locust, ant and kingfisher came to have their unique physical characteristics. The three got together to have a picnic. For lunch, the locust and kingfisher were to supply some fish and the ant was to provide the rice. The ant got the rice by biting a woman carrying a basket of rice on her head. When she dropped the basket, the ant carried it off. The locust sat on a leaf floating in the pond, and soon a fish came along and gobbled both the locust and leaf right up. The kingfisher swooped down and caught the fish and carried it back to the picnic site. The locust popped out of the fish's mouth and began congratulating himself on catching the fish. The kingfisher flew into a great fury, arguing that HE had caught the fish. The ant laughed so hard that his middle became quite thin, just as it is today. The locust grabbed the kingfisher's bill and wouldn't let go, so that the kingfisher's bill grew long, just as it is today. And the kingfisher crunched his long bill down onto the locust's head, forever giving it the flattened shape that it has today.

Koreans have traditionally used special drawings called *pujok* as charms in and around their houses to bring them luck and ward off evil.

5 ● RELIGION

There is a great deal of diversity in South Korean religious life. Koreans have traditionally combined elements from different belief systems, such as Taoism, Confucianism, and Buddhism. Today, the majority of South Korea's religious population are either Buddhist (over 11 million followers) or Christian (more than 6 million Protestants and almost 2 million Roman Catholics).

The South Koreans also have many newer religions that combine Christianity with native pre-Christian beliefs. The most widespread is Ch'ondogyo (the Heavenly Way), founded in 1860.

6 ● MAJOR HOLIDAYS

The New Year is one of South Korea's most important holidays. Three days are set aside for family celebrations. These include honoring parents and grandparents, shooting off firecrackers to frighten away evil spirits, and eating holiday foods. Although New Year's Day legally occurs on January 1, many Koreans still celebrate the traditional lunar New Year, which usually occurs in February.

The birthday of the Buddha (usually early in May) is an important holiday for Korean Buddhists. They hang lanterns in the courtyards of Buddhist temples throughout the country. These lanterns are then carried through the streets in nighttime processions.

Tano, held in early June, is a major holiday in rural areas. It is the traditional time to pray for a good harvest. It is celebrated with a variety of games and competitions, including wrestling matches for men and swinging contests for women. The holiday is also called Swing Day.

Other national holidays include Independence Movement Day (March 1), Arbor Day (April 5), Children's Day (May 5), Memorial Day (June 6), Constitution Day (July 17), Liberation Day (August 15), National Foundation Day (October 3), and Christmas (December 25).

7 ● RITES OF PASSAGE

Traditionally, Korean marriages were arranged, especially among the rich and powerful. Today, however, the popularity of arranged marriages, particularly in urban areas, has declined, although many Koreans still follow the practice in a modified form.

SOUTH KOREANS

0   250   500   750 Miles

0   250 500 750 Kilometers

RUSSIA

Yichun

Sapporo

Sea of Okhjotsk

MONGOLIA

Sea of Japan

JAPAN

NORTH KOREA

Tokyo

P'yòngyang

Kyoto

Seoul

Osaka

Beijing

SOUTH KOREA

Hiroshima

PACIFIC OCEAN

Xi'an

Huang

East China Sea

CHINA

Wuhan

Yangtze

Fuzhou

T'aipai

TAIWAN

Parents and other relatives locate prospective marriage partners, but the young people have the final say in approving their choices. Among the urban upper classes, the services of highly paid semiprofessional matchmakers are also becoming increasingly popular.

Ancestor worship plays a prominent role in Korean folk belief. This system regards death as a rite of passage to a new state rather than an ending. Christian, Buddhist, and Confucian concepts also affect Korean attitudes toward death.

8 ● RELATIONSHIPS

Respect for parents, and for elders in general, is a central value for Koreans. There are detailed and elaborate rules governing one's speech and actions in the presence of older persons. These rules, however, are less rigidly observed now than in the past.

Even when not in the presence of their elders, Koreans are generally very courteous and emotionally reserved. Proper etiquette forbids strong displays of either happiness, distress, or anger.

When at home, Koreans traditionally sit on the floor, although today chairs are common. The most formal and polite posture when seated on the floor is to kneel with one's back kept straight and one's weight on the balls of both feet.

9 ● LIVING CONDITIONS

Most South Koreans in urban areas live in high-rise, multistory dwellings. Most homes are built of concrete. Houses are generally built low, with small rooms. In order to keep out the cold, there are few doors and windows.

The Koreans have a unique heating system called *ondal*. Heat is carried through pipes installed beneath the floors. This is geared toward the traditional Korean custom of sitting and sleeping on mats or cushions on the floor.

Health care in Korea has improved substantially since the 1950s. Average life expectancy has risen from fifty-three to seventy-one years. Traditional causes of death, such as tuberculosis and pneumonia, have been replaced by conditions more typical of industrialized societies, such as cancer, heart disease, and stroke.

10 ● FAMILY LIFE

The typical South Korean household consists of a nuclear family with two children.

Young children are nurtured and indulged. Respect for one's parents—and one's elders, generally—is a central value in Korean life. Fathers in particular exercise a great degree of authority over their sons. Although divorce was not tolerated in the past, today it has become quite common.

11 ● CLOTHING

The majority of South Koreans wear modern Western-style clothing most of the time. Historically, people wore clothes in colors that reflected their social class. Kings and other royalty wore yellow, but common people indicated their modesty by wearing mainly white.

The traditional costume or hanbok is a two-piece outfit for both men and women. Women wore a *chogori,* or short top, with long, rectangular sleeves. This was accompanied by a *ch'ima,* or wrap skirt, made from a large, rectangular piece of fabric with long sashes attached to the skirt to form a waistband. The skirt was traditionally tied high around the chest, just under the arms. Women would carry babies and small children in a *cho'ne,* a large rectangle of quilted fabric with two long sashes. The ch'one is wrapped around the baby on the mother's back and the sashes are tied securely around the mother's body.

The traditional costume for Korean men was a chogori top similar to the one worn by women. Loose-fitting pants, known as *paji,* accompany the chogori. Men who rode horses for hunting preferred paji with narrow legs, but looser paji were preferred for sitting on the floor at home.

Recipe

Kimchi

Kimchi must ferment for at least two days to develop its full flavor.

Ingredients

1 cup coarsely chopped cabbage
1 cup finely sliced carrots
1 cup cauliflower florets, separated
2 Tablespoons salt
2 green onions, finely sliced
3 cloves garlic, finely chopped, or 1 teaspoon garlic granules
1 teaspoon crushed red pepper
1 teaspoon finely grated fresh ginger or ½ teaspoon ground ginger

Directions

1. Combine cabbage, carrots, and cauliflower in colander and sprinkle with salt. Toss lightly and set in sink for about one hour and allow to drain.
2. Rinse with cold water, drain well, and place in a medium-sized bowl.
3. Add onions, garlic, red pepper, and ginger. Mix thoroughly.
4. Cover and refrigerate for at least two days, stirring frequently.

Yields about four cups.

On their first birthday, Korean children are dressed in bright clothing. Their outfit often includes quilted socks with bright red pompons on the toes.

12 ● FOOD

The Korean national dish is *kimchi,* a spicy, fermented pickled vegetable mixture whose primary ingredient is cabbage. It is prepared

EPD Photos

The kayagum, or kayakum, has strings of red twisted silk. The musician sits on the floor to play it. Courtesy of the Center for the Study of World Musics, Kent State University.

in large quantities in the fall by families throughout Korea and left to ferment for several weeks in large jars buried in the ground.

A typical Korean meal includes soup, rice served with grains or beans, and kimchi served as a side dish. (A recipe for kimchi

follows.) Other common dishes include *bulgogi* (strips of marinated beef), *kalbi* (marinated beef short ribs), and *sinsollo* (a meal of meat, fish, vegetables, eggs, nuts, and bean curd cooked together in broth).

Koreans eat with chopsticks and a spoon, often at small, collapsible tables that can be moved to any room of the house.

13 ● EDUCATION

Koreans have a great reverence for education and 90 percent of South Koreans are literate. Education is free and required between the ages of six and twelve. The great majority of students go on to six more years of middle school and high school. Discipline is strict, and children attend school five-and-a-half days per week.

South Korea has over 200 institutions of higher education, including both two- and four-year colleges and universities. Ewha University is one of the world's largest women's universities. The leading public university in South Korea is Seoul National University.

14 ● CULTURAL HERITAGE

Chinese art, Confucianism, and Buddhism have all had a major influence on the arts in Korea. About 80,000 art objects are collected in the National Museum. Outstanding examples of Korean architecture can be seen in historic palaces and Buddhist temples and pagodas.

The National Classic Music Institute trains its graduates in traditional Korean music. Korean folk painting *(min'hwa)* is still popular. Western art forms have been very influential in South Korea. The Korean

National Symphony Orchestra and the Seoul Symphony Orchestra perform in Seoul and Pusan. Western-style drama, dance, and motion pictures have also become very popular among South Koreans.

15 ● EMPLOYMENT

About 15 percent of South Korea's labor force are employed in agriculture, forestry, and fishing, and 25 percent in manufacturing. Various types of government employment supply most of the nation's remaining jobs.

South Koreans have traditionally expected to have jobs for life. In 1997, however, the economy suffered a drastic collapse. For the first time in a generation workers are facing massive layoffs.

16 ● SPORTS

Koreans enjoy a variety of internationally popular sports, including baseball, volleyball, soccer, basketball, tennis, skating, golf, skiing, boxing, and swimming. Baseball is especially popular. South Korea has a professional baseball league. Its games are broadcast on television, as are competitions at the college and high school levels.

The best-known traditional Korean sport is the martial art of *tae kwon do,* taught by Koreans to people throughout the world as a popular form of self-defense.

The 1988 Summer Olympic Games were held in Seoul.

17 ● RECREATION

Both traditional Korean forms of recreation and modern Western pastimes are enjoyed in South Korea. Age-old games and ceremo-

Make a Shield Kite

Materials

five 2-foot bamboo sticks
butcher paper or other strong paper at least 18 inches wide
kite string
strong packing tape
crepe paper or plastic grocery bags for streamers

Directions

1. Cross two of the bamboo sticks at the center to make an X and tie with string.

2. Connect two sides of the X with two more of the sticks and tie the four corners. (Shape will resemble an hourglass.)

3. Tie the fifth stick across the top of the shield and fasten at the corners.

4. Cut a piece of paper at least 2 inches larger than the frame. (Two pieces may be required to cover the frame completely.)

5. Mark a circle in the center of the paper to allow the air to pass through. The circle must be one-half the total width of the kite. (Twelve-inch circle for a 24-inch wide kite, for example.) Cut the circle out.

6. Decorate the kite paper with your name, birth date, and a good-luck wish.

7. Attach the paper to the frame by wrapping the paper neatly around the frame and fastening it securely. Strong packing tape works best.

8. Cut streamers of crepe paper or plastic grocery bags and attach to the lower edge of the kite using tape or glue.

9. The kite may be launched or hung on the wall. (To prepare for launching, cut four 18-inch lengths of string. Tie one to each corner of the kit. Tie the four ends together, and attach them to the flying string.)

nial dances are still performed at festivals and other special occasions. These include mask dances *(Kanggangsuwollae)* and the *Chajon Nori* (juggernaut) game, in which participants ride in wooden vehicles. Also popular are mass tug-of-war games involving as many as a hundred people.

Children and adults enjoy kite-flying. On the first full moon of the year, home-made kites were launched to bring good luck for the new year. Each kite-maker would write his or her name, birthdate, and good luck wishes on his or her kite, and launch it into the air.

Among modern forms of entertainment, television is enjoyed throughout the country. Outside the home, South Koreans enjoy gathering in the country's numerous coffee-houses and bars.

A traditional Korean instrument, the *kayagum,* is played by a musician sitting on the floor. The strings are made of twisted silk, and pass through the bridges on the body of the instrument. Modern Koreans enjoy Western music—especially classical music—and their country has produced many fine performers. They are especially fond of singing. It is common for Koreans to sing for each other at dinners and other social occasions.

18 ● CRAFTS AND HOBBIES

Fine Korean furniture is valued by collectors worldwide. Korean craftspeople are also known for their celadon ceramics, a term that refers to a type of greenish glaze that originated in China.

19 ● SOCIAL PROBLEMS

The most pressing social concern today is the collapse of the South Korean economy that occurred in 1997. It is expected that the huge companies that dominate the economy will have to lay off hundreds of thousands of workers.

In the 1980s, growing numbers of Koreans began to use the illegal substance crystalline methamphetamine, known as "speed" in the United States. By the end of the decade there were thought to be as many as 300,000 using the drug. This included many ordinary working people attempting to cope with high-pressure jobs and long work hours.

20 ● BIBLIOGRAPHY

Faurot, Jeannette, ed. *Asian Pacific Folktales and Legends.* New York: Simon and Schuster, 1995.

Gall, Timothy, and Susan Gall, eds. *Worldmark Encyclopedia of the Nations.* Detroit, Mich.: Gale Research, 1995.

Hoare, James. *Korea: An Introduction.* New York: Kegan Paul International, 1988.

McNair, Sylvia. *Korea.* Chicago, Ill.: Children's Press, 1994.

Oliver, Robert Tarbell. *A History of the Korean People in Modern Times: 1800 to the Present.* Newark, N.J.: University of Delaware Press, 1993.

WEBSITES

Embassy of Korea, Washington, D.C. [Online] Available http://korea.emb.washington.dc.us/new/frame/, 1998.

Samsung SDS Co., Ltd. Korean Insights Kidsight. [Online] Available http:korea.insights.co.kr/forkid/, 1998.

Kuwait

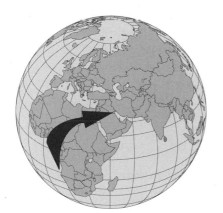

The people of Kuwait are called Kuwaitis. Forty percent of the residents of Kuwait are citizens of the country; the remainder are divided roughly in half between Arabs and non-Arabs.

Kuwaitis

PRONUNCIATION: koo-WAIT-eez

LOCATION: Kuwait

POPULATION: 1.6 million (40 percent of whom are Kuwaiti citizens)

LANGUAGE: Arabic (official); English

RELIGION: Islam (Sunni Muslim, 70 percent; Shi'ah Muslim, 30 percent)

1 ● INTRODUCTION

People have lived in present-day Kuwait for thousands of years. Modern Kuwait was founded in 1722 by the Utub tribe. The name *Kuwait* is a form of the Arabic word for "fortress built near water."

A small but wealthy state, Kuwait has suffered continual conflicts with its larger neighbors, Iraq and Iran. On August 2, 1990, Saddam Hussein led an Iraqi invasion of Kuwait, occupying the country until February 26, 1991. Other countries, including the United States, responded militarily to the invasion, sparking the Persian Gulf War.

The war ended with Iraq's withdrawal from Kuwait.

2 ● LOCATION

Kuwait is located in the desert on the north-western coast of the Arabian (or Persian) Gulf. It is bordered to the north and west by Iraq, to the south and southwest by Saudi Arabia, and to the east by the gulf. Directly across the gulf is Iran. It is just slightly smaller than the state of New Jersey.

The climate in Kuwait is hot and humid, with summer temperatures reaching as high as 120°F (49°C) or more. Frequent sandstorms occur from May to July, and August and September are extremely humid. Winters are cooler, with temperatures ranging from 50° to 60°F (10° to 16°C).

Kuwait's total population is about 1.6 million people, of whom only 656,000 are Kuwaiti citizens. The rest are foreign workers, mostly in the oil industry. Foreign workers are not allowed citizenship, even if they work in Kuwait all their adult lives.

3 ● LANGUAGE

Arabic is the official language of Kuwait. Kuwaiti students are taught English as a second language.

"Hello" in Arabic is *marhaba* or *ahlan,* to which one replies, *marhabtayn* or *ahlayn.* Other common greetings are *as-salam alaykum,* "peace be with you," with the reply of *wa alaykum as-salam,* "and to you peace." *Ma assalama* means "goodbye." "Thank you" is *shukran,* and "you're welcome" is *afwan;* "yes" is *naam* and "no" is *la'a.* The numbers one to ten in Arabic are *wahad, ithnayn, thalatha, arba'a, khamsa, sitta, saba'a, thamanya, tisa'a,* and *ashara.*

4 ● FOLKLORE

Kuwaiti folk beliefs and rituals are strongly linked to Islam. Kuwaitis turn to Islam for daily guidance, as well as for explanations for many aspects of their current lives and past history.

5 ● RELIGION

When the Islamic revolution swept through the Middle East in the seventh century AD, virtually all Kuwaitis converted to Islam. Today, about 70 percent of Kuwaiti citizens are Sunni Muslim. Thirty percent are Shi'ah Muslim.

6 ● MAJOR HOLIDAYS

Secular holidays in Kuwait include New Year's Day (January 1) and National Day (February 25). Liberation Day (February 26) commemorates the withdrawal of Iraqi forces from Kuwait. It is not recognized as an official holiday, but Kuwaitis treat it as one.

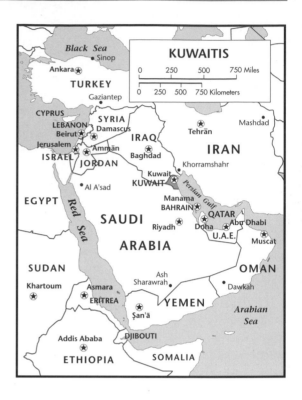

The main holidays in Kuwait are Muslim religious holidays. *Eid al-Fitr* is a three-day festival at the end of the holy month of Ramadan. *Eid al-Adha* is a three-day feast of sacrifice at the end of the month of pilgrimage to Mecca (*hajj*). During this feast families who can afford it slaughter a lamb and share the meat with poorer Muslims. The First of *Muharram* is the Muslim New Year. *Al-Mawlid An Nabawi* is the Prophet Muhammad's birthday. *Eid al-Isra wa Al-Miraj* is a feast celebrating Muhammad's nocturnal visit to heaven.

7 ● RITES OF PASSAGE

Births are the occasion for celebration, particularly if the child is a boy. Kuwaiti boys are circumcised on the seventh day after their birth. This is usually accompanied by a banquet. Sheep are slaughtered, and relatives and friends are invited. After giving birth, a mother is expected to stay in bed for forty days to recuperate and regain her strength.

Weddings are perhaps the most elaborately celebrated occasions, with great feasts and dancing. In the past, girls could be married at the age of fourteen. Today, the typical age for marriage is twenty to twenty-five. Kuwaiti society is built on the importance of the family. Marriages are often arranged between families with long-established ties.

Respect toward the dead is very important. Burial takes place on the same day as the death. The body is washed and wrapped in a white shroud. It is then taken to a nearby mosque, where special prayers (*Salat al-Janaza*) are recited. After the burial, relatives, friends, and acquaintances gather at the home of the grieving family to pay their respects. They also read aloud parts of the Koran (the sacred text of Islam). Mourning lasts for three days

8 ● RELATIONSHIPS

Men and women do not mix socially, except in family groups. Shi'ah and Sunni Muslims also have little to do with each other.

Diwaniyas are private clubs for men. They function as meeting places where men sit and talk while drinking coffee or tea. Discussion topics include business and government policy. During the Iraqi occupation of Kuwait, the diwaniyas became the hub of the resistance movement. Men gathered there (and in mosques) and organized their resistance efforts against the Iraqis.

When talking, Arabs touch each other much more often, and stand much closer together, than Westerners do. People of the same sex will often hold hands while talking or walking.

In earlier days, members of the opposite sex, even married couples, never touched in public; this is changing today. Arabs talk a great deal. They talk loudly, repeat themselves often, and interrupt each other constantly. Conversations are highly emotional and full of gestures.

9 ● LIVING CONDITIONS

Kuwaitis are among the richest people in the world. About one-fourth of all Kuwaitis own a car, usually an expensive one. Housing for ethnic Kuwaitis is partially or completely paid for by the government. Many families have maids.

Health care and education—through the university level—are free to all Kuwaiti citizens. Foreign workers are entitled to some of the benefits but are restricted from receiving to others. The government sponsors social welfare programs for disabled persons, the elderly, students' families, widows, unmarried women over eighteen, orphans, the poor, and prisoners' families. Telephone services are free. Television broadcasting began in 1961, with satellite communications established in 1969.

During the Iraqi invasion and occupation (1990–91), conditions in Kuwait were terrible. For those who remained in Kuwait (many, including the royal family, fled when

Kuwait Information Office

Kuwaiti children ready to participate in Guirgian, a tradition similiar to the Western Halloween, that occurs mid-way through the holy month of Ramadan.

they had the chance), life was extremely difficult and dangerous.

10 ● FAMILY LIFE

The family unit is more important to Kuwaitis than is the individual, the larger community, or the government. Families tend to be large. The government encourages large families in its effort to increase the percentage of ethnic Kuwaitis (they make up less than half the people in the country). The government pays more than $7,000 to couples who marry.

Extended families usually live together, except in some urban areas where the houses are too small. A typical Kuwaiti household consists of a husband, his parents, his wife, his sons and their wives and children, and his unmarried sons and daughters. Parents arrange marriages, usually between extended-family members. First cousins are the preferred match. Marrying and having children, particularly sons, increases a woman's status in society.

Most girls marry young. Almost a third of Kuwaiti women are married by the time they are twenty years old. Women are more independent in Kuwait than in most other Arab countries. However, they are still usually segregated from men and are not allowed to vote.

11 ● CLOTHING

In Kuwait's urban centers, Western-style clothing is becoming popular, particularly with young people. However, many Kuwaitis still wear traditional Arab clothing. This includes the *dishdasha* (ankle-length robe) with a *ghutra* (head scarf). It is usually white, worn over a skull cap, and held in place with an *aqal* (wool rope) for men. Women are veiled according to Islamic law. Both men and women love perfume and wear it most of the time.

12 ● FOOD

Kuwaiti cuisine offers a variety of dishes that reflect its Bedu (also called Bedouin) tradition (the Bedu are the traditional Arab nomadic desert herders), as well as its long history of contacts with other cultures such as those of India, Iraq, and Iran. In addition to the simple Bedu meals of dates and yogurt, Kuwaitis favor meat, fish, and rice. Spices are an essential part of the Kuwaiti diet. Among the most commonly used spices are coriander, cardamom, saffron, and turmeric.

Coffee and tea are the most popular beverages and are often mixed with spices. Coffee is mixed with cardamom, and tea with saffron or mint. Food and drink are always taken with the right hand.

As a wealthy country, Kuwait is able to import foods from all over the world. Their desert climate supports almost no agriculture, making importation absolutely neces-

sary. As Muslims, Kuwaitis cannot eat pork or drink alcohol.

13 ● EDUCATION

Education is required for all Kuwaiti children six to fourteen years of age. Schools teach in Arabic. English is taught as a second language to all students ten years of age and older. Boys and girls attend separate schools. Girls receive training in homemaking and child care, as well as vocational training for jobs considered "acceptable" for women. These include secretary, receptionist, teacher, and so forth. Women are not encouraged to take engineering or mechanical courses, but they may become medical doctors. About one-third of all Kuwaiti doctors are women. Every child is trained to become computer-literate in primary and early secondary school.

Education is free through the university level. The government also pays for students to study abroad. All expenses, including books, tuition, transportation, uniforms, and meals, are paid by the government. The government also pays families of students an allowance to help cover any other education-related expenses.

14 ● CULTURAL HERITAGE

To help promote and encourage the arts in Kuwait, the government founded the National Council for Culture, Arts, and Letters in 1974. Painting and sculpture are relatively recent developments on Kuwait's cultural scene. Compared to that of other Gulf states, the Kuwaiti theater is highly professional.

The National Museum building used to contain the Al-Sabah Collection. Named for

Kuwait Information Office

An outdoor swimming pool at a Kuwaiti sports club.

the ruling family, it was considered one of the most important collections of Islamic arts in the world. During the Iraqi invasion, however, the entire museum was looted by the occupying forces.

Arab music is rich and diverse. The *oud*, a popular instrument, is an ancient stringed instrument that is the ancestor of the European lute. Another traditional instrument is the *rebaba,* a one-stringed instrument. The sea chantey is the most distinctive Kuwaiti folk song. Chanteys were traditionally sung as work songs on pearling ships.

Islam forbids the depiction of the human form, so Kuwaiti art is based on geometric and abstract shapes. Calligraphy is a sacred art, with passages from the Koran being the primary subject matter. Muslim visual art finds its greatest expression in the decoration of mosques.

The Islamic reverence for poetry and the poetic richness of the Arabic language shape much of Kuwait's cultural heritage.

15 ● EMPLOYMENT

The main source of employment and income in Kuwait is the oil industry. At the

Kuwait Information Office

Kuwaiti men enjoying a game of Dama.

current rate of production, proven reserves are expected to last another 250 years. Along with the oil are huge reserves of natural gas.

Even with these sources of substantial guaranteed income, Kuwait is trying to encourage the development of other industries. The government offers low-interest loans, tax breaks, and subsidies for electricity and water to new businesses. Other industries remain small, however. Fishing is one of the oldest industries in Kuwait, as are pearling and shipbuilding.

Trade unions are not permitted in Kuwait, and the oil industry is totally government-run. While over 40 percent of non-

Kuwaiti women in Kuwait work outside the home, fewer than 15 percent of native Kuwaiti women do. Islamic traditions and restrictions prevent most native Kuwaiti women from having outside employment.

16 ● SPORTS

Football (what Americans call soccer) is the most popular sport in Kuwait. The national team has won both Arab and international competitions. Kuwait has also had international success in the traditional sport of horse racing.

Other traditional sports include falconry and camel racing. Water sports are popular in the Persian Gulf, although jellyfish prevent swimming there. Kuwaitis swim in pools. Government-run sports clubs have facilities for swimming, tennis, and other sports.

17 ● RECREATION

Kuwaitis, as well as tourists to Kuwait, spend a great deal of time relaxing on the beaches along the gulf coast. Water sports (except for swimming, because of the jellyfish) are a popular form of recreation.

One of the biggest attractions in Kuwait is Entertainment City, modeled after Disneyland in the United States. It houses both recreational and educational facilities and exhibits. There are several movie theaters in Kuwait cities, which show Arab, Indian, Pakistani, and English-language films.

18 ● CRAFTS AND HOBBIES

The best-known folk art in Kuwait is that of the Bedu (or Bedouins), particularly weavings done with brightly colored wool on a loom called a *sadu*.

19 ● SOCIAL PROBLEMS

Even before the destruction caused by the Iraqi invasion and occupation (1990–91), Kuwait suffered from severe ecological problems. These were caused by human population growth and industrialization. But the most damage has been done by the oil industry. About 250,000 barrels' worth of oil spills into the Persian Gulf each year. Only three out of twenty-seven species of mammals in Kuwait are not endangered, and they are the house rat, brown rat, and house mouse.

Since the Iraqi retreat from Kuwait in 1991, the ecological problems have worsened greatly. The Iraqis deliberately spilled 4 to 6 million barrels of oil into the gulf. This was the largest oil slick ever on the planet. The Iraqis also bombed 749 oil wells, many of which caught fire. It took almost a year to put out the flames. The plume of oil smoke from the burning wells rose about 22,000 feet (over 6,700 meters) into the air. When the fires were still burning, everything in Kuwait was covered with oil and soot, including the people. Children who played outside became black with grime. It was impossible to keep clean.

Since the Iraqi invasion, another division has occurred in Kuwaiti society. This division is between the "insiders"—those who stayed in Kuwait during the occupation, and the "outsiders"—those who fled the country and have since returned. Insiders feel that they should have more say in the running of the country now, since they stayed to defend their homes. Outsiders include the royal family and ruling members of the government, who are reluctant to give up much of their power. The government did finally allow elections for a new National Assembly in 1992, giving the people a greater say in their governance.

20 ● BIBLIOGRAPHY

Canby, Thomas Y. "After the Storm." *National Geographic* 180, no. 2 (August 1991): 2–32.

Kuwait in Pictures. Minneapolis, Minn.: Lerner Publications Co., 1989.

Sluglett, Peter, and Marion Farouk-Sluglett. *Tuttle Guide to the Middle East.* Boston: Charles E. Tuttle Co., 1992.

Vine, Peter, and Paula Casey. *Kuwait: A Nation's Story.* London: Immel Publishing, 1992.

WEBSITES

ArabNet. [Online] Available http://www.arab.net/kuwait/kuwait_contents.html, 1998.

Embassy of Kuwait in Canada. [Online] Available http://embassyofkuwait.com/, 1998.

Kuwait Ministry of Information. [Online] Available http://www.kuwait.info.nw.dc.us/, 1998.

Kyrgyzstan

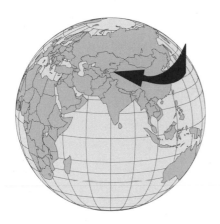

The people of Kyrgyzstan are called Kyrgyz. Ethnic Kyrgyz (people who trace their ancestry to Kyrgyzstan) make up more than 50 percent of the population. The rest are Russians, 22 percent; Uzbeks, 13 percent; Ukrainians and Germans, 2.5 percent each; and Tatars, about 2 percent. For more information on the Russians and Tatars, see the chapter on Russia in Volume 7; for the Germans, see the chapter on Germany in Volume 4; and for the Ukrainians and Uzbeks, see the chapters on Ukraine and Uzbekistan in Volume 9.

Kyrgyz

PRONUNCIATION: KIR-ghiz

LOCATION: Kyrgyzstan; China

POPULATION: 2.5 million

LANGUAGES: Kyrgyz; Russian; English

RELIGION: Islam (Sunni Muslim)

1 ● INTRODUCTION

The Kyrgyz people were nomads throughout much of their history, initially living in the region of south-central Russia between the Yenesei River and Lake Baikal about 2,000 years ago. The ancestors of the modern Kyrgyz were probably not Turks, like most people in the area are. The ancestors of the Kyrgyz exhibited European-like features (such as fair skin, green eyes, and red hair). At some time between the twelfth and sixteenth centuries, they settled in the Tien Shan Mountains.

In modern times, the Kyrgyz people have seen much of their land taken by Russians as the Russian empire spread east. From 1917 to 1991, the Kyrgyz lived in the Soviet Union as residents of the Kirghiz Soviet Socialist Republic. With the collapse of the Soviet Union, the Kyrgyz people became independent and created their own country.

Since 1991, Kyrgyzstan has been led by an elected president and parliamentary form of government. The government has concentrated on elevating the status of Kyrgyz culture in Kyrgyzstan without alienating persons of other ethnic backgrounds (a citizen of Kyrgyzstan does not need to be Kyrgyz). However, there have been conflicts between Kyrgyz and Uzbeks, as well as periodic clashes between Kyrgyz and Tajiks along the border with Tajikistan.

2 ● LOCATION

There are approximately 2.5 million Kyrgyz living throughout the former Soviet Union,

KYRGYZ

0   250   500   750 Miles
0 250 500 750 1000 Kilometers

RUSSIA

KAZAKSTAN

Zaysan

UZBEKISTAN

Almaty
(Alma-Ata)

TURKMENISTAN

Tashkent

KYRGYZSTAN

Ashkhabad   Tejen
Dushanbe   TAJIKISTAN

IRAN   AFGHANISTAN   CHINA

Kabul

Zaranj

Saindak   Islāmābād

PAKISTAN

Indus

Pasni   New Delhi   NEPAL   BHUTAN

Ganges   Kāthmāndu

Gulf of Oman

Arabian
Sea   Lakhpat   INDIA

Surat   BANGLADESH   Dhaka

about 88 percent of them in Kyrgyzstan. Ethnic Kyrgyz constitute slightly more than half of the population of Kyrgyzstan.

Kyrgyzstan is located in Central Asia, along the western range of the Tien Shan Mountains. The boundaries with neighboring countries (Kazakstan, China, Tajikistan, and Uzbekistan) run along mountain ranges, and about 85 percent of Kyrgyzstan itself is mountainous.

The largest mountain lake, Issyk-Kul, is located high in the mountains of eastern Kyrgyzstan. Many Kyrgyz fishing villages are located around the edge of the lake.

3 ● LANGUAGE

Most Kyrgyz people speak the Kyrgyz language, which is a distinct Turkic language with Mongol influences. Although the Kyr-

gyz language is spoken in the home, most Kyrgyz also speak Russian, which is the language of business and commerce. English is the third language of communication.

The Kyrgyz people have many proverbs and sayings related to horses, such as: "A horse is a person's wind."

4 ● FOLKLORE

The telling of epic oral tales dates back about 1,000 years among the Kyrgyz people. One of the most famous epics tells the saga of Manas, the father of the Kyrgyz people; his son Semetey; and his grandson Seytek. The entire poem is incredibly long (about twice as long as the *Iliad* and the *Odyssey* combined). It can take up to three weeks to recite and was not written down until the 1920s. In the epic, the forty Kyrgyz tribes strive for freedom and unity. Under the leadership of Manas, the Kyrgyz people who were the slaves of various tribes are gathered as a nation. Manas is believed to be buried at a small mausoleum near the town of Talas, in western Kyrgyzstan near the border with Kazakstan.

5 ● RELIGION

Horses figured prominently in the traditional spiritual beliefs of the early Kyrgyz. It was believed that a horse carried the spirit of a dead person to a higher world. Most Kyrgyz today are followers of Islam (Sunni Muslim), but many ancient traditions persist.

Since the eighth century AD, Islam has been the dominant religion in the Fergana River Valley in southwest Kyrgyzstan. Even so, it did not gain a strong presence among all the Kyrgyz until the nineteenth century.

The Kyrgyz are generally more secular (nonreligious) in daily life than some of the other peoples in the area. Kyrgyzstan also has a large population of non-Muslims. The government has made no moves to use Islamic law.

6 ● MAJOR HOLIDAYS

New Year's Day (January 1) and Orthodox Christmas (January 7) are official holidays in Kyrgyzstan. The spring equinox (around March 21) is called *Nawruz* and is an important holiday among the Kyrgyz people because it marks the start of the Muslim new year. *Kurban Ait* (Remembrance Day, June 13) and Independence Day (August 31) are also official Kyrgyzstan holidays.

7 ● RITES OF PASSAGE

Kyrgyz rites of passage include large birthday parties with many friends and relatives. These feasts often last five or six hours. Celebrations are held for a birth, for a baby's fortieth day of life, for the first day of school, and for school graduation.

A wedding serves to honor the married couple and assemble an extended family or clan. Traditionally, marriages were arranged by the parents, and a dowry payment was expected. Many modern Kyrgyz young people want to influence the selection of their spouse.

8 ● RELATIONSHIPS

Kyrgyz women typically greet one another with handshakes or hugs. Male-female relations among the Kyrgyz are less formal and

EPD Photos

A Kyrgyz newspaper.

less rigid than among their neighbors, the Uzbeks or Tajiks. Men and women eat together and share some household tasks.

Like many other peoples of Central Asia, the Kyrgyz are very hospitable. Kyrgyz often honor their guests by serving them a cooked sheep's head.

9 ● LIVING CONDITIONS

The traditional Kyrgyz home is a *yurt* or *yurta*—a round, felt-covered structure built upon a collapsible wooden frame. Most Kyrgyz today live in individual permanent homes, but about 40,000 Kyrgyz still live in yurts. The arched opening of a yurta is called the *tundruk*. The flag of the Republic of Kyrgyzstan features a tundruk.

Life in the city has some challenges. There is a lack of housing, and public transportation does not run on schedule. In Bishkek, for example, evening bus service is not reliable. There are taxis in the city, but people looking for a ride will often stop a private car and pay the driver because it is cheaper than using a taxi.

EPD Photos

The ak-kalpak *(white hat) is a symbol of Kyrgyz culture. The basic design of the hat–dome-shaped, white felt with a black brim, black piping, abstract curved stitching, and a black tassel on top–has been the same for generations.*

10 ● FAMILY LIFE

Women in Kyrgyz society still perform the bulk of household chores. Women in the cities are encouraged to be professionals as well as mothers. Both men and women may marry more than one spouse. It is more common for a man to have more than one wife. A husband must provide each wife with her own separate house, and must support her children. In order for a woman to have multiple husbands, she must have substantial wealth or influence.

Kyrgyz families are large, with an average of four to six children. In the capital city of Bishkek, families are slightly smaller. In the countryside, it is common for three generations to live together. As many as ten to twelve people may share a home during the cold months. It is very important to the Kyrgyz to know about ancestors. Some people are able to recount their ancestors as far back as seven generations or 200 years.

11 ● CLOTHING

Traditional everyday clothes were made of wool, felt, and fur. Ornate silks were, and still are, used for special occasions and ceremonies. By the 1990s, cotton denim and other fabrics had become popular for everyday wear.

Headgear figures prominently in Kyrgyz culture. During the Soviet era, women were prohibited from wearing their large traditional hats, which were a symbol of Kyrgyz culture. There is also a traditional hat proudly worn by men as a symbol of Kyrgyz culture, the *ak-kalpak* (white hat).

12 ● FOOD

Because many Kyrgyz live in areas with little rain, the variety of crops grown depends on irrigation from the mountains. Sugar beets and cereal grains are the main crops. Livestock are an important source of food, with sheep, goats, cattle, and horses most common. Pigs, bees, and rabbits are also raised.

Examples of traditional Kyrgyz food include *manti* (mutton dumplings), *irikat* (a type of pasta salad made with noodles, carrots, and radishes), and *koumiss* (fermented mare's milk).

A great Kyrgyz delicacy reserved especially for guests is a combination plate of fresh sliced sheep liver and slices of sheep tail fat. It is often boiled and salted and tastes far more delicious than it sounds.

At the breakfast table, one often finds bountiful amounts of yogurt, heavy cream, butter, and honey served with bread and tea. Dairy products are an essential part of Kyrgyz life.

13 ● EDUCATION

For the most part, Kyrgyz people have been influenced by Russian culture. Most Kyrgyz cannot speak or understand their own native language very well, except for people living in rural areas. Most high school and university instruction is in Russian. Although this is slowly beginning to change, rural Kyrgyz (who are less likely to learn Russian) have a hard time competing at the national level on university entrance exams.

Parents tend to favor a broad education for their children. It is often not possible for parents to send their children to universities and technical schools because education is not free in independent Kyrgyzstan. When Kyrgyzstan was part of the former Soviet Union (1917–91), university education was free.

14 ● CULTURAL HERITAGE

The *kyiak* and *komuz* are traditional musical instruments used by the Kyrgyz. The kyiak

resembles a violin and is played with a bow but has only two strings. The three-stringed komuz is the favorite folk instrument among the Kyrgyz.

The Kyrgyz have several titles of honor that are given to various musical performers. A *jïrchïï* is a singer-poet, whereas an *akin* is a professional poet and musician-composer. The jïrchïï is primarily a performer of known music, while the akin is a composer who plays original compositions as well as traditional music.

A special performer called a *manaschï* performs the famous saga of Manas (see Folklore section). There are also several types of Kyrgyz songs, such as *maktoo* (eulogies), *sanat* and *nasiyat* (songs with a moral), and *kordoo* (social protest tunes).

15 ● EMPLOYMENT

Work hours vary. Most often work runs from 8:00 AM to 5:00 PM. Mills and factories operate on a relay system, with shifts set up by the management. Retail shops are usually open from 7:00 AM to 8:00 PM, with an afternoon lunch period. Department stores, bookstores, and other shops usually open according to the hours set by government offices. Bazaars (street markets) are open from 6:00 AM until 7:00 or 8:00 PM.

16 ● SPORTS

Equestrian sports (sports with horses) are very popular among the Kyrgyz. Racing and wrestling on horseback are especially enjoyed. Wrestling on horseback for a goat's carcass, called *ulak tartysh* or *kok boru,* is a common game among the Kyrgyz. (*Kok boru* means "gray wolf.") The game may have its origin in ancient times, when

Jeannine Davis-Kimball

The jïrchïï is a Kyrgyz musician who performs songs and poetry.

herds of cattle grazed in the steppes (plains) and mountains and were exposed to the threat of attack by wolves. Shepherds would chase after a wolf on horseback and beat it with sticks and whips, and then try to snatch the dead carcass away from each other for fun.

Kok boru was later replaced with ulak tartysh, played with a goat's carcass on a field measuring about 328 yards by 164 yards (300 meters by 150 meters). The two goals are at opposite ends of the field. A goat carcass, usually weighing 60 to 90 pounds (30 to 40 kilograms), is placed in the center of the field. Each game lasts fifteen minutes. The object is to seize the goat carcass while on horseback and get it to the goal of the other team. Players may pick up the carcass from any place within the limits of the field, take it from opponents, pass or toss it to teammates, carry it on the horse's side, or suspend it between the horse's legs.

Falconry (the sport of hunting with trained falcons) while on horseback is another part of Kyrgyz culture that has been practiced for centuries. In addition to falcons, golden eagles are also trained for the sport. *Jumby atmai* is a game that involves shooting at a target while galloping on horseback. *Tyin enmei* is a contest to pick up coins from the ground while riding at full speed on horseback.

17 ● RECREATION

The capital city, Bishkek, has large parks, public gardens, shady avenues, and botanical gardens enjoyed by people traveling on foot. Opera, ballet, and national folklore groups are also popular forms of entertainment. The most popular form of relaxation

Jeannine Davis-Kimball

Falconry (the sport of hunting with trained falcons) has been practiced by Kyrgyz for centuries.

for city dwellers is to spend a weekend at a country cottage. Tens of thousands of these cottages are located on the outskirts of Bishkek. There are no bars or shows in Bishkek, so the city becomes quiet after 11:00 PM.

18 ● CRAFTS AND HOBBIES

The Kyrgyz are best known for crafting utensils, clothes, equipment, and other items used in everyday life and making them beautiful. Many articles are made of felt: carpets *(shirdak and alakiyiz),* bags for keeping dishes *(alk-kup),* and woven patterned strips of carpet sewn together into bags or rugs *(bashtyk).* Ornate leather dishes called *keter* are also made.

19 ● SOCIAL PROBLEMS

After years of life under the Soviet system (1917–91), the transition to a market economy is a difficult undertaking for the Kyrgyz. The poor service and uninspired work ethic that were results of the Soviet era will take a long time to change. Alcoholism and public drunkenness are now a visible social problem, partly because of rising unemployment.

20 ● BIBLIOGRAPHY

Allworth, Edward, ed. *Central Asia: 130 Years of Russian Dominance, A Historical Overview.* Durham, N.C.: Duke University Press, 1994.

Çagatay, Ergun. "Kyrgyzstan: A First Look." *Aramco World* (Houston: Aramco Services Company) 46, no. 4 (1995): 10–21.

Geography Department. *Kyrgyzstan.* Minneapolis, Minn.: Lerner Publications Co., 1993.

Thomas, Paul. *The Central Asian States—Tajikstan, Uzbekistan, Kyrgyzstan, Turkmenistan.* Brookfield, Conn.: Millbrook Press, 1992.

WEBSITES

Embassy of Kyrgyzstan, Washington, D.C. [Online] Available http://www.kyrgyzstan.org/, 1998.

World Travel Guide, Kyrgyzstan. [Online] Available http://www.wtgonline.com/country/kg/gen.html, 1998.

Laos

The people of Laos are called Laotians. There are officially 68 ethnic groups in Laos. Among the largest are the Kammu, believed to be the original inhabitants of Laos. About 6 percent of all Laotians are Lao-lum, or lowland Lao; they are related to the people of Thailand (see Volume 9). Other groups include the Lao-theung, or slope dwellers, who form about one-third of the population; and the Lao-soung, or mountain dwellers, who constitute about one-tenth of the population.

Lao

PRONUNCIATION: LAH-OO
LOCATION: Laos; Thailand
POPULATION: About 23 million
LANGUAGE: Lao
RELIGION: Theravada Buddhism; animism

1 ● INTRODUCTION

The Lao originated in southern China and moved southward into present-day Laos, forming a kingdom in the Mekong River valley in the fourteenth century and pushing the earlier inhabitants of the area, the Kammu, into more mountainous areas. After three centuries, however, disputes over succession to the throne and foreign invasions split the country into three rival kingdoms in the north, center, and south. Caught between the growing power of the Siamese and the Vietnamese, the Lao lost power and territory so that today most Lao people live in Thailand (formerly Siam).

Laos was colonized by the French in the 1890s and treated as the hinterland to their colonies in Vietnam. Laos was unified after World War II and achieved independence within the French Union in 1949 and full independence in 1953. However, regional divisions were replaced by political ones. The Lao were divided into three factions: a right-wing group backed by the United States; a neutralist group in Thailand; and a communist group backed by Vietnam, the Soviet Union, and China. After a devastating civil war fought with heavy American bombing on behalf of the right, and with Vietnamese troops on behalf of the left, the communist Pathet Lao (Lao Nation) took control of the country in 1975, abolished the monarchy, and established the Lao People's Democratic Republic (LPDR). In the political, economic, and social upheavals that fol-

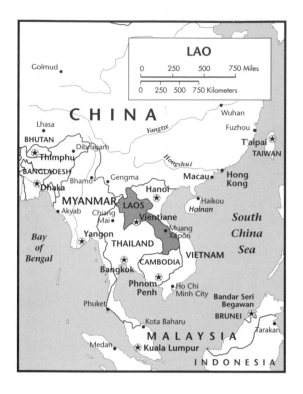

(240 to 320 kilometers) across. The country is extremely mountainous, with only about 4 percent of the land suitable for farming. It has a tropical monsoon climate and most people engage in subsistence rice agriculture. The Lao make up two-thirds of the population, or somewhat over 3 million of the population of almost 5 million. They occupy the most desirable land in the river valleys and live clustered along the Mekong River across from northeast Thailand, most of whose people are Lao, and in the southern plateau. The Lao of northeast Thailand, together with Lao groups in northern Thailand, represent one-third of the whole population of Thailand, or about 20 million people—several times the number of Lao in Laos itself.

After the communists seized power in Laos in 1975, about 360,000 refugees left the country. Refugees were predominantly Lao, but included many Hmong and smaller numbers of other minority groups. Many of the French-speaking elite went to France, but most Lao went to the United States. They live scattered across the country, although southern California is a favorite location because of the warmer climate. Canada and Australia also received thousands of Lao refugees while thousands of others stayed illegally in Thailand, blending in with the Lao population of northeast Thailand.

lowed, about 10 percent of the population fled as refugees, draining the country of skilled and educated people. Although the aging Lao leadership maintains one-party control and continues to assert communist ideology, it has loosened social and economic controls and now invites foreign investment and tourism.

2 ● LOCATION

Laos is a small landlocked country in Southeast Asia bordering on Thailand, Myanmar (Burma), China, Vietnam, and Cambodia. Laos has an area of about 91,400 square miles (236,800 square kilometers), roughly the size of Idaho. It runs about 700 miles (1,126 kilometers) from north to south and averages about 150 to 200 miles

3 ● LANGUAGE

Lao belongs to the Tai family of languages and is related to Thai, but Lao has its own alphabet and numbers. Many words have Sanskrit and Pali roots, especially terms relating to religion, royalty, and government. Most Lao words have one syllable and the grammar is very easy. However, Lao is difficult for Westerners to speak because it is a tonal language. There are six tones, and words that sound similar to a Western ear may be very different depending on the tone. For example, the word *ma* in mid tone means "come"; *ma* in a high tone means "horse"; and *ma* in a rising tone means "dog."

Lao is written from left to right, but no space is left between words, only between phrases or sentences. Readers must know where one word ends and the next word starts. Vowels can appear before, after, above, or below the consonants they go with, or in various combinations thereof. Relatively few people, probably only just over 2 million, can read Lao. While the Lao in Thailand speak Lao, their education is in Thai, so they are literate (can read and write) in that language.

Girls are often given names of flowers or gems, while boys might be given names that suggest strength. However, many have simple names like Daeng (red) or Dam (black), or might be called by nicknames like Ling (monkey). Family names were made compulsory in 1943 but aren't as important as first names. The phone book is alphabetized by first names, and a man named Sitha Sisana would be addressed as Mr. Sitha.

Some common expressions are: *sabai dee* (greetings), *la kon* (goodbye); *khob jai* (thank you); *kin khaw* (eat—literally, "eat rice," the most important food); *bo pen nyang* (it doesn't matter, never mind, it's nothing).

4 ● FOLKLORE

A Lao legend explains the origins of the Lao and Kammu, the original inhabitants of the land:

> Once upon a time three chiefs settled the earth and began rice farming with their water buffalo. After a few years the water buffalo died, and from his nostrils grew a creeping plant that bore three gourds which grew to enormous size. Hearing a loud noise from inside the gourds, one of the chiefs took a red hot iron and pierced each gourd. Crowds of men came squeezing out of the narrow openings. The chief then used a chisel to carve out new openings for the men. This is the origin of the different people in Laos. The Kammu, a dark skinned people who wore their hair in chignons, came out the holes made with the red hot iron; and the Lao, a lighter skinned people who wore their hair short, came out the openings made by the chisel.

Lao proverbs give us an idea of their cultural attitudes.

> To judge an elephant, look at its tail;
> To judge a girl, look at her mother.

> Flee from the elephant and meet the tiger;
> Flee from the tiger and meet a crocodile.
> (Their version of "out of the frying pan into the fire.")

> When the water level falls, the ants eat the fish;
> When the water level rises, the fish eat the ants.

5 ● RELIGION

The first Lao king, Fa Ngum (1316–73), made Buddhism the state religion in the fourteenth century, and almost all Lao are

Theravada Buddhists. Buddha is regarded as a great teacher—not a god, a creator, or a savior. He taught that suffering is caused by desire, anger, and illusion. Each person is responsible for his own salvation. A person's karma, the balance of good and bad deeds, will affect this life and future reincarnations.

When the communists took over in 1975, they did not dare eliminate something so central to Lao identity as Buddhism. Rather, they continued state control of the Buddhist hierarchy and tried to manipulate religion for political purposes. Many monks fled as refugees or disrobed rather than promote government policies. In recent years government controls have eased and there has been a revival of Buddhism.

Animism, belief in spirits, coexists with Buddhism. Ancestor spirits, the local guardian spirits of each village, are appealed to at the beginning of the agricultural year for successful crops. These spirits should also be informed of major changes in a person's life—sickness, a move, a marriage.

The Lao believe the body contains thirty-two spirits, and illness can result if a spirit leaves the body. A *baci* ceremony is held to call the spirits back to the body in order to cure illness, to protect someone about to make a major life change, or to bring health, happiness, and prosperity. A beautifully decorated tray filled with ritual offerings is presented to the spirits. Cotton strings are tied around the wrists of the person who is sick or who is being honored, and blessings are recited when the strings are tied.

6 ● MAJOR HOLIDAYS

The most important Lao holiday is Songkarn, the Lao New Year, celebrated from April 13 to 15. After several months of drought, the first rains of the year begin in April, bringing the start of the agricultural year. Water is poured over Buddha images and elders as a blessing. After this is done very decorously, Songkarn turns into one big water fight, with water splashed on everyone in sight. Since the temperature is over 90°F at that time of year, the water feels good. People try to return to their home villages for Songkarn to visit friends and relatives and to join in the fun.

The Rocket Festival is a popular traditional Lao holiday, although not an official holiday. Today it is celebrated on *Wisakha Bucha,* the day celebrating the birth, enlightenment, and death of Buddha. The Rocket Festival is based on a fertility rite that predates Buddhism in the area. Village men build bamboo rockets packed with gunpowder, and villages compete to see whose rocket can fly the highest. The men hold boat races on the rivers, and the village women hold folk dance contests. This holiday is based on the lunar calendar and falls sometime in May.

Independence Day on July 19 celebrates the granting of autonomy, or independence, from the French Union in 1949; National Day on December 2 celebrates the proclamation of the Lao People's Democratic Republic in 1975, a one-party communist state.

The *That Luang Festival* occurs on the day of the full moon in the twelfth lunar

Cory Langley

Lao children help with farm chores from an early age, and young girls help with child care.

month and celebrates the most sacred Buddhist monument in Laos.

7 ●RITES OF PASSAGE

The main rite of passage for a Lao man is ordination as a Buddhist monk. In the past, most Lao men spent at least one three-month period of Buddhist Lent as a monk, learning about religion, chanting Pali texts, and practicing self-control and meditation. To be ordained, a man reenacts the life of Prince Gautama, who renounced the world and became Buddha, the Enlightened One. The initiate is dressed in finery and escorted with pomp to the monastery, where his head and eyebrows are shaved. He then changes into a simple robe, renounces the world, and

takes his vows as a monk. There is no set length of time for ordination, so a monk can disrobe and return to lay life at any time. Fewer men become ordained today and often for shorter periods, but it is believed that a man gains maturity by doing so, and women consider it desireable for a male to be ordained. There is no ordination for women.

8 ●RELATIONSHIPS

The Lao are a fun-loving people. They work hard when they have to, but they believe that life should be enjoyed. Lao are personable and friendly and have a good sense of humor. They enjoy having people around and are quick to invite them to share a meal

Cory Langley

Man pushing a cart with two pigs. Most Lao are engaged in agriculture, and agricultural practices have changed little over the centuries.

or sit and talk. They try to avoid confrontation and appreciate a person with self-control.

It is considered improper for men and women to touch in public. However, if men hold hands with each other or women hold hands with other women, it is considered friendly and there are no sexual connotations.

In the past both the spoken language and body language showed relative social position, with the inferior person bowing to the superior person, but the communist government insisted on more egalitarian relations, at least overtly. Still, however, a Buddhist

will prostrate himself and bow his head to the floor three times in front of a Buddha image or a monk as a sign of respect.

9 ● LIVING CONDITIONS

Laos is one of the poorest countries in the world with an estimated income in the late 1990s of about $2,000 per year. The population is mainly rural with 85 percent depending on agriculture, mostly subsistence rice cultivation. The Lao are largely engaged in wet rice agriculture, depending on seasonal rains to flood their fields.

Water buffalo are used to plow, and agricultural practices have changed little over the centuries. Mechanization in the form of water pumps and small tractors is just beginning.

Rural homes are built on stilts to avoid flooding. They are made of wood or bamboo, often with walls of bamboo matting, and roofs of thatch or corrugated tin. Lao houses usually have little or no furniture. People sit, eat, and sleep on mats on the floor. Village houses are built close together, and farmers walk to their fields outside the village. There are no secrets in a small village, and gossip is a potent weapon to keep people in line.

Villages rarely have electricity or running water. Laos has great potential for hydroelectric power and currently exports electricity to Thailand. But the Lao buy electricity back from the Thai for their cities across the Mekong River from northeast Thailand, as Laos has no national power grid.

There are few roads, and some of these are impassable quagmires in the rainy season. Most transportation is by boat along the rivers. Ox carts are still common.

Health facilities are limited. Malaria, dysentery, malnutrition, and parasites are major problems. Life expectancy is about fifty for men and fifty-three for women. The Lao undoubtedly do better than minority (mainly rural) populations, as they are more likely to live in or near the cities or along transportation routes, and they continue to favor themselves at the expense of minorities.

10 ● FAMILY LIFE

Lao families are close and children are welcome. The LPDR government had banned birth control devices until recently, but few people have access to birth control services. Women have many children but there is a high rate of infant and child mortality.

There is no dating, but groups of young men in the village go from house to house in the evening to call on families with young women and engage in banter with them and their parents. Traditionally, the young man is expected to pay a bride price and move in with the wife's family on marriage. When the next daughter marries, the couple might set up housekeeping on their own with help from the wife's parents. Ultimately the youngest daughter is left to take care of the parents and inherit the family home and remaining farm plot.

Women are responsible for much heavy work—hauling water for the household and, in the absence of rice mills, pounding the rice in big mortars of hollowed out logs to husk it. The men plow and deal with draft animals, while women tend to be responsi-

ble for pigs and poultry and vegetable gardens. The animals usually live under the house. Everyone, including the children, helps with transplanting and harvesting rice.

Children rarely have toys but enjoy catching fish, frogs, and insects to supplement the family diet. Boys are skillful with slingshots and blowguns in hunting small birds. Young girls help with child care and often carry a younger sibling astride a hip while they play with their friends.

11 ● CLOTHING

When the communist government came to power in 1975, it tried to ban blue jeans, calling them bourgeois Western decadence. It even tried to do away with the sin, the traditional sarong-like women's lower garment, but the government soon had to back down. The sin is a very practical garment—one size fits all. It is a tube of cloth folded with a pleat to fit the waist and secured with a belt or a tuck in the waist. Worn above the breasts, it makes a useful garment for bathing in the public stream or well, which is necessary since few village homes have bathrooms. A dry garment is slipped over the wet garment, which is then dropped without any loss of modesty. Lao women continue to wear the sin, sometimes adapted into a skirt, with a blouse. On special occasions women wear handwoven silk sin with beautiful tie-dyed patterns and a colorful woven and embroidered strip added to the hem.

Lao men wear shirt and pants, but bathe and relax around the house in a phakhawma, a cloth about two yards long and thirty inches wide that can be worn as a skirt-like garment or wrapped into shorts. Little chil-

Recipe

Papaya Salad

Ingredients

3 cups shredded green papaya (shredded cabbage, rutabaga, sliced green beans, or grated carrots may be substituted)
2 to 3 cloves garlic
2 to 3 fresh, small, hot, Thai chilis
cherry tomatoes
fresh lime juice
fish sauce (salt may be substituted)
1 teaspoon sugar

Directions

1. Grind garlic and chilis in a bowl with a mortar.
2. Add vegetables and cherry tomatoes and mix well.
3. Sprinkle lime juice and fish sauce over the top to taste.
4. Sprinkle entire mixture with sugar and mix well.

Lao Papaya Salad is hot, sour, salty, and sweet all at once. Serve with lots of rice.

dren often go naked or wear only a shirt. It is common for people to go barefoot or wear rubber sandals. In the cities, of course, Western dress is common.

12 ● FOOD.

The staple food of the Lao is sticky rice, also known as glutinous rice or sweet rice. The rice must be soaked for several hours before being steamed in a basket over a pot of boiling water. It is then put in another basket that serves as a serving dish or lunch pail. Sticky rice is eaten with the fingers, so one doesn't need dishes or silverware. People take a bit of rice from the basket and shape it into a small ball. It is then dipped into the serving dish for whatever other food is offered, most likely a hot sauce of chilis, garlic, fish sauce, and lime. The Lao have two categories of food—rice and "with rice." Foods other than rice are limited and are served more as condiments, something to add flavor, so they tend to be very hot or very salty so that one will eat a lot of rice with them.

Dried salty beef is a favorite dish if meat is available. Beef is sliced thin and liberally doused with fish sauce (a salty liquid made from salt and fish) or salt, and placed on a tray to dry in the sun to preserve it. The meat can also be deep-fried to cook it and remove most of the moisture

13 ● EDUCATION

The literacy rate (percentage of the population who can read and write) in Laos is estimated at 45 percent. The Lao are much more likely to be literate (able to read and write) than minority peoples, and men are more likely to be literate than are women. The LPDR is the first government to make a serious effort to extend education beyond the Lao areas to minorities. However, with the loss of about 90 percent of its most educated population (who fled the country as refugees), education has perhaps been set back a generation, and already low standards have declined further. Universal primary education by the year 2000 is the government's goal but seems beyond reach given current progress. Many village schools have only one or two grades and little in the way of books, paper, or school supplies. Teachers are paid little and often infrequently, so they often have to farm or hold a second job to support their families. School sessions, therefore, tend to be sporadic.

There are five years of primary school, but probably only half of primary school-age children finish fifth grade. This is followed by three years of lower secondary school and three years of upper secondary school. Secondary schools are few in number and are located in cities and provincial capitals. One must pass a test to enter secondary school. School uniforms and supplies are expensive, the distances are great, and village education too rudimentary for many village children to continue their education. There are a few colleges and technical institutes in Vientiane, the capital.

In the early days of the LPDR, teenagers from "bad" family backgrounds, as defined by the communists (children of officials from the old regime or of shopkeepers), were often denied entrance to secondary education. Some teens fled the country on their own, risking being shot or drowning as they swam the Mekong River to Thailand. They were hoping to resettle abroad and continue their education.

Recently private schools have been allowed and are preferred over public schools by parents who can afford the fees. Lack of financial resources and trained teachers remains a problem for Laos.

14 ● CULTURAL HERITAGE

The most distinctive Lao musical instrument is the *khaen*. According to a popular saying, "those who eat sticky rice, live in

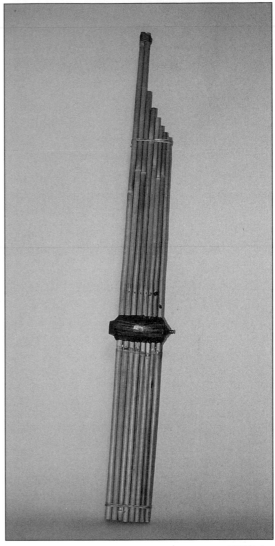

EPD Photos

An example of a khaen, a free-reed mouth organ, featuring 16 bamboo pipes. Courtesy of the Center for the Study of World Musics, Kent State University.

dwellings mounted on piles, and listen to the music of the khaen are Lao." The khaen is a collection of bamboo pipes of different lengths, each with a small hole for fingering and a metal reed, preferably of silver, all attached to a mouthpiece. There are six-hole, fourteen-hole, and sixteen-hole instruments. A khaen musician accompanies a *mohlam* performance, a traditional Lao entertainment that usually involves two singers, a man and a woman, and offers courting poetry, suggestive repartée, and dance. The songs and poetry represent oral literature passed on to performers by their teachers. Relatively few have been written down. Ability to add witty and rhyming repartée on the spot is valued. Males and females never touch in Lao dance.

A great work of Lao literature is *Sin Xay,* an epic poem. Sin Xay (which translates to "he who triumphs through his merits"), the hero, is rejected by his father, the king. He sets out to rescue his aunt, the beautiful Sumontha, from a giant who has carried her off. After many trials and combat with giants, demons, monstrous beasts, and magical beings, plus treacherous attacks by six half-brothers, Sin Xay rescues his aunt and reunites her with her brother, Sin Xay's father. The king regrets his previous rejection of Sin Xay and recognizes his nobility of character.

15 ● EMPLOYMENT

The vast majority of people are engaged in agriculture, especially subsistence rice farming on small family plots. Children help with farm chores from an early age, and most are engaged full-time in farming after leaving primary school. There is little industry. With the New Economic Mechanism (a policy of loosening of controls by the LPDR government), some people have gone into business and there is increasing interest in developing tourism and handi-

craft. The Lao predominate in the government bureaucracy.

16 ● SPORTS

Few Lao have time for sports, but those who do enjoy soccer, volleyball, and *takraw*—a Southeast Asian sport that involves keeping a rattan ball in the air without touching it with the hands. The feet and head are used as in soccer.

17 ● RECREATION

The biggest entertainment for the Lao in Laos, especially in the cities, is tuning in to Thai radio and television stations from across the Mekong River. The Lao government worries that Lao language and culture is being corrupted by the popularity of these programs and that youth are learning the wrong values from the commercialism of Thailand. The media in Laos is under tight Communist Party control and tends toward heavy-handed propaganda. They have nowhere near the impact of Thai mass media. In Thailand itself, mass media are spreading Thai language and culture to Lao-speaking areas.

18 ● CRAFTS AND HOBBIES

The Lao are becoming increasingly known for their exquisite handwoven textiles in cotton and silk with intricate tie-dyed designs. Basketry is another Lao specialty.

19 ● SOCIAL PROBLEMS

Discrimination by the Lao against the minority groups that make up one-third of the population of Laos remains a problem. In Thailand, on the other hand, the central Thai feel superior to the Lao of the Northeast. Human rights are an issue as the LPDR government will not tolerate criticism of the one-party communist control. Dissatisfaction is widespread among the aging ideologues who hold power and an increasingly corrupt bureaucracy and military. The youth seem particularly disillusioned and attracted to the alternate vision of society offered by Thai television. Even the communist leadership of Laos is now calling for a return to Buddhist values. Poverty and lack of health and education will continue to hamper development and make life difficult, especially in the rural areas.

20 ● BIBLIOGRAPHY

Cordell, Helen. *Laos*. Santa Barbara, Calif.: Clio, 1991.

De Berval, Rene. *Kingdom of Laos*. Saigon: France-Asie, 1959.

Diamond, J. *Laos*. Chicago: Children's Press, 1989.

Savada, Andrea Matles, ed. *Laos: A Country Study*. Washington, D.C.: Library of Congress, 1995

Stuart-Fox, Martin. *Buddhist Kingdom, Marxist State: The Making of Modern Laos*. Bangkok: White Lotus, 1996.

White, Peter T. "Laos Today." *National Geographic* (June 1987): 772-795.

WEBSITES

Embassy of Laos. Washington, D.C. [Online] Available http://www.laoembassy.com/, 1998.

World Travel Guide. Laos. [Online] Available http://www.wtgonline.com/country/la/gen.html, 1998.

Kammu

PRONUNCIATION: kah-MOO
ALTERNATE NAMES: Khamu; Khmu
LOCATION: Laos
POPULATION: About 500,000
LANGUAGE: Kammu
RELIGION: Animism; some Buddhism and Christianity

1 ● INTRODUCTION

The Kammu (also written Khamu and Khmu) are believed to be the original inhabitants of Laos, and they make up its largest minority today. They are an Austro-Asiatic people who moved north from the area of Indonesia in prehistoric times. The Kammu practiced paddy rice agriculture in the valleys along the Mekong River until they were displaced around the fourteenth century by the Lao moving southward from what is today southern China. The Kammu then settled on mountain slopes and in small, narrow upland valleys in northern and central Laos and in northern Thailand.

The Lao were contemptuous of the Kammu, referring to them as *kha,* or slaves. Roads, schools, and government services were basically designed for the Lao people and ignored minorities. Many Kammu joined the communist Pathet Lao (Lao Nation) movement and the Lao People's Liberation Army during the Lao civil war, for the communists promised them respect and education and technical training in Vietnam if they joined the cause. Some Kammu areas were heavily bombed by the United States during this period, as the civil war was linked to the war in Viet Nam, which was also being fought in Laos. After the

Pathet Lao won control of the country in 1975, some Kammu communist cadres had risen to power, but most were soon replaced by ethnic Lao with better training and more skills.

The Lao People's Democratic Republic (LPDR), established in 1975, has tried to do away with ethnic labels and now refers to lowland, midland, and upland Lao. The Kammu are classified as midland Lao because they tend to live on the mountain slopes. The LPDR government has tried to end slash-and-burn agriculture and has encouraged the Kammu to resettle in lowland areas. Some Kammu had already relocated during the war to escape the fighting and bombing. The Kammu, like other midland Lao, are among the poorest people in what is already a very poor country. Their low levels of education and geographic isolation, together with continued prejudice from the ethnic Lao, have been barriers to their integration.

2 ● LOCATION

As the Kammu are the earliest inhabitants of Laos, they are in their homeland, even if they have been displaced and treated as outsiders by the Lao, who took over the land. There are roughly one-half million Kammu in Laos and smaller numbers of Kammu in northern Thailand, northern Vietnam, and southern China. A few thousand Kammu fled as refugees after the communists came to power in 1975, and they have resettled mostly in the United States.

The Kammu live in scattered villages in mountainous areas of north and central Laos and in mountainous border regions of neighboring countries. Often villages are small, with only twenty or thirty families, but some villages can include several hundred households. Neighboring villages may belong to different ethnic groups lumped together with the Kammu as midland Lao, but with their own cultures and languages that are mutually incomprehensible. Young Kammu men often leave their mountain homes to find unskilled jobs in towns and cities for a few years to earn money for a bride price. During the Lao civil war, many young men went to Thailand to escape the draft. All the countries where Kammu are settled have tried to get them to switch to stationary lowland farming rather than shifting slash-and-burn cultivation, but they have not always been offered good land for farming.

3 ● LANGUAGE

The Kammu have their own language that belongs to the Mon-Khmer family of languages, but it is not a written language. Consequently, the Kammu have no written history of their own and little mention is made of them in the histories of dominant groups in the countries where they reside. Variation in the Kammu language is common, as the Kammu are spaced over a wide area with limited contact with more distant settlements. The language includes an increasing number of loan words from Lao.

Most people are illiterate, as few have had access to education. Thus agreements are oral and are made before the village elders, who memorize the terms and will arbitrate any disputes.

Children use their father's first name as their last name, so last names change every generation. Once a person becomes a parent, he or she is referred to as the father or mother of their child.

4 ● FOLKLORE

The Kammu have a rich folklore that has been transmitted orally. They are well regarded by other groups for their knowledge of folk medicines made from plants gathered in the forest.

The Kammu consider Luang Prabang, which served as the Lao royal capital, as their city, and they have a legend that explains how the city was founded by a Kammu.

The old people say that long, long ago people wished to build the city of Luang Prabang, but an enormous tree grew on the site. Nobody was able to cut it down. Each man that tried fell ill and fled. Then a man by the name of Wang said, "I will cut the tree if you will taboo [prohibit] the day of my death forever." The people promised and Wang cut the tree, but he dropped dead when the tree fell. Once they buried Wang, the Kammu began to build the city of Luang Prabang.

When the city was finished, they looked for a man to be their king. They all went to a cliff overlooking the place where the Ou River flows into the Mekong River, and the people said, "Any man brave enough to jump off this cliff, we will elect king."

The people boarded seven boats and seven rafts in the waters below the cliff and called for the men who wished to be king to jump. Looking down from the dizzying heights, one man after another was afraid and ran away. Finally just one man remained, a rela-

tive of Wang, who had cut the tree. This man had tucked a quiver into his belt, and as he leaned over to look down from the top of the cliff, his quiver struck against something and he lost his balance and fell into the river. The people hurried to help him get in a boat, and they praised his courage and elected him king. To this day the Kammu taboo the day Wang cut the tree and the day Wang was buried, and on these days no work is undertaken.

The Kammu played a significant role in annual ceremonies in the Lao court of Luang Prabang until fairly recent times. The ceremonies in effect indicated the Kammu's prior claim to the land and supported the legitimacy of the Lao, who now hold sway over the land. A symbolic payment was made to the Kammu representatives, who in turn acknowledged the legitimacy of the King of Luang Prabang.

5 ● RELIGION

The Kammu are mostly animists, people who believe in spirits, although a few are Buddhist or Christian. The Kammu believe there are hundreds of different spirits in the jungle, many of which are harmful but some of which are helpful.

Each village has its own shaman to propitiate the spirits that cause illness and accidents, and a priest (lkuun) to perform the village ceremony for the ancestor spirits. A shaman can be either male or female, but the priest holds a hereditary office passed on to the eldest son of the priestly family, even if the individual is only a child at the time. One becomes a shaman by apprenticing to a shaman and learning the magic formulas to be recited on different occasions.

Cory Langley

The Kammu generally don't buy food, but make do with what they can grow or hunt or trade. Besides rice, they grow corn and other vegetables.

The shaman must also be a person of good character who follows many specific rules or the magic formulas will not work to drive away evil spirits.

Living far from health centers and access to modern medicine, the Kammu often attribute illness to evil spirits and call on a shaman to exorcise them and bring back the soul of the patient. Minor, easily recognizable diseases are treated by a medicine man, an expert in herbal remedies.

The Kammu calendar operates on a sixty-day cycle. Certain days are considered particularly favorable for some activities and unfavorable for others. There are many taboo days when various kinds of work cannot be done and strangers cannot enter the village.

There are small rituals to be obvserved for many activities. For example, before setting out traps or beginning to hunt, a man must perform a small ceremony to ask permission from the spirit of the place.

6 ● MAJOR HOLIDAYS

The biggest holiday for the Kammu is the three-day series of ceremonies once a year to sacrifice to the village ancestor spirits, remake the village common house where the spirits reside, and ritually renew the village. The village spirits are considered benign, helping people to have good and happy lives so long as proper rituals are observed. There is no set day to sacrifice to the village spirits, but the ceremony is usually performed just after sowing the rice so the spirits will bring rain, or just before harvest, so they will chase away evil spirits such as the spirits of accidents or the spirits of waste. The house where the spirits are believed to reside is cleaned and remade with a new thatched roof, then a black pig is killed and its blood smeared on the altar. The spirits are offered pork, rice, and rice wine, and then the whole village eats and drinks.

The next day a sacrifice is made to the water spirits. Villagers dress up and parade to the village well with drums and gongs. There is a ritual cleaning of the well, and fresh water is fetched from the well in a decorated container and placed in the house of the spirits.

On the third day each family places a basket under the water container, which the priest shoots with an arrow from a crossbow. Those baskets that get sprinkled with a lot of water are considered a sign of luck and a good harvest. There is then a procession to a stream to float away the bad spirits. The young people engage in horseplay with mud fights and pushing each other in the water. A communal meal is eaten at noon and, in the evening, the villagers parade home and celebrate with lots of food and rice wine.

7 ● RITES OF PASSAGE

For most men the main rite of passage is preparing for marriage, usually by leaving home to work as a laborer for a few years to get money for a bride price. Each family has a totem and is grouped by totems (plants, birds, four-legged creatures) into a system of marriage alliances. There are three such groups in each village, with a pattern of one group taking wives from a second group and giving wives to a third group. The man can choose a bride only from the wife-giving group in his marriage alliance system, or it is believed dire misfortune will result. Ideally there is matrilineal cross-cousin marriage, in which a man marries his mother's brother's daughter (the brother might be a real brother or a clan brother). Within the constraints of the marriage alliance system, the bride and groom are free to choose a partner, but their parents will negotiate the bride price. Sometimes a man can work for his bride's parents for a few years in lieu of a bride price.

8 ● RELATIONSHIPS

Interpersonal relations tend to be based on one's family lineage. The eldest man in the family is treated with great respect. The marriage alliance system also involves patterns of respect, with the wife-givers having a higher ritual status than the wife-takers because the wife brings children to the family. A father-in-law must be treated with great respect. Indeed, it is common to call an elderly man "father-in-law" as a term of respect.

Living as they do in isolated villages, the Kammu must depend upon each other for mutual help—so relations are relatively egalitarian. Although most families farm individually-owned plots, in some Kammu villages the land was owned collectively.

9 ● LIVING CONDITIONS

Living conditions are harsh for most Kammu. They tend to be among the poorest people in each country where they reside. Governments have been slow to extend roads, education, and health services to the hill areas. Diseases like malaria, dysentery, and pneumonia are common, and there are very high infant death rates. Most Kammu suffer from malnutrition. There is endless concern about having enough to eat, and most of each day is spent in farming or hunting, fishing, and gathering. People don't go into the forest alone, however, because they worry about wild animals, snakes, and accidents.

Kammu houses are built close together in the village, located on a hilltop or halfway up a mountain. The village is usually surrounded by a thick band of old forest, which separates it from their fields. The large old trees are believed to have souls, and they serve to protect the village from storms and from fire when the fields are burned off. Houses are built on piles 3 to 7 feet (1 to 2 meters) above the ground, usually with frame and floors of wood, walls of bamboo matting, and a roof of thatch. There is an open porch on one side of the house and a kitchen hearth built over a box of dirt toward the back. The area underneath the house is fenced in for the pigs and poultry. There is no running water or electricity, nor are there any sanitary facilities. There is rarely any furniture.

10 ● FAMILY LIFE

A household usually numbers six or seven people but can be much larger. Ideally a dwelling would have parents, children, wives of married sons, and grandchildren. Much of the work of the household is gender-specific, with women working longer hours than men and responsible for the hard work of hauling water and firewood and husking the rice. Traditionally, young boys left the family home between age six and eight, to live in the nearest village common house with older boys, unmarried men, and male guests in the village. However, newer villages set up in lowland areas have dispensed with common houses for men. Children are engaged in helping the family get enough food from an early age. Boys learn to fish and make snares to catch rodents and small game. Girls help their mothers garden and go in a group to the forest to look for edible shoots, tubers, and other plants. Women would be embarrassed if the house ran out of water or firewood, while men would be embarrassed if the family ran out of meat or fish. The family could not function without the labor of all, so there is mutual respect for the contribution each person makes to the household.

11 ● CLOTHING

In the past, clothing was most often rough homespun cloth made from their own cotton, but today manufactured fabric or store-bought clothes are increasingly common. Women wear a long-sleeved blouse that fastens to one side and a sarong, while men wear a shirt and pants. Rubber sandals serve as shoes. Both sexes may carry woven or knit bags that the women make. Some people have special clothes for ritual occasions.

12 ● FOOD

The staple food of the Kammu, as for the Lao, is sticky (glutinous) rice, which is eaten at every meal. The Kammu generally don't buy food, but make do with what they can grow or hunt or trade. Besides rice, they grow corn and other vegetables. The men fish, hunt small game with rifles and crossbows, and set snares for rats and other small animals. Frogs and various insects are also eaten. Fish and meat are smoked and dried over the fires that are kept going around the clock in the men's common houses. Large game is usually shared. The women gather bamboo shoots, mushrooms, and other wild plants in the forest. Deforestation (cutting trees for logging) has made supplementing their diet through hunting and gathering more difficult. Although most families have a water buffalo or cow, these animals are rarely eaten except on ceremonial occasions, when an animal is sacrified to please the spirits. Fruit trees, like bananas, citrus, and jackfruit, are planted around the village. Eggs are considered a special food, and gifts of eggs are given to wife-givers. Black sticky rice is used for traditional ceremonial meals. It represents safety, so a small packet of black sticky rice is always carried by people when they travel. Kammu meals tend to be rather simple fare seasoned with salt and chilis.

13 ● EDUCATION

Few Kammu have had any education at all, and those few have had to study in the Laos national language, a foreign tongue to them. Although schools are being extended into Kammu areas, these are still relatively few and tend to have very low standards. Teachers sent to Kammu areas often consider the assignment a hardship or a punishment. Compulsory school attendance laws, such as those in Thailand, are rarely enforced and don't apply in any case to children living at a great distance from a school. Kammu are much less likely than the majority population to have a primary school education. Kammu boys are more likely to be sent to school than are girls. Extremely few Kammu would be able to pass entrance exams to go to high school or have the financial means or family network in a city with a high school to make such attendance possible.

Parents and older siblings provide children with on-the-job training for life in a Kammu village. Boys learn from older residents of the men's common houses. Because of the pattern of males leaving the village to work in cities or in northern Thailand for a few years, men are more likely to speak a national language like Thai or Lao.

14 ● CULTURAL HERITAGE

The Kammu have a musical tradition, but instruments are usually played for ceremonial purposes in conjunction with prayer and sacrifice. Their instruments include long wooden drums, kettlegongs, knobbed gongs, cymbals, bamboo beaters, flutes, and buffalo horns. Musical instruments are often ritual gifts. Bamboo clappers are a gift from wife-givers to wife-takers, while the highly valued long wooden drum is usually a gift from the wife-taker to the wife-giver.

There are songs appropriate to various ritual occasions, and different types of music for every season of the farming year. Music thus plays a ritual role in securing a sufficient supply of food.

15 ● EMPLOYMENT

Work tends to be gender-specific. Men clear and burn the swidden fields, weave baskets, repair farm tools, care for large animals, trap, and hunt. They are also more likely to be involved in trade, selling livestock, forest products, and, more recently, scrap metal left over from the war. Women cook, care for children, husk rice, haul water, and firewood, care for gardens and pigs and poultry, gather edible plants, weave cloth, and sew. They may engage in trade of vegetables and chickens.

Children help their parents, and both boys and girls may help with care of young siblings. When the rice develops ears in the autumn, young people stay in small field huts for days to scare away the birds and wild animals that come to eat the rice. Teenagers enjoy this period away from the village and grownups. Grandparents help with cooking, childcare, and small chores near the house.

16 ● SPORTS

The Kammu do not engage in organized sports. Play tends to involve preparation for adult work. Thus, boys like to go fishing, catch insects, and practice with bows and arrows. Children like to swim in the streams.

17 ● RECREATION

Singing and storytelling are popular entertainments. Chanted poems give vent to emotions like sorrow at a friend's departure. Folktales include creation stories, tales of magic and the supernatural, stories of why animals and plants are the way they are, and tales of rascals and tricksters. Kammu in lowland areas also have access to films and concerts.

18 ● CRAFTS AND HOBBIES

The Kammu are very skillful in the use of bamboo, which they use to make a wide variety of items including baskets, musical instruments, water containers, snares and even houses.

19 ● SOCIAL PROBLEMS

Because of their lack of education and their geographic isolation, the Kammu are not progessing as quickly as the majority of the population. No government approves of their slash-and-burn agriculture, and they are being pressured to give up their traditional way of life and settle in lowland areas. They usually have no official titles to their land, so government officials can arbitrarily force them to move. Corrupt officials in league with illegal loggers also seek to force them out so the old growth forests near their villages can be cut. They still face prejudice and discrimination and many ethnic Lao still casually use the pejorative term "slave" in speaking of the Kammu.

20 ● BIBLIOGRAPHY

Damrong Tayanin. *Being Kammu: My Village, My Life*. Ithaca, N.Y.: Cornell University, 1994.
Lindell, Kristina, et al. *The Kammu Year: Its Lore and Music*. London: Curzon Press, 1982.
Lindell, Kristina, et al. *Tribe Kammu of Northern Laos and Thailand: Folklore and Folkliterature*. Taipei: Chinese Association for Folklore, 1984.

WEBSITES
Embassy of Laos. Washington, D.C. [Online] Available http://www.laoembassy.com/, 1998.
World Travel Guide. Laos. [Online] Available http://www.wtgonline.com/country/la/gen.html, 1998.

Latvia

The people of Latvia are called Latvians. More than half the population trace their ancestry to Latvia. The remainder of the population is Russian, 33 percent; Belarusan, 4 percent; Ukrainian, 3 percent; Polish, 2 percent; and Lithuanian, a little more than 1 percent. For more information on the Polish and Russians, see the chapters on Poland and Russia in Volume 7; on the Belarusans, the chapter on Belarus in Volume 1; and on Ukrainians, the chapter on Ukraine in Volume 9.

Latvians

PRONUNCIATION: LATT-vee-uhns
ALTERNATE NAMES: Letts
LOCATION: Latvia
POPULATION: 2.8 million (52 percent are ethnic Latvians)
LANGUAGE: Latvian (Lettish)
RELIGION: Christianity (Lutheran, Roman Catholic, Russian Orthodox, Baptist, Old Believers, Pentecostal, Adventist); Judaism

1 ● INTRODUCTION

Like many peoples, the Latvians have been ruled by foreigners for centuries. Often, these foreigners treated them terribly and tried to destroy their culture. The Latvians have been ruled by the Germans, Swedes, and Poles. Their most brutal foreign rulers by far were the Russians, however. Russia annexed the independent country of Latvia in 1940. They did so for many reasons, but one of the more important reasons was because they needed a port that was not iced over for most of the year. After taking over the country, the Russians began taking ethnic Latvians from their homes and moving them thousands of miles away to Central Asia. Many thousands more were simply killed.

During the first year of the Russian occupation, 35,000 ethnic Latvians and other Latvian citizens (including Jews) were arrested, murdered, or deported. Some 16,000 alone were sent into exile on the nights of June 13 and 14 in 1941. As a result, there are still a few of these exile Latvian communities scattered in the Russian part of Central Asia and Siberia.

Latvian campaigns for democracy and independence did not begin in earnest until October 1988, with the formation of the Popular Front of Latvia. Latvians finally won independence in August 1991 after the collapse of communism and the Soviet government in Moscow.

LATVIANS

2 ● LOCATION

The population of Latvia is approximately 2.8 million. Of these, 52 percent are ethnic Latvians. About 34 percent are ethnic Russians. At the close of World War II (1939–45), thousands of Latvians fled their homeland to escape the returning Russian troops. There are now many ethnic Latvians and their descendants living in the United States (over 100,000), Australia, and elsewhere.

Latvia is on the Baltic coast and borders Estonia to the north, Lithuania to the south, the Russian Republic to the east, and Belarus (which was part of Poland before World War II) to the southeast. Latvia is slightly larger than the state of West Virginia. The coastline is mostly flat, but inland and eastward the topography

becomes hilly, with more forests and lakes. Reznas Lake is the largest of Latvia's 2,300 lakes.

The climate is generally temperate, but with considerable temperature variations. Summer and winter can be intense, but spring and autumn are mild. Precipitation is distributed throughout the year, with the highest amount occurring in August.

3 ● LANGUAGE

Modern Latvian shows the influences of former conquerors. Words are taken from Swedish, German, and Russian. There are three main Latvian dialects: Central (which is used as the basis for written Latvian), East, and Livonian. Mainly because of the Russian occupation, only about half of the population in Latvia speaks Latvian today. In 1989 the government made Latvian the official language, requiring it in governmental use.

Latvian first names for males always end in the letter "s." They include names such as Andris, Ivars, Jānis, Kārlis, Vilnis, and Visvaldis. Female first names usually end in the letter "a" and include names like Aina, Laima, Māra, Ausma, Ieva, Ināra, Maija, and Zinta. Examples of everyday Latvian words include *Sveicinati!* (How do you do?), *lūdzu* (please), *paldies* (thank you), and *uz redzēšanos* (goodbye).

4 ● FOLKLORE

Latvian folk songs are popular and are known as *dainas*. These beautiful verses have been written over many centuries. They are rich in experience, feeling, and folk wisdom. Here is a daina describing the dawn:

Sidrabina gailis dzied
Zeltupītes maliņā,
Lai ceļās Saules meita
Zīda diegu šķeterēt.

Translation:

A silver rooster crows
Beside a golden stream,
To make the Sun's daughter rise
To twine her silken yarn.

Modern dainas are typically philosophical and are revered as Latvian lyric poetry. Efforts to preserve traditional Latvian folklore began late in the nineteenth century, and several volumes of traditional Latvian myths and folk songs were compiled and published. Modern scholars have catalogued more than a million traditional Latvian folk songs.

One of the most famous figures of Latvian myth is Lacplesis the Bear-Slayer. The legend of Lacplesis tells how he could break a bear's jaw with his fist and even get bears to pull his plow. Although Lacplesis wanted to help others, he often did not know his own strength and would end up breaking peoples' tools.

According to legend, Lacplesis was finally defeated by a vicious three-headed monster. The monster's mother told her son that Lacplesis would lose his great strength if his ears were cut off. The battling Lacplesis and the monster plunged into the Daugava River and were swept out to sea.

5 ● RELIGION

Christianity spread through Latvia during the ninth through twelfth centuries, with Russian Orthodoxy dominant in the east and Roman Catholicism in the west. Most people in the cities are Lutheran. There are also small communities of other faiths, such as Baptist, Old Believers, Pentecostal, Adventist, and Jewish.

6 ● MAJOR HOLIDAYS

Three Christian holidays that have become prominent in Latvian culture are Christmas (December 25 or January 7), Easter (late March or early April), and Whitsuntide (the week of Pentecost in May). At Christmas, Latvians attend church services, decorate spruce trees with ornaments and lights, and exchange presents. Easter traditions include coloring eggs and making decorations from onion skins and herbs. Another popular activity at Easter is to build a swing and swing high, from the traditional belief that such an activity will repel mosquitoes from biting in the summer. Many homes are decorated with birch branches for Whitsuntide. The national holiday of Latvia is on November 18, to commemorate the proclamation of the republic.

Ligo svētki is a traditional midsummer festival that celebrates the summer solstice on June 23 and *Jāņi* (St John's Day) on June 24. Ligo svētki activities include many old customs that are believed to bring the aid of good spirits into the home, barn, field, and forest. These spirits also protect the crops from witches and devils. It is a night of singing, dancing, lighthearted merriment, and fortune telling. Men, women, and children dress in colorful folk costumes.

Other Latvian traditions include two All Fool's days. One is on April 1 and the other on April 30. Every Latvian also celebrates not only a birthday but a namesake day. For an individual's namesake day, specific male

Cory Langley

An example of Latvian architechture.

and female first names are assigned to each day on the calendar.

Special Harvest Day (Thanksgiving) is celebrated on the first Sunday in October. There are many other celebrations. Among these are church festivals, district fairs, monthly market days, 4H Club exhibitions, gigantic open air performances of theater plays, dances, and choir songfests. Especially popular is the *Dziesmu svētki* (Song Festival).

7 ● RITES OF PASSAGE

Latvian baptisms are marked by families getting together for a feast. Weddings are celebrated as the most important Latvian rite of passage. They can go on for as long as three days. Owning a car was rare in Latvia throughout the Soviet years (1940–91), so learning to drive as a teenager was not common. However, Latvians could legally only ride a bicycle in the cities with a bicycle driver's license. These were not available until age sixteen. Passports in Latvia are issued at age twenty-one.

8 ● RELATIONSHIPS

Handshaking is customary, and most standard European courtesies are observed. Latvians are somewhat reserved and formal in public but are usually very hospitable in private.

9 ● LIVING CONDITIONS

Many Latvians enjoy local mineral spas. One of the most famous is in Kemeri, near Riga. The local mineral water and mud have been used for medicinal therapy for almost 300 years.

Since the winters are cold, housing is built accordingly, with firewood as the main source of heat. Government-operated railroads are the primary way for people to get around in Latvia.

10 ● FAMILY LIFE

Latvian culture has always emphasized strong family ties. Men have the role of provider and women are homemakers in traditional Latvian culture. The typical family includes two to four children.

11 ● CLOTHING

Most Latvians dress in standard European clothes for everyday wear. During folk dances and traditional ceremonies, many women wear the traditional Latvian costume. This consists of a large, colorful, pleated skirt worn with a white blouse and a short, round hat.

12 ● FOOD

Traditional Latvian soups include cabbage soup and buckwheat soup. These are usually served with boiled pork, onions, potatoes, and barley. Traditional dishes include grilled pork ribs, smoked fish (including salmon and trout), gray peas (navy beans) with fried fat, and *piragi* (pastries filled with bacon and onions).

A popular sweet pastry is *Alexander Torte,* which is filled with raspberries or cranberries. Other popular national dishes include *zemnieku brokastis* (peasant's breakfast), which is a large omelet with potatoes and mushrooms. *Maizes zupe ar putukrejumu* is cornbread soup with whipped cream. *Skābe putra* is a drink made from pearl barley or rye flour and whey. *Silķe, biezpiens ar kartupeļiem un krejumi* is a dish made of salt herring, cottage cheese, potatoes, and sour cream.

13 ● EDUCATION

Since independence from the Soviet Union in 1991, the Latvians have thoroughly changed the organizational structure and curricula that were part of the Soviet education system. Primary education lasts for nine years, and secondary education lasts for three years. There are now private as well as public universities available for those who pass entrance exams.

As for Latvians outside the homeland, over half of ethnic Latvians in the United States have a college degree. There are some 600 Latvian scientists and scholars teaching at American universities, and about as many physicians and dentists practicing in the United States.

14 ● CULTURAL HERITAGE

Latvian folk history preservation is a popular activity. Several folk dance troupes, such as Ilgi, Skandinieki, and Dandari, are well known for their performances that preserve Latvian heritage. Ballet is popular among Latvians.

The *kokle* is the most celebrated of the Latvian folk instruments. A small board zither, the kokle is related to a larger family of similar stringed instruments found throughout the Baltic region. The kokle was usually played by men to accompany folk dances. It is now favored by young female ensembles and is also played in large modern orchestras. There are soprano, alto, tenor, and bass models available.

The popular *Dziesmu svētki* (Song Festival) is an event that occurs every four years. The first Song Festival took place in 1873 with 1,003 singers. By 1938 the event had grown to 16,000 singers with an audience of over 100,000. Latvian Song Festivals are also held every four years in the United States, Canada, Australia, and Europe.

15 ● EMPLOYMENT

The Soviet government controlled the Latvian economy for decades. During this time the Latvians worked with little incentive under a system of price controls and quotas. Since independence, the Latvian government has reformed the system. However, the transition has been difficult for many workers. As a result, many Latvians (especially women) have suffered unemployment in recent years. Latvians not in school can begin working at age sixteen.

16 ● SPORTS

Soccer, volleyball, and basketball are popular outdoor activities among Latvians. Latvia has many organized sports clubs and organizations for these and other sports. Bobsled and motor racing are popular spectator sports. Latvian athletes have occasionally won medals at the Olympics.

17 ● RECREATION

In 1772 the Riga Opera-Theater house opened. Going to the theater is still popular among Latvians today. Many productions are dramas, but musicals have become popular in recent years. Circuses are also popular, and Riga has had a permanent circus building since 1889.

18 ● CRAFTS AND HOBBIES

Interest in folk arts and crafts is expressed through jewelry making, intricate sewing, and embroidering of the traditional Latvian folk dress. Workshops in ceramics, woodworking, and leather craft are also common.

19 ● SOCIAL PROBLEMS

As in many other places in the world, there is ethnic tension in Latvia. Latvians and Russians have deep resentments against each other. Major problems have to do with language and with the fact that many Latvians' houses were stolen by Russians. The new Latvian government reinstated Latvian as the official language. They also gave Russians seven years to return stolen property.

In the Soviet era, environmental protection in Latvia did not exist. Air pollution became concentrated in industrialized areas. The rivers and lakes were used as open sewers for sloppy industrial waste-disposal methods. As a result, even the Baltic Sea is not safe for swimming. In many places even the ground water is contaminated.

20 ● BIBLIOGRAPHY

American Latvian Association. *Latvia: Country, People, Liberty.* Rockville, Md.: American Latvian Association, 1976.

The Baltic States. Tallinn, Estonia: Estonian, Latvian, and Lithuanian Encyclopaedia Publishers, 1991.

Šveics, Vilnis V. *How Stalin Got the Baltic States.* Jersey City, N.J.: Jersey City State College, 1991.

WEBSITES

Embassy of Latvia, Washington, D.C. [Online] Available http: // www.seas.gwu.edu/guest/latvia/, 1998.

Latvia Network. [Online] Available http://www.latnet.lv/, 1998.

World Travel Guide. Latvia. [Online] Available http://www.wtgonline.com/country/lv/gen.htm, 1998.l

Lebanon

The people of Lebanon are called Lebanese. Lebanese are divided into Muslims and Christians. Muslims are divided into Sunnis and Shi'ites. The Christian Maronites make up about one-third of the total population of Lebanon, and are a distinct and significant group.

Lebanese

PRONUNCIATION: leb-un-EEZ
LOCATION: Lebanon
POPULATION: 3.1 million
LANGUAGE: Arabic (official); English; French
RELIGION: Islam; Christianity; Druze; Alawi; Baha'i

1 ● INTRODUCTION

Lebanon is a small, war-torn country on the east coast of the Mediterranean Sea. Located on fertile territory at the crossroads of three continents—Africa, Asia, and Europe—it is a valuable and highly desired territory. Throughout its history, it has been the stage for conflicts between local tribespeople and world powers. After being ruled by the Ottoman Empire and by the French, Lebanon gained full independence in 1943.

The presence of Palestinian refugees and guerrilla bases, and tensions between Christians and Muslims, have led to continuing political instability and warfare in recent decades. However, the Lebanese people have continued to survive in the face of repeated disruptions of their economy and day-to-day life. From 1975 until 1991, civil war ruined Lebanon. Since the early 1990s, the government has gradually regained power but there are still incidents of political violence, especially in the south near Israel.

2 ● LOCATION

Lebanon is a tiny country. Its area is only a little more than 4,000 square miles (10,400 square kilometers)—about the size of the state of Connecticut. Lebanon has two mountain ranges, a coastal strip, and an inland plain. In former times it was famous for its cedars. However, due to centuries of deforestation, very few cedars are left. Those that remain are now protected.

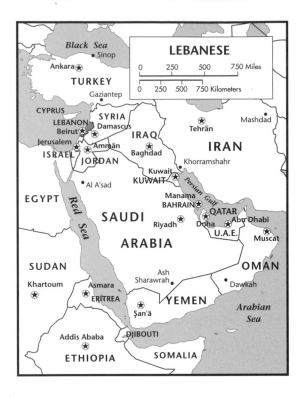

LEBANESE

The population of Lebanon is as varied as its terrain. The official population of Lebanon, excluding Palestinian refugees, is about 3.1 million. Most Lebanese are Arabs.

3 ● LANGUAGE

Arabic is the official language of Lebanon, but many Lebanese also speak English. For some, the French language still has the greatest prestige.

"Hello" in Arabic is *marhaba* or *ahlan,* to which one replies, *marhabtayn* or *ahlayn.* Other common greetings are *as-salam alaykum* ("peace be with you"), with the reply of *walaykum as-salam* ("and to you peace"). *Ma'assalama* means "goodbye." "Thank you" is *shukran,* and "you're welcome" is *afwan.* "Yes" is *na'am* and "no" is *la'a.* The numbers one to ten in Arabic are: *wahad, itnin, talata, arba'a, khamsa, sitta, saba'a, tamania, tisa'a,* and *ashara.*

4 ● FOLKLORE

One of the most popular characters in Arab folklore is Jeha the Fool. He figures in many stories, from teaching tales to purely humorous anecdotes. Also popular are the real-life lovers, Ablah and Antar. Antar was a sixth-century Arab who was born a slave but became a heroic warrior and a poet. Antar and Ablah, the chief's daughter, fell in love. But of course a slave could not marry the chief's daughter. Eventually, after many tragic struggles, Antar was given his freedom, and he and Ablah married.

The story of the Greek hero Adonis takes place at Byblos, in Lebanon. Also, Saint George, who later became the patron saint of England, lived in Lebanon. He fought the famous sea-dragon at the mouth of a river near Beirut. Most likely, the Christian Crusaders took Saint George's tale back with them to the West.

The Lebanese are very fond of proverbs and can quote one for almost any situation. Examples include "Better blind eyes than a closed mind," and "The one who took the donkey up to the roof should be the one who brings it down."

5 ● RELIGION

Christianity arrived in Lebanon during the Byzantine Roman era (AD 4–636). Its followers have since divided into a variety of sects including Maronite, Roman Catholic, Greek Catholic, Greek Orthodox, Armenian Catholic, Armenian Orthodox, and Protestant. Islam was introduced in the seventh century ad. Muslims are now divided into Sunnis, several types of Shi'ites (including Ismaeli), and Sufis (Muslim mystics).

The Lebanese government keeps a record of every citizen's religious affiliation. A person may belong to any religion, but each person must belong to one. It is estimated that a little more than half of the Lebanese population is Muslim. The rest are mostly Christian. Seats in the government are based on religious representation.

6 ● MAJOR HOLIDAYS

The Lebanese celebrate both the Christian and Muslim holy days, plus a couple of secular public holidays. The major Muslim holidays are Ramadan, celebrated by complete fasting from dawn until dusk for an entire month; *Eid al-Fitr,* a three-day festival at the end of Ramadan; *Eid al-Adha,* a feast at the end of the *hajj* (the pilgrimage month to Mecca); the First of *Muharram,* the Muslim New Year; *Ashura,* a Shi'ite commemoration and day of mourning; and the Prophet Muhammad's birthday.

Two Easters are celebrated in Lebanon (both in late March or early April)—the Greek Orthodox date, and the date for the rest of the Christian population. Other Christian holidays include New Year's Day (January 1); St. Maroun's Day (the patron saint of Maronite Christians, February 9); the Day of the Ascension (May 15); the Feast of the Assumption (August 15); and Christmas and Boxing Day (December 25 and 26).

Three secular public holidays in Lebanon are: Labor Day (May 1); Martyrs' Day, which honors patriots killed by the Turks during World War I (May 6); and Independence Day (November 22).

The Christian New Year's Day (January 1) is celebrated in Beirut by shooting tracer bullets out over the Mediterranean Sea. It is also customary to go "strolling" along the coast road in one's car after midnight on New Year's. Such "strolling" is a Lebanese tradition for almost any festival.

Both Muslim and Christian children play a game with colored (hard-boiled) eggs at Easter time. One child taps the tip of his or her egg against the tip of another child's egg. The child whose egg stays intact while cracking everyone else's eggs wins the game. The children then eat their eggs.

7 ● RITES OF PASSAGE

Most Lebanese mark major life events, such as birth, marriage, and death, within the Islamic or Christian religious traditions.

8 ● RELATIONSHIPS

The Lebanese lifestyle is relaxed, but by no means lazy. Opinions are strongly held and fiercely defended with vigorous gestures in heated discussions. At the market, the same vigor is used to haggle prices, something the average Lebanese is quite good at doing. A favorite Lebanese pastime is to sit and discuss politics or other hot topics—loudly. The same attitude prevails on the road, where there are few (if any) traffic signals or stop signs, and drivers simply "get ahead" as they need to. Pedestrians also cross the road whenever and wherever they choose, leaving it to drivers to stop for them.

Recipe

Baked Kibbeh

Ingredients

2 cups cracked wheat (bulgur)
4 cups cold water
2 pounds lean ground beef or lamb
1 medium onion, very finely chopped
1½ teaspoons salt
½ teaspoon pepper
½ teaspoon allspice (optional)
¼ cup melted butter

Directions

1. Place cracked wheat in a large mixing bowl and cover with the cold water. Let stand 5 minutes, and then drain. Press on grains to remove water.
2. Add remaining ingredients and mix well.
3. Process in batches in a food processor fitted with the chopping blade.
4. Butter a 9x12-inch baking pan. Spread the mixture into the pan, smoothing the top with wet hands. Cut into 2-inch squares.
5. Pour melted butter over the top. Bake at 375°F for 50 minutes. Serve with pita bread.

Adapted from Salloum, Mary. *A Taste of Lebanon.* New York: Interlink Books, 1988, p. 102.

Traditional Arab hospitality reigns in Lebanon. Hosts provide feasts for their guests, then smoke the *nargile* (a water pipe) after dinner. Visits are usually not planned in advance. Lebanese are very affectionate with friends and family. They touch each other often, hold hands, and men may kiss each other on the cheeks. An Arab will never ask personal questions, as that is considered rude.

9 ● LIVING CONDITIONS

Until recently, Lebanon was a war-torn nation. Much of the capital city of Beirut was in ruins. So was a great deal of the rest of the country. Rebuilding is now under way in order to address a lack of housing, as well as unreliable gas and water supplies.

In rural areas, farmhouses are made of stone or concrete with tile floors. They have only a few necessary pieces of furniture. A small wood-burning or kerosene stove is used for heat in the winter. Most rural houses have running water.

10 ● FAMILY LIFE

Most city families are small, averaging two children each. Children usually live with their parents until they get married. Most businesses are family-owned and -run. The revenue sent back by family members working abroad has kept the Lebanese economy afloat during the recent, difficult war years.

Rural families generally live on small farms. They have many children to provide help with the farmwork—often as many as ten or fifteen. Women on the farms have a very busy life. They do all the cooking, cleaning, and laundry (in old-fashioned washtubs, with no electric dryers). They also work in the fields when needed.

11 ● CLOTHING

Western-style fashions are popular in Lebanon's cities. Urban women are very fashion-conscious. More-traditional clothes are still worn in some villages. These include long dresses for women, and black pants and jackets for men. Men's pants are full and baggy from the waist to the knee, then tightly fitted from the knee to the ankle. Their jackets have fancy, brightly colored, embroidered trim. Some older rural men continue to wear the traditional short, cone-shaped, brown felt hat. Most modern Lebanese men, however, have traded it in for a *keffiya,* the common Arab head scarf

12 ● FOOD

Lunch is the big meal in Lebanon. Almost everything is eaten with bread. Two types of unleavened Lebanese bread are *khub,* which resembles pita bread, and *marqouq,* which is paper-thin. Lebanese do not eat fish and dairy in the same meal. *Mezze* are popular in Lebanon, as elsewhere in the Middle East. Similar to appetizers, mezze basically consist of any food served in small portions. An entire meal can consist solely of mezze. The Lebanese national dish is *kibbeh* (or *kibbe),* made of either lamb or beef and cracked wheat (bulghur, or *birghol).*

Common ingredients in Lebanese cooking include *laban* (similar to yogurt), rice, lentils, grape leaves (which are served with various stuffings, such as rice or meat), pine nuts, rose water, sesame seeds, chickpeas, tahini (sesame paste), and mint.

Wine has been made in Lebanon for thousands of years. A unique Lebanese alcoholic creation is *arak,* a colorless, 100-percent-alcohol beverage flavored with anise. Other popular beverages are coffee served very thick, tea with lots of sugar and no milk, and locally bottled spring water from the mountains.

AP/Wide World Photos

Lebanese girls at the entrance to their school. Education is highly valued by the Lebanese. However, each school emphasizes a different type of learning, so Lebanese don't receive a standard education.

13 ● EDUCATION.

Education is highly valued in Lebanon. There are five years of required education, with an attendance rate of over 90 percent. A major problem in Lebanon is a lack of standard education across the nation. Many Lebanese send their children to private schools. Each school emphasizes a different type of learning, so children receive vastly different educations.

14 ● CULTURAL HERITAGE

Lebanon has long been known for its high-quality book publishing. A flourishing film industry produces high-quality films. A revival of folk art, music, and dance began in the late 1960s. The national folk dance of Lebanon is the *debki,* a line dance. People hold hands and step and stomp to the beat of a small drum called a *derbekki.* Belly dancing is also popular.

15 ● EMPLOYMENT

Lebanon has a high proportion of skilled labor among its labor force. However, there is a shortage of jobs for them. Many work outside the country or are unemployed. Business dealings are based on friendship. A great deal of "wining and dining" is done to establish connections before any business is conducted.

16 ● SPORTS

Soccer, basketball, and volleyball are popular. Cross-country running, particularly in the mountains, and the martial arts are widely practiced. Skiing, rock-climbing, and cave exploration are also enjoyed in the mountains. Many Lebanese go swimming and fishing in the lakes, rivers, or Mediterranean Sea. In the city, pigeon-shooting is a favorite sport.

17 ● RECREATION

The Lebanese love television. There are over fifty television stations in Lebanon, all of them commercial. Lebanese cinemas tend to show violent, sexy American and European films. Live theater is popular, as are nightclubs and pubs. At home, besides watching television, Lebanese enjoy playing board games (especially Monopoly), chess, checkers, card games, and backgammon. The Lebanese enjoyment of good conversation is so great that talking could even be called the national pastime.

The social center of rural life is the foorn, the village bakery where women bake their loaves of bread.

18 ● CRAFTS AND HOBBIES

Traditional Lebanese crafts include basketry, carpet weaving, ceramics and pottery, copper- and metalworking, embroidery, glass-blowing, and gold- and silversmithing. Lebanon is also known for its finely crafted church bells. Wine making can also be considered an art, one that dates back thousands of years.

19 ● SOCIAL PROBLEMS

Warfare has caused widespread destruction throughout the country. At least 120,000 people were killed in the recent civil war and 300,000 were wounded, most of them civilians. Another 800,000 or so left the country, mostly the wealthy and well-educated. As many as 1,200,000 Lebanese—almost half the population—had to move from their homes and neighborhoods during the war.

The "Green Line" dividing Muslim Beirut and Christian Beirut is now the center of major urban reconstruction.

20 ● BIBLIOGRAPHY

Bleaney, C. H. *Lebanon.* Santa Barbara, Calif.: Clio Press, 1991.

Eshel, Isaac. *Lebanon in Pictures.* Minneapolis, Minn.: Lerner Publications Co., 1988.

Foster, Leila Merrell. *Enchantment of the World:*

Lebanon. Chicago, Ill.: Children's Press, 1992.

Marston, Elsa. *Lebanon: New Light in an Ancient Land.* New York: Dillon Press, 1994.

WEBSITES

ArabNet. [Online] Available http://www.arab.net/lebanon/lebanon_contents.html, 1998.

Embassy of Lebanon, Washington, D.C. [Online] Available http://www.erols.com/lebanon/, 1998.

World Travel Guide, Lebanon. [Online] Available http://www.wtgonline.com/country/lb/gen.html, 1998.

Maronites

PRONUNCIATION: MA-ruh-nites
LOCATION: Lebanon
POPULATION: 1.2 million
LANGUAGE: Arabic; French; English
RELIGION: Maronite (Uniate Catholicism)

1 ● INTRODUCTION

The Maronites believe that their heritage dates back to the time of Jesus. They were one of the Christian sects in the Middle East to remain intact after the Islamic revolution of the seventh century AD. At first the Maronites welcomed the Muslims as saviors from the hated Byzantine rulers. However, when the European Crusaders attacked Alexandria, the Maronites supported them. This caused the Muslims to question Maronite loyalty and punish them along with the rest of the Christians. The Maronites eventually fled to the hills of Mount Lebanon to escape persecution by the Ottoman Turks in the fifteenth century. They stubbornly survived there for centuries. Taking refuge in small, isolated communities, the Maronites became clannish and fiercely self-protective.

In the mid-nineteenth century, the Ottomans divided Lebanon into two states, one Christian and one Druze (a Muslim sect). The French supported the Maronites in their war with the British-supported Druze. The French again allied themselves with the Maronites from 1920 to 1943. This cemented the Maronite identification with the West, particularly France. This "Western" identity has led to a sense of separateness from other Arabs, and resentment on the part of their neighbors. Recently, however, Maronites have become more comfortable with their Lebanese identity.

The Maronites have campaigned for an independent homeland since the seventh century AD. However, they are no longer attempting to convert Lebanon into a Maronite state.

2 ● LOCATION

After surviving in the high mountains of northern Lebanon for many centuries, the Maronites spread southward during the eighteenth and nineteenth centuries. By the mid-nineteenth century, the Maronite Church owned one-fourth to one-third of all the land in Mount Lebanon. During the twentieth century, some Maronites began to move out of the mountains to the cities and coastal plains, especially to Beirut.

During the recent Lebanese civil war, more than 600,000 Maronites were driven out of their homes and off their lands. The Maronite population is about 1.2 million people. Maronites are concentrated in East Beirut, while Muslim Shi'ites live primarily in West Beirut.

3 ● LANGUAGE

Although Arabic is the official language of Lebanon, many Maronites also speak French. Syriac is used for the church liturgy, but Maronites have used Arabic for church records since their beginnings.

4 ● FOLKLORE

The door of the Maronite church in the town of Bayt Meri near Beirut is never locked because it is believed that the hand of any thief there would be miraculously paralyzed.

5 ● RELIGION

The Maronites are Uniate Catholics. They recognize the authority of the Roman Catholic pope, but they have their own form of worship. Their priests can marry, and monks and nuns are housed in the same building. The Maronites have continued to use the Syriac language for their liturgy instead of Latin. The Maronites hold the orthodox view that Christ has two natures, one human and one divine, that are inseparable yet distinct. Christ is at one with God in his divine nature, and at one with humanity in his human nature. The Qadisha (Holy) Valley is the Maronites' spiritual center.

6 ● MAJOR HOLIDAYS

The Maronites celebrate the usual Christian holidays, such as Christmas (December 25), Easter (in March or April), the Feast of the Ascension (May 15), and the Feast of the Assumption (August 15). On the Festival of the Cross (September 14), Maronites set fires on high places all over Mount Lebanon and light candles at home and in churches. A special Maronite holy day is St. Maroun's Day (February 9), the feast of the Maronites' patron saint, St. John Maroun, who lived in the fifth century AD.

7 ● RITES OF PASSAGE

The Maronites mark major life events, such as birth, marriage, and death, within the traditions of Christianity.

8 ● RELATIONSHIPS

Living for centuries in isolated mountain communities has led the Maronites to develop both clan loyalties and fierce feuding.

9 ● LIVING CONDITIONS

Maronite homes are small and simple, yet elegant, often with a balcony overlooking the mountains or the Mediterranean Sea. During the recent Lebanese civil war, many Maronites fled from the cities (especially Beirut) back to their ancestral homes in Mount Lebanon. As a result, business there boomed, housing construction soared, and the area became quite prosperous.

10 ● FAMILY LIFE

The Maronites, like other Arabs in Lebanon, still have a strong sense of extended family. Men spend quite a bit of time at home with the women and children. There is some intermarriage between Maronites and members of other religious groups. Divorce is forbidden by Maronite law.

11 ● CLOTHING

Maronites wear Western-style clothing, as do other cultural groups in Lebanon. The more-devout Maronites tend to wear conservative clothing.

12 ● FOOD

Maronites eat typical Middle Eastern and Mediterranean food. For example, breakfast might consist of either Lebanese flatbread or French croissants with cheese and coffee or tea. Lunches and dinners usually consist of meat with onion, spices, and rice. Mutton (lamb meat) is often ground and served as meatballs or in stews. It is also mixed with rice and vegetables and rolled in grape leaves. Maronites like to eat *mezze* (small portions of a wide variety of foods). Also popular is *arak,* the anise-flavored alcohol produced in the region.

13 ● EDUCATION

Most Maronites today still receive their primary and secondary schooling in French-language schools. Then they generally go to the University of St. Joseph in Beirut, founded by French Jesuits in 1875.

Today all Lebanese students must know Arabic in order to graduate from secondary school. Many older Maronites, however, speak only French.

14 ● CULTURAL HERITAGE

The Maronites have strong cultural ties to the West. In 1585 a religious school for Maronite men was established in Rome. A short time later, European Catholic missionaries settled in Lebanon and began schools there.

15 ● EMPLOYMENT

Maronites have long held powerful positions in Lebanese government, business, and education. Many are wealthy. With the aid of the French, the Maronites developed Mount Lebanon's greatest moneymaking venture of the past—the silk industry. The mountainsides are dotted with old silk-reeling factories.

16 ● SPORTS

Soccer, basketball, and volleyball are popular. Cross-country running, particularly in the mountains, and the martial arts are widely practiced. Skiing, rock climbing, and cave exploration are also enjoyed in the mountains. Maronites enjoy swimming and fishing in the lakes, rivers, or Mediterranean Sea.

17 ● RECREATION

Lebanon has over fifty television stations, all of them commercial. One station shows all Christian programming, another all Muslim. Lebanese cinemas show American and European films. Lebanon itself also has an active filmmaking industry. Like other Lebanese, Maronites enjoy going to the theater. They particularly like comedies that poke fun at government leaders and Lebanese society.

Maronites play board games (especially Monopoly), chess, checkers, card games, and backgammon, which is called *tawleh* (literally, "table").

18 ● CRAFTS AND HOBBIES

Traditional crafts include basketry, carpet-weaving, ceramics and pottery, copper- and metalworking, embroidery, glass blowing, and gold- and silversmithing. Lebanon is also known for its finely crafted church bells.

19 ●SOCIAL PROBLEMS

Within the Maronite community, centuries of clannish mountain life have led to perpetual feuding, continuing today among the different Maronite militias.

20 ●BIBLIOGRAPHY

Bleaney, C. H. *Lebanon.* Santa Barbara, Calif.: Clio Press, 1991.

Eshel, Isaac. *Lebanon in Pictures.* Minneapolis, Minn.: Lerner Publications Co., 1988.

Foster, Leila Merrell. *Enchantment of the World: Lebanon.* Chicago, Ill.: Childrens Press, 1992.

Marston, Elsa. *Lebanon: New Light in an Ancient Land.* New York: Dillon Press, 1994.

WEBSITES

ArabNet. Lebanon. [Online] Available http://www.arab.net/lebanon/lebanon_contents.html, 1998.

Embassy of Lebanon, Washington, D.C. [Online] Available http://www.erols.com/lebanon/, 1998.

World Travel Guide. Lebanon. [Online] Available http://www.wtgonline.com/country/lb/gen.html, 1998.

Lesotho

The people of Lesotho are called Sotho (or Basotho).

Sotho

PRONUNCIATION: SOH-toh
LOCATION: Lesotho; South Africa
POPULATION: 5.6 million in South Africa; 1.9 million in Lesotho
LANGUAGE: Sotho language, or Sesotho
RELIGION: Traditional beliefs (worship of Modimo); Christianity

1 ● INTRODUCTION

The Sotho people are an ethnic group living in Lesotho and South Africa. There are two major branches, the southern Sotho and the northern Sotho (also called the Pedi). Southern Sotho people make up about 99 percent of the population of Lesotho. The southern Sotho and the northern Sotho taken together are the second largest ethnic group in South Africa.

Sotho society was traditionally organized in villages ruled by chiefs. The economy was based on the rearing of cattle and the cultivation of grains such as sorghum. In the early nineteenth century, several kingdoms developed as a result of a series of wars that engulfed much of southern Africa. During this period, southern Sotho people as well as other ethnic groups sought refuge in the mountainous terrain of what is now Lesotho. A local chief named Moshoeshoe (pronounced mow-SHWAY-shway) emerged as a skillful diplomat and military leader who was able to keep his country from falling into the hands of Zulu and, later, white Afrikaner forces. After Moshoeshoe's death in 1870, this independence was weakened, and English authorities from the Cape Colony tried to administer Lesotho as a conquered territory. The people resisted this attempt at control, however, leading to the Gun War of 1880–81 in which the Cape Colony was defeated.

The northern Sotho suffered at the hands of African armies during the wars, but several chiefdoms were able to recover. After 1845, the Pedi also had to contend with an

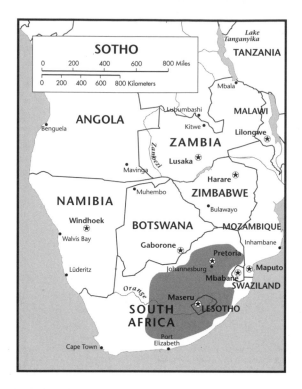

SOTHO

0   200   400   600   800 Miles
0   200   400   600   800 Kilometers

TANZANIA

Lake
Tanganyika

Mbala

ANGOLA

Benguela

Lubumbashi

Kitwe

MALAWI

Lilongwe

ZAMBIA

Lusaka

Mavinga

Harare

Muhembo

ZIMBABWE

NAMIBIA

Windhoek

Bulawayo

Walvis Bay

BOTSWANA

MOZAMBIQUE

Gaborone

Inhambane

Lüderitz

Pretoria

Johannesburg

Maputo

Mbabane

SWAZILAND

Orange

Maseru

SOUTH
AFRICA

LESOTHO

Port
Elizabeth

Cape Town

influx of white Afrikaner settlers, some of whom seized Pedi children and forced them to work as slaves. The Pedi were finally conquered by British, Afrikaner, and Swazi forces in 1879. The northern Sotho then lost their independence and fell under the political control of white authorities. Northern Sotho lands were turned into reserves, and Sotho people were forced to relocate to these reserves, causing great hardship.

In 1884, Lesotho became a British protectorate. Unlike the Pedi kingdom, therefore, Lesotho was not incorporated into South Africa. Lesotho became an independent country in 1966, completely surrounded by South Africa. South Africa's former system of apartheid (the governmental policy of racial segregation and discrimination) hindered Lesotho's development.

The nation also has had trouble establishing democracy. The first democratic elections after independence were voided by the government of Leabua Jonathan. Jonathan ruled Lesotho from 1970 until he was overthrown in a coup in 1986. In the 1990s, Lesotho began a new period of elective government.

2 ● LOCATION

According to 1995 estimates, there were about 5.6 million people who identified themselves as southern or northern Sotho in South Africa. In Lesotho there were about 1.9 million southern Sotho.

The home of most of the southern Sotho is in Lesotho and in South Africa's Free State Province. There are also many Sotho who live in South Africa's major cities. Lesotho is a mountainous country that is completely landlocked within the borders of South Africa. It has an area of about 11,700 square miles (about 30,350 square kilometers). The Free State is a highland plain, called a *highveld* in South Africa, bordering Lesotho to the west. The eastern section of Lesotho is also a highveld, with plateaus similar to those found in the American Southwest. The Maloti and Drakensberg mountains are in the central and western parts of the country. The Drakensberg Mountains form sharp cliffs that drop off dramatically to South Africa's KwaZulu-Natal Province. The climate of South Africa is temperate, but the mountains make for cold winters. In winter, snow sometimes falls in the Lesotho highlands.

The region considered a traditional home by many rural Pedi is between the Olifants and Steelpoort rivers in South Africa's Northern Province. It is bounded by the

Rob Wayss

Sotho women wearing traditional blankets return from a meeting.

Leolo Mountains on the east and by dry plains to the west. This region and neighboring arcas of the Northern Province are also home to other ethnic groups, including the Lovedu, Tsonga, Ndebele, Venda, Zulu, and Afrikaners. The Northern Province is much warmer than Lesotho.

3 ● LANGUAGE

The Sotho language, or Sesotho, is a Bantu language closely related to Setswana. Sotho is rich in proverbs, idioms, and special forms of address reserved for elders and in-laws.

The division between southern and northern Sotho people is based on the dif-
ferent dialects of the two groups. The southern form of Sotho is spoken in Lesotho, and the northern form is spoken in the Northern Province. The northern dialect is called Sepedi. Southern Sotho utilizes click consonants in some words, while Sepedi does not have clicks. Currently, southern Setho has two spelling systems, one in use in Lesotho and another in South Africa. For example, in Lesotho a common greeting is *Khotso, le phela joang?* (literally, "Peace, how are you?"). In South Africa, the word *joang* (how) is written *jwang,* and *khotso* is written *kgotso.*

Names in Sotho generally have meanings that express the values of the parents or of the community. Common personal names include *Lehlohonolo* (Good Fortune), *Mpho* (Gift), and *MmaThabo* (Mother of Joy). Names may also be given to refer to events. For example, a girl born during a rainstorm might be called *Puleng,* meaning "in the rain." Individuals may also be named after clan heroes. Surnames are taken from relatives on the father's side of the family.

4 ● FOLKLORE

According to one Sotho tradition, the first human being emerged from a sea of reeds at a place called Ntswanatsatsi. However, little is known or said about the events of this person's life.

Sotho has a rich tradition of folktales (*ditsomo* or *dinonwane)* and praise poems (*diboko).* These are told in dramatic and creative ways that may include audience participation. Folktales are adventure stories which occur in realistic and magical settings. One of the best known of the folktales is about a boy named Sankatana who saves the world from a giant monster.

Praise poems traditionally describe the heroic real-life adventures of ancestors or political leaders. Here is the opening verse of a long poem in praise of King Moshoeshoe:

> You who are fond of praising the ancestors,
>
> Your praises are poor when you leave out the warrior,
>
> When you leave out Thesele, the son of Mokhachane;
>
> For it's he who's the warrior of the wars,
>
> Thesele is brave and strong,
>
> That is Moshoeshoe-Moshaila.

5 ● RELIGION

The supreme being that the Sotho believe in is most commonly referred to as Modimo. Modimo is approached through the spirits of one's ancestors, the *balimo,* who are honored at ritual feasts. The ancestral spirits can bring sickness and misfortune to those who forget them or treat them disrespectfully. The Sotho traditionally believed that the evils of our world were the result of the malevolent actions of sorcerers and witches.

Today, Christianity in one form or another is accepted by most Sotho-speaking people. Most people in Lesotho are Catholics, but there are also many Protestant denominations. Independent African churches are growing in popularity. The independent churches combine elements of African traditional religion with the doctrines of Christianity. They also emphasize healing and the Holy Spirit. One of these churches, the Zion Christian Church, was founded by two Pedi brothers. It has been very successful in attracting followers from all over South Africa. Each spring there is a "Passover" meeting in the Northern Province that attracts thousands of people to the church's rural headquarters.

6 ● MAJOR HOLIDAYS

Lesotho has a number of holidays that recognize its history. These holidays include Moshoeshoe's Day (March 12) and Independence Day (October 4). Moshoeshoe's Day is marked by games and races for the nation's young people. Independence Day is celebrated by state ceremonies that often include performances by traditional dance groups.

Rob Wayss

A typical family compound.

7 ● RITES OF PASSAGE

Women give birth with the assistance of female birth attendants. Traditionally, relatives and friends soaked the father with water when his firstborn child was a girl. If the firstborn was a boy, the father was beaten with a stick. This ritual suggested that while the life of males is occupied by warfare, that of females is occupied by domestic duties such as fetching water. For two or three months after the birth, the child was kept secluded with the mother in a specially marked hut. The seclusion could be temporarily broken when the baby was brought outside to be introduced to the first rain.

There are elaborate rites of initiation into adulthood for boys and girls in Sotho tradition. For boys, initiation involves a lengthy stay in a lodge in a secluded area away from the village. The lodge may be very large and house dozens of initiates *(bashemane)*. During seclusion, the boys are circumcised, but they are also taught appropriate male conduct in marriage, special initiation traditions, code words and signs, and praise songs. In Lesotho, the end of initiation is marked by a community festival during which the new initiates *(makolwane)* sing the praises they have composed. In traditional belief, a man who has not been initiated is not considered a full adult.

Initiation for girls *(bale)* also involves seclusion, but the ritual huts of the bale are generally located near the village. Bale wear masks and goat-skin skirts, and they smear their bodies with a chalky white substance. They sometimes may be seen as a group near the homes of relatives, singing, dancing, and making requests for presents. Among some clans, the girls are subjected to tests of pain and endurance. After the period of seclusion the initiates, now called *litswejane*, wear cowhide skirts and anoint themselves with red ocher. Initiation for girls does not involve any surgical operation.

In Lesotho, a period of working in a mine was once considered a kind of rite of passage that marked one as a man.

When someone dies, the whole community takes part in the burial. Speeches are made at the graveside by friends and relatives, and the adult men take turns shoveling soil into the grave. Afterward, all those in attendance go as a group to wash their hands. There may also be a funeral feast.

8 ● RELATIONSHIPS

In Sesotho, the words for father *(ntate)* and mother *(mme)* are used commonly as address forms of respect for one's elders. Politeness, good manners, and willingness to serve are values very strongly encouraged in children. The general attitude toward childhood is well summarized by the proverb *Lefura la ngwana ke ho rungwa*, which roughly translates as "Children benefit from serving their elders."

The standard greetings in Sotho reflect this attitude of respect towards age. When greeting an elder, one should always end with *ntate* (my father) or *mme* (my mother). Words for brother *(abuti)* and sister *(ausi)* are used when one talks to people of the same age. A child who answers an adult's question with a simple "Yes" is considered impolite. To be polite, the child needs to add "my father" or "my mother."

Hospitality and generosity are expected. Even those who have very little will often share their food with visitors. Of course, those who share also expect the favor to be returned when it is their turn to visit.

Dating was not part of traditional Sotho life. Marriages were arranged between families, and a girl could be betrothed in childhood. Nowadays, most people pick their mates.

9 ● LIVING CONDITIONS

Rural areas in South Africa and Lesotho are marked by poverty and inadequate access to health care. Diarrheal diseases and malnutrition sometimes occur. Malaria is also found in the low-lying regions of the Northern Province.

However, people with access to land and employment enjoy a reasonable standard of living. Lesotho's capital city, Maseru, is a growing city with modern hotels and fine restaurants.

Rob Wayss

Children stand next to a "wind block" used to shelter the fire used for cooking from the wind. Their roofed home stands directly behind them.

Common forms of transportation include buses, trains, and taxis. The "taxis" are actually minivans that carry many riders at one time. Most such taxis are used for short distances in urban areas, but they are also used as a faster alternative to the long-distance routes of buses. There are also personal cars and trucks.

10 ● FAMILY LIFE

In Sotho tradition, the man is considered the head of the household. Women are defined as farmers and bearers of children. Family duties are also organized into distinct domains based on gender for all Sotho, but the Pedi maintain a stricter separation of living space into male and female areas. Polygynous marriages (more than one wife) are not uncommon among the elite, but they are rare among commoners. Marriages are arranged by transfer of *bohadi* (bride wealth) from the family of the groom to the family of the bride. Upon marriage, a woman is expected to leave her family to live with the family of her husband.

The Sotho have clans, many of which bear animal names, such as the *Koena* (crocodile). These clans stress descent

Rob Wayss

Children take a break from their studies for a school-provided lunch of bean soup and corn meal porridge.

through the father's side, but there is flexibility in defining clan membership. A feature of Sotho kinship was that a person was allowed to marry a cousin *(ngwana wa rangoane)* who was a member of the same clan.

Family life for many rural Sotho has been disrupted for generations by migrant labor. Today, many Sotho men continue to live in all-male housing units provided by the gold-mining companies that employ them. With the end of apartheid, some of the families previously separated by the old labor laws now live together in urban areas.

11 ● CLOTHING

Much about Sotho apparel is the same as the apparel of people in Europe and the United States. However, the most acceptable form of clothing for a woman is still the dress, and her hair is expected to be covered with a scarf, head cloth, or hat. The Sotho of Lesotho are identified with the brightly colored blankets that they often wear instead of coats. These blankets have designs picturing everything from airplanes to crowns to geometric patterns. The blankets are store-bought—there is no tradition of making them locally.

12 ● FOOD

Sotho people share many food traditions with the other peoples of South Africa. Staple foods are corn (maize), eaten in the form of a thick paste, and bread. Beef, chicken, and mutton (lamb) are popular meats, while milk is often drunk in soured form. South African beer is made from sorghum rather than barley.

The major mealtimes are breakfast and dinner (in the evening). Children may go without lunch, although there are some school lunch programs.

13 ● EDUCATION

The first Western-style schools for Sotho-speakers were begun by missionaries. Religious institutions and missionaries continue to play a major role in education in Lesotho today. Many of Lesotho's high schools are boarding schools affiliated with churches. In Lesotho, only a minority of students manage to graduate from high school because school fees are high and the work is very demanding. To graduate, one must pass the Cambridge Overseas Examination. Today, Lesotho has an adult literacy rate (percentage of those who can read and write) of about 59 percent.

Under the former system of apartheid, Africans' access to education in South Africa was restricted, and many of the best schools were closed. Today, the government's goal is to provide a tuition-free education for everyone between the ages of seven and seventeen. Literacy and education are now seen as keys to success and are highly valued by most people in Lesotho and South Africa.

14 ● CULTURAL HERITAGE

Sotho traditional music places a strong emphasis on group singing, chanting, and hand clapping as an accompaniment to dance. Instruments used included drums, rattles, whistles, and handmade stringed instruments. One instrument, the *lesiba*, is made from a pole, a string, and a feather. When it is blown, the feather acts as a reed, producing a deep, resonant sound.

Generations of mine labor have led to a distinct migrant-worker subculture in Lesotho. This subculture developed its own song and dance traditions. Some types of mine dances have synchronized high-kicking steps. One song tradition, *difela*, has lyrics relating the travels, loves, and viewpoints of the migrant workers. Other popular music in Sotho includes dance tunes played by small groups on drums, accordions, and guitars.

Sotho written literature was established in the nineteenth century by converts to Christianity. One of the first novels in a South African language was *Chaka*, written in Sotho by Thomas Mofolo in the early years of the twentieth century. It is still read today and has been translated into a number of languages.

15 ● EMPLOYMENT

Wage labor for many rural Sotho has meant leaving home to find employment in the city. In South Africa, Sotho are frequently hired as miners and farm laborers. Women also work as farm laborers, but work in domestic service is more highly valued. Health care, education, and government administration are popular careers for those with high school and college educations.

South Africa's migrant-labor system dramatically altered Sotho social life. Besides putting strains on the family, migrant labor led to the development of new social groups. For example, associations of young men called *Marussia* formed with values that combined urban and rural attitudes. These so-called "Russians" are sometimes criticized as nothing more than criminal gangs based on home ties.

16 ● SPORTS

Many of the games popular among Sotho children are found worldwide. These include skipping rope, racing, swimming, playing catch, dodgeball, and hopscotch. Boys also enjoy wrestling and fighting with sticks. A common pastime for rural boys is making clay animals, especially cattle. Young boys and girls enjoy playing house (*mantlwantlwaneng*). The most popular traditional game among young men and old men is a game of strategy called *morabaraba*. Today, the most popular sport in Lesotho and South Africa is soccer.

17 ● ENTERTAINMENT

Most of the movies seen by the Sotho people are imported from foreign countries. Televisions and videocassette recorders are becoming widespread, although listening to the radio is more common due to the lower cost. Broadcasts in Sotho are restricted to a few hours of the day, with Sotho soap operas being the most popular shows. Music videos of popular South African musical groups are also seen. In rural areas, however, there can be little to do for entertainment.

18 ● CRAFTS AND HOBBIES

Traditions of folk art include beadwork, sewing, pottery making, house decoration, and weaving. Functional items such as sleeping mats, baskets, and beer strainers continue to be woven by hand from grass materials. Folk craft traditions have been revived and modified in response to the tourist trade.

19 ● SOCIAL PROBLEMS

The main social problems among the Sotho include poverty, malnutrition, crime, and divided families. Many of these problems started under South Africa's former system of apartheid, which only ended in the early 1990s. The rural lands of the northern and southern Sotho people became heavily eroded, overpopulated, and overgrazed. Competition for scarce resources in South Africa also led to conflict with other ethnic groups, particularly the Xhosa.

20 ● BIBLIOGRAPHY

Bardill, John E., and Jame H. Cobbe. *Lesotho.* Boulder, Colo.: Westview Press, 1985.

Carpenter, Allan. *Lesotho.* Chicago: Childrens Press, 1975.

Hofmeyer, Isabel. *"We Spend Our Years as a Tale That is Told": Oral Historical Narrative in a South African Chiefdom.* Portsmouth, N.H.: Heinemann, 1994.

Mofolo, Thomas. *Chaka.* London: Heinemann, 1981.

Tonsing-Carter, Betty. *Lesotho.* New York: Chelsea House, 1988.

WEBSITES

Internet Africa Ltd. Lesotho. [Online] Available http://www.africanet.com/africanet/country/lesotho/, 1998.

World Travel Guide. Lesotho. [Online] Available http://www.wtgonline.com/country/ls/gen.html, 1998.

Liberia

The people of Liberia are called Liberians. The country has about 28 ethnic tribes, but tribal divisions are becoming less distinct. This is due to intermarriage, and to Liberia's goal of national unification of all Liberians. There are more than 1.5 million Malinke distributed over several African nations, including Liberia.

Malinke

PRONUNCIATION: mah-LING-kay

ALTERNATE NAMES: Mandinka; Maninka; Manding; Mandingo; Mandin; Mande

LOCATION: Territory covering The Gambia, Senegal, Mali, Guinea Bissau, Guinea, Sierra Leone, Liberia, and Côte d'Ivoire (Ivory Coast)

POPULATION: 1.5 million

LANGUAGE: Variations of Mande languages

RELIGION: Islam

1 ● INTRODUCTION

Liberia's population of over 2 million steadily declined in the 1990s. During the 1989–96 civil war, as many as two hundred thousand people died and another seven hundred thousand became refugees. Liberia's population consists of over two dozen ethnic groups, which fall into three main language groups: Kru (east and southeast), Mel (northwest), and Mande (north and far west). The Malinke are a Mande-speaking group.

The Malinke are also commonly referred to as Mandinka, Maninka, Manding, Mandingo, Mandin, and Mande. They live in areas of sub-Saharan Africa that have a history of agricultural settlements dating as far back as 7,000 years.

The Malinke are heirs to the great Mali Empire, a medieval merchant empire that flourished from the thirteenth to the sixteenth century and greatly influenced the history of western Africa. Malinke territories in the northern region of Africa were brought under Muslim control in the eleventh century. The renowned city of Islamic teaching, Timbuctu, was also part of the vast and prosperous Mali Empire. The empire declined in the fifteenth century and was gradually absorbed by the Songhai Kingdom, which extended to the seventeenth century.

MALINKE

Scale:
0 200 400 600 800 Miles
0 200 400 600 800 Kilometers

MOROCCO
Rabat
Oran
ALGERIA
Semara
Chegga
WESTERN SAHARA (Occupied by Morocco)
Canary Is. (SPAIN)
MAURITANIA
MALI
Nouakchott
Néma
Tombouctou
CAPE VERDE
Praia
Dakar
SENEGAL
Bamako
Niger
THE GAMBIA
Banjul
Bissau
BURKINA FASO
GUINEA-BISSAU
GUINEA
Yagaba
Conakry
Freetown
CÔTE D'IVOIRE
SIERRA LEONE
Yamoussoukro
Abidjan
Monrovia
LIBERIA
ATLANTIC OCEAN

As early as 1444, Portuguese traders had enslaved the first Malinke people, and in the next three and a half centuries, thousands of Malinke and other peoples were transported by Portuguese, British, French, and Dutch merchants to the Caribbean and the Americas to work as slaves on plantations. During the nineteenth century the kingdoms of the Malinke peoples were subjugated by the British, French, and Portuguese and were incorporated into their colonial systems.

The Malinke people gained some popular attention when American author Alex Haley published his best-selling book, *Roots* (1974), later made into a television series. The story of Haley's ancestral family and the book's main character, Kunta Kinte of the Mandinka (Malinke) people, personalized the terrible plight of African slaves and their families who were sold into slavery.

The Malinke were not only victims of the slave trade, but they were also perpetrators of the institution, having had a long history of owning and maintaining slaves. There were two distinct kinds of slaves to be found: those who had been captured in battle or purchased; and those who had been born into the slave families of their village. The indigenous slave trade persisted into the nineteenth century.

2 ● LOCATION

Today there are more than 1.5 million Malinke distributed over several African nations within a wide arc that extends 800 miles (1,300 kilometers). The region starts at the mouth of the Gambia River in the northwest and circles around in a bow form, ending in the Côte d'Ivoire (Ivory Coast) in the southeast. The territory includes areas in the nations of The Gambia, Senegal, Mali, Guinea Bissau, Guinea, Sierra Leone, Liberia, and Côte d'Ivoire. There are numerous other African ethnic groups sharing these areas.

3 ● LANGUAGE

The Malinke peoples speak slight variations of the broad Mande branch of the Niger-Congo family of languages. The term "Mande" frequently refers to a group of closely related languages spoken by the Malinke and other west African peoples such as the Bambara, the Soninke, and the Dyula.

4 ● FOLKLORE

Details of the early days of the Mali Empire and the lifestyles of the people have been kept alive for centuries through the epic poem, *Sonjara* (or *Sundiata*; also *Sunjata*), which has been sung for generations by the *griots*, bards or praise-singers of West Africa. In over 3,000 lines of poetry in the oral tradition, the epic tells the story of Sonjara, a legendary leader who, after countless obstacles and trials, unites the Malinke clans and chiefdoms at the beginning of the thirteenth century. Sonjara is unable to walk as a child because of a spell put on him by his father's jealous second wife. Sonjara finally learns to walk and becomes a hunter, giving up his claim to the throne during a long exile with his mother and siblings. A delegation from Mali comes to him and begs him to return and save them from an evil sorcerer-king, Sumanguru. Sonjara organizes an army to regain his throne. With help from his sister, who seduces Sumanguru in order to learn his weaknesses, and after many bloody battles, Sonjara's army defeats the forces of Sumanguru.

5 ● RELIGION

The majority of the Malinke are Muslim (followers of Islam) and have adapted the teachings of Islam into their native beliefs. Most Malinke villages have a mosque. Women sit separate from the men, both in the mosque and during outside religious services. Those villagers who have made the *hajj* (pilgrimage) to Mecca, or even descendants of those who have made the journey, are highly respected.

The principal religious leader is the elected *imam,* an elder who leads prayers at the mosques and has great religious knowledge. The other Islamic clerics who play major roles as healers and religious counselors are the *marabouts*. They are respected as preservers of morality through oral tradition and teachers of the Koran (sacred text of Islam). They are perceived to be experts at preventing and healing ailments or injuries inflicted by mortals or those that are believed to have been inflicted by evil spirits.

6 ● MAJOR HOLIDAYS

The favorite is Muslim holiday is Tabaski, which usually falls in the spring or summer, the day being determined according to the Islamic lunar calendar. Tabaski commemorates the moment when Abraham was about to sacrifice his son Isaac in obedience to God's command, when God interceded and provided a ram instead. It is prestigious to have a very large and fat ram to slaughter for the holiday. On this day people attend the mosque, and there is much eating (especially roasted mutton) and visiting of friends. Other religious holidays include the Feast of Ramadan celebrated at the end of the annual thirty-day Muslim fast, and Muhammad's birthday.

7 ● RITES OF PASSAGE

A week after the birth of an infant, the Malinke hold a name-giving ceremony. A marabout leads prayers during the ceremony, shaves the infant's head, and announces the name of the child for the first time.

Puberty rites and circumcision are very significant in the lives of the Malinke, both male and female. It is the most important rite of passage, for one cannot attain adulthood or marry without it. For boys the rite is held about once every five years and includes novices from six to thirteen years old, who may be in a group of thirty to forty-five boys. Boys are kept secluded for six to eight weeks of instruction before circumcision.

Girls are circumcised in smaller groups, and the ceremonies occur more frequently. The girls stay secluded for ten days to two weeks. During this time they are taught Malinke values and how to work together as a group. In recent years there has been pressure to conduct female circumcisions in clinics or to stop them altogether. In general, however, the older generation is very reluctant to let go of these traditional rituals.

Marriage for a Malinke girl may begin with her betrothal at birth to a boy who may be as old as twelve. The preferred marriage arrangement is for a betrothal between a boy and his mother's brother's daughter. Prior to marriage, the suitor makes several payments of a bride price (including money, kola nuts, salt, and some livestock) to the parents of the prospective bride. The typical Malinke wedding, called a "bride transfer," takes place on a Thursday or Friday—the two holiest days of the week.

For funerals, a corpse is ritually bathed and buried on its right side, head facing east, feet to the north. A fence is built around the grave to protect it from animals; sticks are put over the hole. During the next forty-five days, three mortuary ceremonies are held at which oil cakes and kola nuts are distributed to those attending.

8 ● RELATIONSHIPS

When the Malinke encounter a family member or friend, an extensive ritual exchange of formal greeting questions can take up to a minute. They might say, "Peace be with you," "Is your life peaceful?", "How is everything going?", "Are your family members in good health?", "How is your father?", or "Is the weather treating your crops well?" The questions go back and forth and may end with, "Thanks be to Allah." Even if one is not feeling well or if things are not going well, the answers are usually positive. It is considered very bad manners not to engage in the lengthy greeting exchange.

If a guest drops by at mealtime, he or she will surely be invited to share the meal. Those who have been blessed by Allah (God) with wealth are expected to share some of theirs with others.

9 ● LIVING CONDITIONS

The Malinke who live in the cities have adapted to an urban lifestyle. Most, however, still live in traditional villages of anywhere from a few hundred to a few thousand people. The villages are rather compact, consisting of groups of compounds enclosed by millet-stalk fences. A compound contains several cylindrical houses built of sun-baked bricks or wattle and daub, with a thatched roof; there will also be a granary and a separate cylindrical kitchen with low half-walls and a thatched roof. Houses are grouped around a center courtyard that may contain a well.

For transportation, a bicycle, an occasional motorbike, an ox cart, or a horse cart are used by those who can afford them. More frequently, villagers walk to catch a bus or perhaps share a taxi, or they simply walk to their destination. Women do not have much opportunity to leave their villages, and travel for women is discouraged by the Malinke culture.

10 ● FAMILY LIFE

The Malinke consider large families to be important. A large compound with brothers and their wives will always be bustling with family members of several generations and children of many ages. The Malinke practice polygyny (multiple wives), and Islam permits men to take up to four wives. The expensive bride price and the fact that society requires that all wives be provided for equally means that only prosperous men can afford several wives.

Women are always busy with some kind of work, while it is common to see men sitting under a tree in the village square, chatting with other men and having a smoke and some tea. The household heads have the authority to make all important decisions, although women wield significant power behind the scenes.

The social organization of the Malinke is based on an ancient caste (class) system into which members are born. A Malinke can never change the caste-status into which he or she is born. There is rarely marriage between individuals of different castes. In an average village, however, the differences in wealth or status among the castes is barely visible. The size of the family is often more of an indication of wealth; small families with few children and few extended family members are thought of as poor and unfortunate.

11 ● CLOTHING

Today, Malinke who live in urban centers, especially the men, may have adopted Western-style clothes. Villagers, on the other hand, take pride in their traditional clothing, which is important to them. In fact, one of the obligations of a husband is to give each wife the cloth for at least two new outfits every year.

Women generally wear a loose, scoop-necked smock over a long skirt made by a wrap-around piece of cloth. They often tie a matching piece of cloth around their head in an informal turban, each woman's turban having its own special flair. They use brightly colored cotton prints with splashy, large designs; some also wear tie-dyed, wood-block, or batik prints. The traditional casual dress for men is made with the same bright prints fashioned in an outfit that resembles pajamas.

For formal occasions men and women may wear the *grand boubou*. For women this is a loose dress that extends to ground level and may be trimmed in lace or embroidery. For men it is a long robe-like garment covering long pants and a shirt. Many middle-aged or elder men wear knit caps. Shoes are leather or rubber thongs.

12 ● FOOD

Traditional Malinke are cultivators who grow varieties of millet, sorghum, rice (in the swampy areas), and corn as staple crops. As cash crops they grow peanuts and cotton, and to supplement their diet and gain a bit of income, they grow diverse vegetables in

AP/Wide World Photos

A young Malinke boy carries water home to his family.

garden plots. Some villages have a bakery where small loaves of French-style bread are baked.

The wealthier Malinke own some live-stock—cattle, goats, chickens, and perhaps a horse for plowing. The cattle are used for milk and for the prestige of owning them; they are rarely slaughtered. There is little meat in the diet. Those who live near rivers or lakes may supplement their meals with fish.

A typical breakfast might consist of corn porridge eaten with a spoon made of a small, elongated calabash (gourd) split in half. The midday and evening meals may consist of rice or couscous with sauce (often peanut) and/or vegetables. Couscous can be made of pounded and steamed millet, sorghum, or cornmeal.

Tea-time is an important break for the Malinke. Tea is made by filling a small pot with dried tea leaves and covering these with boiling water. The brewed tea is extremely strong and is served with several small spoons of sugar in tiny glasses. After the first round of tea, the pot is filled with boiling water a second and third time, thus the second and third rounds of tea are a bit diminished in strength.

13 ● EDUCATION

Many villages today have a government school as well aa a Koranic (Islamic) school for learning to recite verses from the Koran. The educational model of the government schools is based on those of the ex-colonial masters, either French or British. Since the nations where the Malinke are found today have many other tribal peoples, it is likely that the school teachers are of a different ethnic group and do not speak the Malinke language. Further, instruction is often in French of English, making it difficult for Malinke children.

Poor attendance and high drop-out rates are common in the village schools. Muslim parents often do not think it is as important for their daughters to get an education as it is for their sons, so the enrollment of boys is much higher than that of girls. Only a small percentage of the village pupils pass the state examination at the end of sixth grade in order to go on to high school. In the countries where the Malinke live, generally less than half the population is able to read and write.

14 ● CULTURAL HERITAGE

Much of the cultural heritage of the Malinke is embedded in the great Mali merchant empire of the thirteenth to the sixteenth centuries and the Islamic religion that was adopted by the chieftains. There was a flourishing trade in gold, and many ornate ornaments, jewelry, and staffs of gold date from that period. Additionally, the cultural heritage has been immortalized in the famous epic poem *Sonjara*, sung by minstrels since the thirteenth century (*see* Folklore).

15 ● EMPLOYMENT

Farming is a respected occupation, and all members of society are given farming tasks. The children, too, guard the fields against wild boar, monkeys, and birds. The Malinke use natural fertilizer, allowing livestock to graze on the fields lying fallow; and children are often seen tending the livestock

Men do the plowing, sowing, planting, and a major part of the harvesting work. Some also engage in hunting and fishing. Women do weeding and tend vegetable plots.

16 ● SPORTS

Boys might be seen playing soccer with a homemade ball. They enjoy listening to soccer matches, both national and international, on the radio, or watching matches on television in town; many Malinke men and boys can recite the names of international soccer stars.

17 ● RECREATION

In addition to the storytelling and music provided by the griots, the Malinke like to listen to the radio. For those living in villages with electricity, a television set is a prized item. It is common for large groups of villagers to gather at the home of the television's owner.

Woaley is a board game similar to backgammon. It is a major pastime for the Malinke as well as for other West Africans. The board is in the form of a rectangle with twelve indentations to hold beans, and two larger indentations at the ends to hold the captured beans. Both spectators and players of all ages enjoy woaley matches. (The game is referred to by many other names—such as *mancala*, and is played all over the world in slight variations.)

18 ● CRAFTS AND HOBBIES

Present-day hobbies of Malinke young men include such things as collecting cassette tapes of their favorite singers (such as reggae singers from Jamaica or American rock stars). Young women enjoy braiding each other's hair, making decorative rows or braiding in long strands of synthetic hair.

19 ● SOCIAL PROBLEMS

Since the Malinke are socialized with a strong sense of responsibility to their family and lineage, many of the social problems that are prevalent in industrialized society are not encountered. AIDS and the spread of venereal diseases by men who have brought these back from urban areas is a problem in some places. There is malnutrition and a lack of understanding of its causes. Some people view the situation of women as a social problem. Women have fewer opportunities for education, fewer rights, and share a husband with co-wives.

20 ● BIBLIOGRAPHY

Haley, Alex. *Roots*. Garden City, N.Y.: Doubleday, 1976.

McNaughton, Patrick R. *The Mande Blacksmiths: Knowledge, Power, and Art in West Africa.* Bloomington, Ind.: Indiana University Press, 1988.

Moss, Joyce, and George Wilson. *Africans South of the Sahara*. 1st ed. Detroit: Gale Research, 1991.

Sallah, Tijan M. *Wolof*. New York: Rosen Publishing Group, 1996.

WEBSITES

Internet Africa Ltd. [Online] Available http://www.africanet.com/africanet/country/liberia/, 1998.

World Travel Guide. Liberia. [Online] Available http://www.wtgonline.com/country/lr/gen.html, 1998.

Libya

The people of Libya are called Libyans. More than 90 percent of the population identify themselves as Arab, with most of the remaining minority composed of Berbers (general name for North Africans) and black Africans.

Libyans

PRONUNCIATION: LIB-ee-uhns
LOCATION: North Africa
POPULATION: 4 million
LANGUAGE: Arabic; English
RELIGION: Islam (Sunni Muslim)

1 ● INTRODUCTION

Libya is located in North Africa, bordered to the east by Egypt and to the west by Algeria. The name *Libya* is taken from an ancient Egyptian name for a local tribe. It was later applied by the Greeks to most of the people of North Africa. For centuries, Libya was ruled by foreign powers. It was colonzied by the Italians. Libya finally achieved independence in 1951.

Today, Libya is a pro-Arab, anti-Western state ruled by a dictator, Colonel Mu'ammar al-Qadhafi (b. 1942). The United States and the United Kingdom consider it to be a criminal country. It has huge amounts of oil, however, so most other countries of the world have avoided being as hostile to it as have the United States and the United Kingdom.

2 ● LOCATION

Libya has a population of over 4 million people, more than half of whom are under the age of fifteen. More than 90 percent of the population identify themselves as Arab, with most of the remaining minority composed of Berbers and black Africans. About three-quarters of the population now live in urban areas concentrated along the coast.

Libya is located in North Africa on the Mediterranean Sea. It is the fifteenth-largest country in the world. Libya is bordered on the west by Tunisia and Algeria, on the east by Egypt and Sudan, and on the south by Niger and Chad. To the north of Libya lies the Mediterranean Sea, with southern Europe at the opposite shore. In all, more than 80 percent of Libya is covered by the Sahara Desert. There are no rivers. There are a few saltwater lakes near the Mediterranean coast.

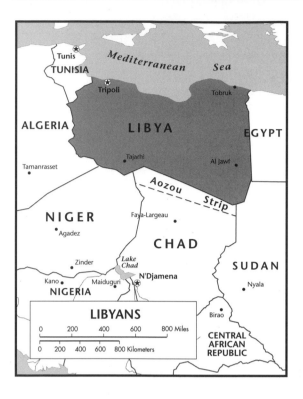

3 ● LANGUAGE

Arabic is the national language of Libya and, although the government officially discourages the use of other languages, English is the most popular second language and is regularly taught in school.

In greeting, a Libyan says *As-salamu `alaykum*, which means "Peace be with you." The response is *Wa `alaykum as-salam*, which means "And peace be with you as well."

Common Libyan female names are *Aysha, Fatima, Amna, Khadija,* and *Asma.* Male names are *Muhammad, Ali, Yusif, Ibrahim,* and *Mukhtar.*

4 ● FOLKLORE

Libya has many legends based on the exploits of Muslim leaders who resisted European invaders. These leaders, such as Umar al-Mukhtar, often come from religious backgrounds and are considered well-learned. They are called *marabouts,* or holy men, and are believed to have *baraka,* or divine grace. This allows them to perform miracles.

Most folklore in Muslim countries tells stories of important figures in religious history. One such story is that of *al-Isra wa al-Miraj.* According to legend, on the twenty-sixth day of the Islamic month of Rajab, the Prophet Muhammad traveled at night from Mecca, Saudi Arabia (then Hijaz), to Jerusalem. From Jerusalem, he rode his wondrous horse, al-Burak, on a nocturnal visit to heaven. This legend is in part responsible for the importance of Jerusalem to people of the Islamic faith.

5 ● RELIGION

The overwhelming majority of Libyans are Muslim. Most Libyans belong to the Sunni school of Islam, which was brought by the original conquering Arabs.

6 ● MAJOR HOLIDAYS

Libya commemorates secular holidays and Muslim religious holidays. One major Muslim holiday is *Eid al-Fitr,* which comes at the end of Ramadan, the month of fasting. During Ramadan, Muslims refrain from eating or drinking during daylight hours. They do this in order to reflect on God and on the plight of the unfortunate who do not have enough food. At the end of the month, Muslims celebrate for three days.

The other major Muslim holiday is *Eid al-Adha,* which commemorates the willingness of Abraham to obey God's command in all things, even when Abraham was told to sacrifice his son.

Other Islamic holidays, celebrated to a lesser degree, are the Islamic New Year, the Prophet Muhammad's birthday, and the Tenth of *Muharram.* This holiday commemorates Moses leading the Israelites out of Egyptian slavery. The Prophet Muhammad instructed all Muslims to fast on this day.

Secular holidays include Independence Day (December 24), and a holiday commemorating the United States withdrawal from Wheeling Air Force base (Evacuation Day) in Libya on June 11, 1970. Army Day is August 9, and Proclamation Day is November 21.

7 ● RITES OF PASSAGE

Male babies are usually circumcised at birth. Some families wait until the boy reaches the age of ten or eleven. Children of both sexes are expected to help with household chores.

The majority of Libyan marriages are arranged by families. Even those who marry for love must have the approval of their families. Weddings take place either in a mosque or in the bride's home. The ceremony is administered by an *imam* (Muslim prayer leader). A marriage contract is signed during the wedding ceremony.

Elderly family members are cared for by their children, and none are put in retirement or old-age homes. Upon death, the deceased's body is washed, clothed in clean linen, and buried with his or her right side facing Mecca. Only men attend the funeral, and women express their grief at the deceased's home by wailing.

8 ● RELATIONSHIPS

Islam is central to Libyan life. This is easily seen in their social practices. Daily life revolves around the five daily prayers Muslims are required to recite. Many Libyan men attend the mosque regularly in keeping with the five prayer times. Libyan women usually pray at home.

A Libyan always greets guests with a cup of coffee or tea. Desert tradition requires that a guest be offered food. Hospitality is part of the Libyan code of honor.

Since alcohol is forbidden by Islam, Libya has no bars or nightclubs. There are many sidewalk cafes, however. Here men drink coffee or tea and socialize. In the evenings, most Libyans can be found at home.

Most Libyans treasure their privacy. This has been particularly true since political opposition to the government became a punishable offense. Libyans avoid making any public comments that can be interpreted as political criticism.

9 ● LIVING CONDITIONS

Living conditions for most Libyans have improved in recent years. Housing shortages, however, continue to be a problem. The typical Libyan family lives in an apartment. Those who can afford them hang Persian carpets on the walls as decoration. It is common to have at least one sofa and a few embroidered floor cushions for seating. Some families can afford television sets.

One-tenth of all families have cars, often Japanese.

10 ● FAMILY LIFE

Libyans live with their extended families in tightly knit communities. A typical household consists of a man, his wife, and his sons with their wives and children. Also included are unmarried daughters and other relatives such as a widowed or divorced mother or sister. At the death of the father, each son establishes his own household and repeats the cycle. Marriages are conducted by negotiation between the families of the bride and groom. Men and women are generally not allowed to mix socially.

The traditional roles of men and women changed noticeably in the 1970s. Then, the government began encouraging women to vote and to work outside the house. Working mothers were offered cash bonuses. Day care was greatly improved. The retirement age for women was set at fifty-five, and laws were passed ensuring equal pay for equal work.

In spite of the government's efforts, some traditional views have been slow to change. For example, women are more likely to be secretaries than engineers. However, by the mid-1980s women had broken into several professional fields, most notably in the health-care arena. Recently, the government has tried to further redefine the role of women and expand its armed forces by making military service required for both sexes.

11 ● CLOTHING

Two styles of clothing are currently common in Libya. In the cities, there is a mixture of Western and traditional clothes. Girls commonly wear brightly colored dresses, and boys wear jeans and shirts. Young men and women wear predominantly modern clothing, but most women continue to cover their hair in keeping with Islamic tradition.

The traditional attire for men is a long, white gown worn over a shirt and pants. Some men wear a black or white Muslim hat on their heads. Traditional women also wear long gowns and hair coverings. Most women's gowns cover both the head and body. In rural areas, traditional dress is very common.

Styles of dress in the cities will often fall along generational lines, and it is not unusual to see people walking side by side in differing styles of garments. Unlike in other parts of North Africa, in Libya dress has not become a political issue.

12 ● FOOD

Before every meal, a Libyan recites the Muslim expression *Bismillah,* or "In the name of God." After finishing the meal, the Muslim then says *Al-hamdu lillah,* which means "Thank God."

Couscous is a very popular food. Couscous is semolina (a type of wheat flour) sprinkled with oil and water and rolled into tiny grains. The grains are steamed and then are ready for use in a favorite recipe. It can be mixed with a number of sauces and then combined with a variety of meats and/or vegetables. Couscous is also combined with honey and milk and served for breakfast. The main meat eaten by Libyans is lamb.

Recipe

Babaghanuj (Eggplant Dip)

Ingredients

1 large eggplant
5 Tablespoons tahini (sesame paste)
1 garlic clove, pressed through a garlic press
3 to 4 Tablespoons lemon juice
½ teaspoon salt
2 Tablespoons olive oil
3 Tablespoons chopped parsley

Directions

1. Heat over to 400°F. Bake whole, un-peeled eggplant on a cookie sheet for 40 minutes until soft. Allow to cool un-til it can be handled.
2. Peel the eggplant and mash the flesh in a bowl. Add the other ingredients, and mash together well.
3. Mound the dip on a plate or in a bowl. Drizzle olive oil over the top, and sprinkle with parsley.

Serve with triangles of pita bread.

Adapted from Coralie Castle and Marga-ret Gin. *Peasant Cooking of Many Lands.* San Francisco: 101 Productions, 1972.

Most Libyan meals are eaten with *kas-rah,* a flat, round, nonyeasted bread. Kasrah is often eaten with dips, such as *babagha-nuj,* a dip made of mashed, roasted eggplant mixed with lemon, tahini (sesame seed paste), and a pinch of salt. A recipe for babaghanuj can be found above.

Dates from palm trees are used in many forms by Libyans. The fruit can be eaten fresh or squeezed to make juice or date honey. Dried dates can be ground into date flour, and date pits can be roasted and ground to make date coffee.

Coffee and mint tea are popular drinks, served throughout the day. Alcoholic bever-ages and pork are forbidden by Islamic law.

13 ● EDUCATION

Before World War II (1939–45), few schools existed in Libya. Less than 10 per-cent of the population could read or write. After the discovery of oil in 1959, Libya invested in new schools, vocational training centers, and universities.

Libya now uses a Western-style educa-tion system that includes six years of pri-mary school, three years of preparatory school, and three years of secondary school. Schooling is required for both boys and girls until the age of fifteen. After comple-tion of secondary school, Libyans may attend either vocational schools or universi-ties.

Libya's first university was established in 1955 in Benghazi. This was followed by universities in Tripoli, Mersa Brega, and Sabha. All schooling, including that at the university level, is free. This includes books, school supplies, uniforms, and meals. Today, about 90 percent of Libyans are literate.

14 ● CULTURAL HERITAGE

Traditional Libyan folk dance is a very pop-ular. Music and dance troupes often perform together at festivals. Line dancing is also popular, with dancers linking arms while swaying, hopping, and gliding across the stage. Singers are often accompanied by musicians who play violins, tambourines, the `ud (a windpipe made of cane), the *tablah* (a hand-beaten drum), and the lyre.

The Libyan government controls the production and distribution of printed matter, and all printing presses are government-owned. Libraries, also government-owned, have abundant collections of old religious writings, but far less modern literature. Material critical of the regime or of Islam is censored.

15 ● EMPLOYMENT

Most workers are employed in the oil industry. It is the largest and most important part of the Libyan economy. Other people work in state-owned manufacturing. These companies produce machinery, appliances, cement and construction equipment, cigarettes, clothing, leather goods, textiles, shoes, fertilizers, and industrial chemicals. They also make processed foods such as olive oil, citrus fruits, tomato paste, tuna, and beverages.

Many farm workers moved to the cities during the 1960s and 1970s following the oil boom and industrial development. Agricultural workers now make up less than one-fifth of the work force. These workers grow citrus fruits, barley, wheat, millet, olives, almonds, dates, onions, potatoes, tomatoes, and tobacco. Many farmers raise sheep, goats, cattle, camels, and poultry, and produce dairy products and honey. Fishermen operating out of Tripoli bring in tuna, sardines, and mullet.

There is a shortage of unskilled laborers. Because of this, many unskilled foreign workers from neighboring countries live in the country. Libya also has hundreds of thousands of foreign technical workers, needed especially to advise on petroleum extraction and to design and construct irrigation systems.

16 ● SPORTS

Libyan sporting events tend to be very strenuous and spirited. Popular sports are camel and horse racing and football (what Americans call soccer). Camel racing and horse racing have been popular events for thousands of years. Competitions are held on racetracks in rural areas. Football is both a spectator sport and a participation sport. Libya has a national football team that competes in regional matches with other Arab and African teams. Other popular sports are basketball and track and field events.

17 ● RECREATION

Radio is a popular form of communication in Libya, with state-sponsored news, religious, and musical programming. There are about one million radios and more than seventeen hours per day of broadcasting. Libyan television began in 1968. There are three stations. Two of these rebroadcast foreign programs with Arabic subtitles. The third is dedicated to explaining the ideas expressed in Qadhafi's *Green Book*. Libyans are expected to have a good understanding of the ideas in this book, although most people pay it little attention. Movie theaters show imported foreign films.

Libya has nine museums housing archeological, religious, and historical exhibits. Chess and dominoes are enthusiastically played, both in cafes and in homes.

18 ● CRAFTS AND HOBBIES

Libyan art, in keeping with Islamic beliefs, does not contain realistic depictions of people or animals. Instead, artists paint designs that are complex, geometric, and abstract. Libyan artisans use intricate lines and geometric shapes in their carpets, embroidered goods, jewelry, leather goods, tiles, and pottery. Islamic words and passages from the Koran (the sacred text of Islam) are often etched in elaborate calligraphy. Libyan architecture has the same restrictions against portraying human or animal figures, and lifelike statues and adornments are not found on buildings.

19 ● SOCIAL PROBLEMS

The greatest problems facing Libya today stem from economic problems and the lack of political freedom. Since the mid-1970s, when Libyans enjoyed a very high standard of living, changes in oil prices have led to serious economic problems. This has caused housing shortages as well as dissatisfaction among young people.

Most crime in Libya is property theft, with relatively few incidents of violent crime. A significant number of convictions are for what the government calls "crimes against freedom, honor, and the public." This could mean anything from public drunkenness to student demonstrations to more serious political offenses.

20 ● BIBLIOGRAPHY

Brill, M. *Libya*. Chicago, Ill.: Children's Press, 1987.

Castle, Coralie, and Margaret Gin. *Peasant Cooking of Many Lands*. San Francisco: 101 Productions, 1972.

Copeland, Paul W. *The Land and People of Libya*. New York: J. B. Lippincott, 1967.

Gottfried, Ted. *Libya: Desert Land in Conflict*. Brookfield, Conn.: The Millbrook Press, 1994.

Metz, Helen C., ed. *Libya: A Country Study*. Washington, D.C.: Federal Research Division, Library of Congress, 1988.

Wright, John. *Libya: A Modern History*. Baltimore, Md.: The Johns Hopkins University Press, 1981.

WEBSITES

ArabNet. [Online] Available http://www.arab.net/libya/libya_contents.html, 1998.

World Travel Guide. Libya. [Online] Available http://www.wtgonline.com/country/ly/gen.html, 1998.

Liechtenstein

The people of Liechtenstein are called Liechtensteiners. Over 60 percent of the population are descended from people of Switzerland and southwestern Germany.

Liechtensteiners

PRONUNCIATION: lick-ten-SHTINE-uhrs
LOCATION: Liechtenstein
POPULATION: 30,000
LANGUAGE: Standard German; Alemannic German; English; French
RELIGION: Roman Catholicism; Protestantism

1 ● INTRODUCTION

Liechtenstein is a tiny, beautiful country located in the heart of Europe. The citizens of this politically neutral principality enjoy a peaceful and prosperous existence in the midst of a scenic Alpine landscape.

The region now known as Liechtenstein has been inhabited since 3000 BC. It was eventually settled by the Alemanni, a Germanic people who arrived in the area in the fifth century AD. It was later divided into two separate entities: the Lordship of Schel-lenberg and the County of Vaduz. Prince Johann Adam of Liechtenstein acquired Schellenberg in 1699 and Vaduz in 1712, uniting the two domains as the Imperial Principality of Liechtenstein. Except for a brief period of French rule under Napoleon, the principality has been independent since 1912.

The principality joined the United Nations in 1991 and applied for membership in the European Community (EC) in 1994. Crown Prince Hans Adam has been Liechtenstein's reigning monarch since 1984.

2 ● LOCATION

Liechtenstein is a landlocked country located in the Rhine River valley between Switzerland and Austria. With an area of roughly 62 square miles (160 square kilometers)—slightly smaller than Washington,

LIECHTENSTEINERS

Bangs

Salez

Ruggell

Schellenberg

Tisis

Gamprin · Mauren

Frastanz

Eschen

Motten

RHEIN VALLEY

Gurtis

Planken

AUSTRIA

L I E C H T E N S T E I N

Schaan

Vaduz

Triesenberg

A L P S

Triesen

Malbun

Rhein

Balzers

SWITZERLAND

SWITZERLAND

3 ● LANGUAGE

Standard German is the official language of Liechtenstein. It is used for official purposes and taught in the schools. However, most people also speak a local Alemannic dialect that resembles the German spoken in Switzerland. The people in the mountain region of Triesenberg speak a unique dialect called Walser. The principal second languages taught in school are English and French.

4 ● FOLKLORE

Some of Liechtenstein's legends date back to the seventeenth century. During this time, a savage wave of witch hunts swept over the principality during the reign of the Count of Hohenems. One legend concerns a fiddler named Hans Jöri, who unknowingly plays at a party thrown by a group of witches. The witches vanish when he disobeys them by drinking a toast to his own health. After this he suddenly finds himself seated on a scaffold holding a bleeding ox's hoof—a symbol of witchcraft—in his hand.

In another tale, a farmer suspects that a witch's spell is preventing his butter from thickening. After he thrusts a red-hot pitchfork into it, it thickens right away. The farmer's suspicions are proven when he is then approached by a witch who has burn marks on her hands shaped exactly like the prongs of the pitchfork.

5 ● RELIGION

Roman Catholicism is the state religion of Liechtenstein, and about 85 percent of the people are Catholic. Approximately 7 percent are Protestant, and the rest belong to

D.C.—it is Europe's fourth-smallest country. The western part of Liechtenstein, situated on the Rhine's eastern bank, is a flat region covering about 40 percent of the country, with mountains occupying much of the larger area to the east.

Liechtenstein has a population of approximately 30,000 people. Of these, about two-thirds are native-born residents of Alemannic descent. The rest are immigrants from Switzerland, Austria, and other countries. Liechtenstein's population is unevenly distributed among the principality's eleven administrative districts, which are called "communes." Vaduz, the capital city, has a population of about 5,000.

other denominations. Freedom of religion is guaranteed by the constitution.

6 ● MAJOR HOLIDAYS

Many of Liechtenstein's holidays are holy days of the Christian calendar. These include Epiphany (January 6), Candlemas (February 2), the Feast of St. Joseph (March 19), Easter (observed from Good Friday through Easter Monday in late March or early April), Ascension Day (in May), Whit Monday (in May), Corpus Christi (in June), the Nativity of Our Lady (September 8), All Saints' Day (November 1), the Immaculate Conception (December 8), and Christmas, which is celebrated December 24–26.

Christmas is the most important holiday of the year, celebrated by putting up Christmas trees, exchanging gifts, and visiting with friends and family. Other holidays include New Year's Day (January 1), Labor Day (May 1), and Liechtenstein's national day (August 15), which is celebrated with speeches and fireworks.

People in rural areas still observe some of the traditional holiday customs passed on for generations. There is the annual Corpus Christi procession. During this procession, the entire village turns out, carrying a variety of devotional objects. They then pass by homes adorned with candles, flowers, and religious paintings.

On Bonfire Sunday, the first Sunday of Lent (in February), boys walk through their villages collecting wood for a large bonfire, which they light in the evening. They then perform an age-old ceremony, tracing patterns in the air with torches they have lit from the flames of the bonfire. After the fire dies out, the boys return home to a traditional pancake supper.

Another rural Lenten custom is "Dirty Thursday," also called "Sooty Thursday," which is observed on the last Thursday before Lent. On this occasion, boys arm themselves with chimney soot, which they rub into the faces and hair of unsuspecting victims. Another traditional prank carried out on this date is stealing a pot of soup from the kitchen of a village house. Some women have been known to even the score by hiding an old shoe in the soup pot.

7 ● RITES OF PASSAGE

Liechtensteiners live in a modern, industrialized, Christian country. Hence, many of the rites of passage that young people undergo are religious rituals, such as baptism, first communion, confirmation, and marriage. In addition, a student's progress through the education system is marked by many families with graduation parties.

8 ● RELATIONSHIPS

Liechtensteiners commonly greet each other by shaking hands. Verbal greetings include *Gruezi* (also used in Switzerland) and the German *Grüss Gott* (these two greetings are used to say "hi"). *Hoi!* is a popular informal greeting used among friends.

9 ● LIVING CONDITIONS

Liechtenstein is a modern, industrialized country whose residents enjoy one of the highest standards of living in the world. Most Liechtensteiners live in single-family homes, although apartment living has become common for young families who cannot afford their own homes. There is sufficient housing for all of Liechtenstein's inhabitants, and dwellings range from wooden houses scattered across picturesque mountain villages to modern multistory apartment buildings in the capital city of Vaduz.

Private automobiles are Liechtenstein's most important mode of transportation, and the principality has a well-developed system of roads and highways. Its main highway runs through the country, linking it with Austria and Switzerland. Low-cost public transportation is provided by postal buses. These carry passengers to destinations within Liechtenstein, and also to Austria and Switzerland. Liechtenstein has one railway, operated by the Austrian Federal Railways. There is no airport within Liechtenstein. The nearest one is Kloten Airport in Zurich, Switzerland.

10 ● FAMILY LIFE

The typical family in Liechtenstein is the nuclear family, composed of parents and, on average, about two children. Most Liechtensteiners marry in their late twenties, preferring to complete their education before taking on the responsibilities of raising a family. It is not unusual for unmarried couples to live together before (or instead of) marrying.

Several distinctive traditional customs are still practiced at weddings in rural villages. When the bride and groom leave the church following the marriage ceremony, they often find their way barred by a rope held by the village children, who must be "bribed" by the best man in order to let the couple pass. Further bribes may have to be paid later, at the wedding feast, if the chil-

dren manage to make off with one of the bride's shoes. Sometimes the groom's friends even "kidnap" the bride herself, and it is then the groom's turn to pay up. Yet another wedding custom is firing guns into the air, a practice that has been banned for safety reasons but is still done occasionally.

Women in Liechtenstein have only had the right to vote nationally since 1984 and are still denied local suffrage in some parts of the country. Many married women work outside the home.

11 ● CLOTHING

The people of Liechtenstein wear modern, Western-style clothing for both casual and formal occasions. They dress neatly and conservatively in public. Their traditional costumes, or *Trachten,* are worn only rarely, for festivals and other special occasions. The women's costume has a gathered waist, a full skirt, and an apron, while men wear knee-length breeches, a flat black hat, and a *loden* (woolen) jacket.

12 ● FOOD

Liechtensteiners eat three meals a day. Coffee and bread with jam are commonly eaten for breakfast (called *Zmorga*). *Zmittag,* eaten at midday, is the main meal of the day and typically includes a main dish, soup, salad, and dessert. A lighter meal *(Znacht)* is eaten at dinnertime, often consisting of an open-faced sandwich made with various kinds of meat and cheese.

Although Liechtenstein is too small to have developed an extensive national cuisine, it does have some distinctive regional dishes. *Käsknöfle* consists of noodles made by squeezing a mixture of flour, water, and eggs through a perforated board. The noodles are then baked with grated cheese and a layer of fried onions and are often served with applesauce or a salad. *Hafaläb*, another favorite, is a dish made with a corn- and wheat-flour dough formed into small loaves. These are then boiled, left out to dry, sliced, and then fried. Corn flour is the principal ingredient of *Törkarebl,* made from porridge that is then fried to create a dumplinglike dish often served with elderberry jam.

13 ● EDUCATION

Virtually all adults in Liechtenstein are literate. Both primary and secondary education are administered by the central government, and all children must attend school from ages seven to sixteen. In addition to government-run public schools, there are also private schools sponsored by the Catholic Church.

After completing their secondary school requirements, students either receive vocational training or prepare for the university entrance examination, known as the *Matura.*

Liechtenstein has no universities of its own. Its young people go to college in Germany, Austria, or Switzerland. Liechtenstein does have an evening technical college that offers courses in engineering and architecture, and a music school, as well as a variety of facilities for adult education.

14 ● CULTURAL HERITAGE

Liechtenstein's great cultural treasure is the art collection of its prince, which dates back to the early 1600s. Housed in the capital city of Vaduz, it is the second-largest private art collection in the world. It is surpassed in size only by that of Britain's royal family. It is also one of the finest art collections—public or private—in the world. Its many masterpieces cover a wide range of periods and schools of art. It includes sculptures, tapestries, silver, and porcelain, as well as paintings by Breughel the Elder, Botticelli, Rembrandt, Rubens, and other masters of Renaissance art.

Liechtenstein also has a strong musical tradition. Brass bands and vocal ensembles are common in rural areas, while the cities of Vaduz and Balzers both have highly regarded operetta companies.

15 ● EMPLOYMENT

Since World War II (1939–45), Liechtenstein has been transformed from a farming society into a modern industrial state. Agriculture once occupied most of the people, but now only about 5 percent of the people farm. Nearly half of all employed adults work in service-sector jobs.

Liechtensteiners put in a long workday. It lasts from 8:00 AM to 6:30 PM with a midday lunch break lasting an hour or longer. Over a third of Liechtenstein's labor force commute to work from Switzerland or Austria. Liechtenstein's major industries include metal finishing, ceramics, pharmaceuticals, and electronic equipment.

16 ● SPORTS

Most Liechtensteiners are sports enthusiasts. Over a third of the population belong to the National Sports Union. The principality's downhill ski resorts are world-famous, especially those at Malbun and Steg. The Steg resort also has a popular cross-country ski course with a 1 mile (1.7-kilometer) stretch that is lit with floodlights, allowing for nighttime skiing. Summer sports include hiking, bicycling, and soccer.

17 ● RECREATION

Cultural pursuits—such as performing in choirs and bands—are popular. Many people belong to social clubs. Television is a common form of recreation. Liechtenstein has about one television set for every three people. All television programming is received from abroad. Radio broadcasts originating in Liechtenstein began in 1994.

18 ● CRAFTS AND HOBBIES

Historically, Liechtenstein's major crafts included basket weaving, coopering (barrel-making), clog carving, and the fashioning of elaborate rakes. Today these activities have largely been replaced by the modern crafts of pottery, sculpture, and woodcarving, all areas in which Liechtenstein's artisans have a distinguished reputation throughout Europe.

Liechtenstein is world-famous for its beautiful postage stamps. They are valuable collector's items that provide a significant source of government revenue. Many are based on paintings found in the prestigious art collection of Liechtenstein's prince.

19 ● SOCIAL PROBLEMS

Concern about the large number of foreign residents in Liechtenstein—over one-third of the population—has led to restrictive immigration policies. These were passed because the presence of so many foreigners was causing Liechtenstein to lose the cultural unity that distinguishes this tiny nation from its neighbors.

However, increased numbers of foreign workers from neighboring German-speaking countries continue to commute to jobs in Liechtenstein, and foreigners still account for approximately 60 percent of the principality's work force.

20 ● BIBLIOGRAPHY

Carrick, Noel. *Let's Visit Liechtenstein.* London: Pegasus House, 1985.

Gall, Timothy, and Susan Gall, ed. *Worldmark Encyclopedia of the Nations.* Detroit, Mich.: Gale Research, 1995.

Meier, Regula A. *Liechtenstein.* Santa Barbara, Calif.: Clio Press, 1993.

WEBSITES

World Travel Guide. Liechtenstein. [Online] Available http://www.wtgonline.com/country/li/gen.html, 1998.

Lithuania

The people of Lithuania are called Lithuanians. The native-born population is about 80 percent of the total. Russians are about 9 percent; Poles, 7 percent; Belarusans, 2 percent; and Ukrainians, 1 percent. For more information on these groups, consult the chapters on Russia and Poland in Volume 7; the chapter on Belarus in Volume 1; and the chapter on Ukraine in Volume 9.

Lithuanians

PRONUNCIATION: lith-oo-ANE-ee-uns

LOCATION: Lithuania

POPULATION: 3.7 million (total population of country; 80 percent are ethnic Lithuanians)

LANGUAGE: Lithuanian

RELIGION: Roman Catholicism; Old Believers; Russian Orthodox Church; Lutheranism; Judaism

1 ● INTRODUCTION

It is likely that the first people to live in the area now known as Lithuania came from Asia around 4,000 to 10,000 years ago. During the fifteenth and sixteenth centuries, Lithuania and Poland were part of a large empire that dominated eastern Europe. By 1795, Russia had taken over all of Lithuania. During World War I (1914–18), the German army occupied Lithuania. Lithuania was recognized as a sovereign (self-governing) state following the war, but independence did not last long.

During World War II (1939–45), Germany occupied Lithuania, and sent about 160,000 Lithuanians to die in concentration camps. After the war, the Russians returned to Lithuania and claimed it as a part of the Soviet Union. (At that time Russia was one of the states of the Soviet Union.)

When the Soviet Union fell apart in late 1991, the Lithuanians were finally free to govern themselves for the first time since 1940. The last foreign army units left Lithuania on August 31, 1993.

2 ● LOCATION

Lithuania, along with Estonia and Latvia, is one of the Baltic States that border the Baltic Sea. It is located in the western part of eastern Europe, along the basin of the Nemunas River. Water travel has long been an important means of transportation in Lithuania. The 2,833 lakes in Lithuania

occupy about 1.5 percent of the surface area of the nation. The rivers and lakes are frozen over for about three months each winter.

There are millions of Lithuanians living outside Lithuania, including over 800,000 people of Lithuanian heritage living in the United States, and another 15,000 in Canada.

3 ● LANGUAGE

The Lithuanian language was formalized at the end of the nineteenth century. There are many dialects (variations on the language) spoken throughout Lithuania.

Lithuanian first names for males end in *as* or *us*. Typical first names include *Algimantas, Jonas, Darius,* and *Vytautas*. Female first names often end in the letter *a* and include *Rasa, Daiva, Laima, Ruta,* and *Aldona*.

Family names reflect gender, and for females, their position. For example: Antanas Butkus is the husband and father. His wife, Birute, uses a feminine variation of his family name—Butkiene—to indicate that she is his wife. His unmarried daughter, Ruta, uses another variation—Butkute—to indicate her status. His sons are entitled to use the name Butkus.

Examples of everyday Lithuanian words include:

English	Lithuanian	Pronunciation
Hello	sveiki	SVAY-kih
Good-bye	sudiev (literally "with God")	SU-dyo
Thank you	aciu	ah-CHUH
Yes	taip	TYPE
No	ne	NEH
Please	prašom	PRAY-shoh

4 ● FOLKLORE

The old Lithuanian *dainos* (songs) are famous for their beauty and variety. The dainos were created by women doing farm work or celebrating festivals. They were also created to mark mournful occasions. Romantic love and leave-taking are important themes.

Many folk songs have been harmonized or used in compositions by modern composers. Folk song festivals and performances by choral groups are an important part of cultural life. Folk music is played solo or by instrumental groups. Popular instruments include *kankles* (zither), *skuduciai* (pan-pipe), *lamzdelis* (recorder), *ragas* (horn), *smuikas* (fiddle), *birbyne* (folk clarinet), and *skrabalai* (cow bells).

5 ● RELIGION

The ancient Lithuanians worshiped many gods and believed that forests and fires were sacred. The most popular gods that they worshiped were Perkūnas (god of thunder), Velnias (the devil, the guardian of wizards), Medeina (goddess of forests), and Zvorūne (goddess of hunting).

About 80 percent of Lithuanians who have religious beliefs are Roman Catholic. Most of the rest are Russian Orthodox, Old Believers (a seventeenth century breakaway Russian Orthodox sect), Lutheran, and Jewish.

6 ● MAJOR HOLIDAYS

Independence Day commemorating the 1918 declaration of independence is February 16. The Day of Independence Restored, celebrated on March 11, commemorates the date in 1990 when Lithuania declared its independence from what was then the Soviet Union.

Easter is the most important religious holiday among Lithuanians. Lithuanians begin celebrating Easter by attending a church service before sunrise with their immediate family. The service is followed by a festive breakfast. Beginning in the late afternoon and on Easter Monday, groups of young men call on their neighbors, singing and asking for *marguciai* (decorated Easter eggs). It is considered inhospitable to refuse the carolers' requests. General merrymaking on the second day of Easter includes the rolling of Easter eggs, games to test one's strength, and swinging on swings. Adults

travel to visit relatives and friends. On the third day of Easter, the dead are remembered and cemeteries are visited.

7 ● RITES OF PASSAGE

Traditionally, couples to be married participated in a series of pre-wedding rituals and customs. Most of these placed great emphasis upon the bride's leaving her parents and her childhood home. Customary ceremonial songs, dances, and verse accompanied each of these events. They included *vakarynos* (the last evening) when the bride's friends braided her hair for the last time. They also sang to her of past happiness and future worries.

Jaunojo sutiktuves (greeting the bridegroom) included the exchange of gifts. During the *svocios pietūs* (dinner for the bride), the bride's wreath was exchanged for a married woman's headdress. At the *nuotakos išleistuves* (taking leave of the parental home), the bride kissed the table, the crucifix, and a loaf of bread and bid farewell to her parents and other family.

8 ● RELATIONSHIPS

An old greeting still used in some rural areas of Lithuania is *Garbe Kristui* (Praise Christ). The traditional response is *per amzius amen* (forever amen). It was also customary to greet someone working in the fields or in gardens with *Dieve padek* (May God help you).

Lithuanians have long prided themselves on their hospitality. A visit to a Lithuanian home is sure to include a warm response, a richly laid table, and perhaps storytelling and singing.

EPD Photos

Traditional Lithuanian folk costume, more frequently worn by folk dancers today. The young women model necklaces made from amber found on the shores of the Baltic Sea.

9 ● LIVING CONDITIONS

The Lithuanian government is developing a new health-care program to improve health conditions. Cancer is the leading cause of death in Lithuania, and diseases related to alcoholism are also common. The average life expectancy for a Lithuanian born now is about seventy-two years, which is relatively high among eastern European and former Soviet nations.

During World War II (1939–45), many Lithuanian towns and villages were completely destroyed. After the war, many stan-dardized housing projects were constructed. They were often built in large sections from prefabricated materials. Many of these units today are in poor condition.

10 ● FAMILY LIFE

Large families, with ten to twelve children, were historically common in Lithuania. Though traditionally the father was the head of the family, the mother also commanded respect within the family structure. Roman Catholicism was the fundamental force in family life.

Modern Lithuanian families tend to be much smaller, with one or two children the norm. In the 1990s, women outnumber men in Lithuania, leaving more women unmarried than in the past. It typically takes a young couple fifteen to twenty years to save enough money to buy a house or an apartment. A young couple must often turn to their parents for financial help. The number of single-parent families is on the rise, as is alcoholism. Two-income households have become common. The divorce rate has increased as well, having reached about 20 to 25 percent of all marriages. Alimony is awarded to a woman only if the children are minors at the time of the divorce.

11 ● CLOTHING

Lithuanians dress in modern, Western-style clothes. Traditional clothing is worn only for festivals. A traditional costume for women consists of a woven, colorful full skirt, embroidered blouse, vest, and headpiece with ribbons. Jewelry made from amber found on the shores of the Baltic Sea is treasured.

Recipe

Grybuka
(Honey Mushrooms)

Ingredients

For cookies
1 cup flour
2 egg yolks plus 1 whole egg
¼ cup butter
1 cup honey
1 cup brown sugar
1 teaspoon baking soda
2 Tablespoons sour cream
½ teaspoon cinnamon
¼ teaspoon each of allspice, ground cloves, and ground ginger
For icing
1 cup powder sugar
1 egg white
pinch of creme of tartar
2 teaspoons cocoa or chocolate powder

Directions

1. Combine cookie ingredients in a mixing bowl. Stir with a wooden spoon until a thick dough forms.

2. Divide the dough in half. With one half, form mushroom caps from walnut-sized pieces of dough by making a ball and flattening one side. Make a small indentation on the flat side for the mushroom stem. Put the mushroom caps, flat side down, on cookie sheet.

3. With the other half of the dough, form mushroom stems about the thickness of a finger and 1½ inches long. Place stems on cookie sheet.

4. Preheat oven to 325°F. Bake for 25 to 30 minutes. Turn off the oven.

5. Make icing. Beat egg white with powdered sugar and creme of tartar.

6. Assemble mushrooms by using the icing to glue the caps and stems together. Frost the stems with icing.

7. When the stems are frosted, tint the remaining icing brown with the cocoa powder. Frost the caps with the brown icing.

8. Return the frosted cookies to a warm oven for 15 minutes to harden and dry the icing.

12 ● FOOD

Food has always been treated with great respect by Lithuanians. It is seen as a gift from God. Until the early 1900s, eating was a very serious and even holy act. The family dinner table was not the place for talking or child's play. In traditional Lithuanian culture, meals were presided over by the male head of the household. He led the family in a short prayer before dividing the bread and meat. Other dishes would then be served by the wife.

Sour cream is an important part of Lithuanian dishes. *Varske* (curd or dry cottage cheese) is also important. It is used as a filling in such dishes as *varskeciai* (rolled pancakes with sweetened curd), *cepelinai* (large, blimp-shaped potato dumplings), and *virtinukai* (ravioli-like dumplings). The latter two dishes commonly feature a filling of meat and are topped by a large mound of sour cream or fried bacon bits.

A very popular summer dish is the refreshing *saltibarsciai,* a cold soup of sour cream and buttermilk or sour milk, with sliced beets, cucumbers, green onions, boiled'eggs, and parsley. It is usually eaten with a hot boiled potato. Among the large variety of pancakes, potato pancakes form a separate category. Roasts of pork, veal, beef, or poultry, as well as pork chops, are more common on Lithuanian home and restaurant tables than are beef steaks. The seasoning of Lithuanian dishes is mild.

13 ● EDUCATION

Education starts at age six. There are three types of public schools: elementary (grades one through four), nine-year (grades one through nine), and secondary (up to grade twelve). There are also professional, technical, and specialized secondary schools. Higher education in Lithuania is available at sixteen institutions.

14 ● CULTURAL HERITAGE

The oldest known folk songs are the *dainos,* which were sung by Lithuanian women during the Middle Ages. The most popular instruments for playing Lithuanian folk songs are *skrabalai* (cow bells), *dambrelis* (jaw harp), *kankles* (zither), *smuikas* (fiddle), *skuduciai* (panpipe), *lamzdelis* (recorder), *ragas* (horn), *daudyte* (long trumpet), and the *birbyne* (folk clarinet).

Musical elements of the traditional folk songs are often used in modern compositions as well. Choral singing is an important part of cultural festivals in Lithuania. Every five years, Vingis Park in Vilnius is the site of a huge folk music festival. The stage is big enough to hold 20,000 performers. The costumed performers demonstrate ancient Lithuanian folk songs and dances.

In 1706, Aesop's fables became the first nonreligious work published in Lithuanian. Antanas Baranauskas was a famous poet of the mid-nineteenth century, whose lyrical romantic poem *Anykšciu šilelis* (The Forest of Anykšciai) is a milestone in Lithuanian literature. Lithuanian literature has long been linked with nationalism and the liberation movement, especially the literature of the late nineteenth and early twentieth centuries.

15 ● EMPLOYMENT

During the decades of Soviet rule, the government controlled the economy. The independent Lithuanian government has begun to replace that inefficient system with one that allows businesses and individuals to make their own decisions. However, the transition toward a market economy has been difficult for many workers.

16 ● SPORTS

Lithuanians are sports enthusiasts. Riding and hunting are traditional activities. A popular traditional game is *ripkos,* involving the

Arvydas Sabonis and Sarunas Marciulionis, have found success in the American National Basketball Association. Sabonis and Marciulionis also helped lead the Lithuanian team to Olympic bronze medal victories in 1992 and 1996.

Other popular sports in Lithuania include cycling and canoeing. Soccer is also very popular. Most recently, baseball and field hockey have entered the Lithuanian arena of sports as new favorites. Vilnius, Klaipeda, and Kaunas have the largest of Lithuania's forty-one stadiums.

17 ● RECREATION

From the ancient past until today, Lithuanians have maintained a love of traditional song and dance. The arts are especially supported in the capital city, Vilnius.

Lithuanians also enjoy the outdoors. In summer, beaches along the Baltic Sea, seaside resort towns, and lakes, forests, and campgrounds in the countryside are visited by vacationing Lithuanians. Health resorts are equally popular. Time spent in a sauna or steam bath is considered a necessary luxury by Lithuanians. World travel for the citizens of Lithuania was forbidden until 1993, but by the late 1990s it had become a popular activity.

Local cafes, movie theaters, and video arcades attract young people, as do nightclubs and rock concerts. Numerous health clubs have opened their doors since 1993 and are gaining in popularity. There are few carnival rides or amusement parks in Lithuania.

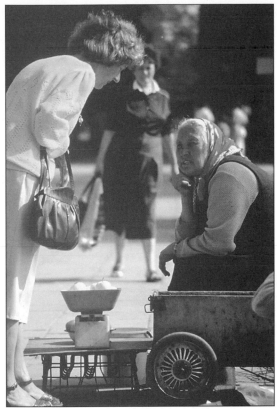

Cory Langley

A woman buys produce from a street vendor.

throwing and hitting of a wooden disk. Over fifty types of sports are practiced and played in Lithuania, including rowing, boxing, basketball, track and field, swimming, handball, and table tennis.

Basketball is the most popular sport in Lithuania today. It was introduced by a Lithuanian American named Stasys Darius after World War I (1914–18). The sport caught on rapidly, and the Lithuanian team won the European basketball championship twice before World War II (1939–45). Today, two Lithuanian players in particular,

18 ● CRAFTS AND HOBBIES

Lithuanian folk art frequently involves the decoration of common household items. Bed and table linens, towels, window treatments, wooden trim, and ceramics are objects that are often decorated. Themes in paintings and sculptures typically focus on religion, work, and everyday life.

19 ● SOCIAL PROBLEMS

After Lithuania gained its independence from the Soviet Union in 1993, many large factories closed, creating a sudden rise in the unemployment rate. Young people are often tempted to seek work in other countries.

Crime has increased in Lithuania. Mugging, robbery, car-jacking, and murder have become more commonplace. Prisons and juvenile detention centers are overcrowded.

20 ● BIBLIOGRAPHY

Bindokiene, Danute Brazyte. *Lithuanian Customs and Traditions*. Chicago: Lithuanian World Community, Inc., 1989.

Chicoine, Stephen. *Lithuania: The Nation That Would Be Free*. New York: Cobblehill Books, 1995.

Lithuania. Minneapolis, Minn.: Lerner Publications Co., 1992.

Kagda, Sakina. *Lithuania*. New York: Marshall Cavendish, 1997.

Stasys, Yla. *Lithuanian Family Traditions*. Chicago: Lithuanian Library Press, Inc., 1978.

Tamošaitis, Anatas, and Anastasia Tamošaitis. *Lithuanian National Costume*. Toronto: Time Press Litho Ltd., 1979.

WEBSITES

Embassy of Lithuania, Washington, D.C. [Online] Available http://www.ltembassyus.org/, 1998.

World Travel Guide. Lithuania. [Online] Available http://www.wtgonline.com/country/lt/gen.html, 1998.

Luxembourg

The people of Luxembourg are called Luxembourgers. Those who are native-born consider themselves a distinct nationality. About one-third of the population consists of immigrants.

Luxembourgers

PRONUNCIATION: lucks-ehm-BOOR-guhrs
LOCATION: Luxembourg
POPULATION: 401,000
LANGUAGE: Letzebürgesch; French; German
RELIGION: Roman Catholicism; small numbers of Protestants and Jews

1 ● INTRODUCTION

The Grand Duchy of Luxembourg is a tiny but prosperous nation in Western Europe. For 400 years Luxembourg was ruled by its Western European neighbors, including France, Spain, and Austria. However, the country retains a distinct identity of its own. The Luxembourgers' pride in their identity is expressed in their motto: *Mir woelle bleiwe wat mir sin* (We want to remain what we are).

Luxembourg became an independent, neutral state in 1867. It has had its own ruling dynasty since 1890. With the discovery of iron ore around 1860, the country began the transition to a modern, industrialized nation.

2 ● LOCATION

Luxembourg has an area of only 998 square miles (2,586 square kilometers). The northern third of the country is known as the Oesling. This forested upland region is dotted with the ruins of historic castles. Luxembourg's southern two-thirds are called "The Good Land" (*Gutland* in German and *Bon Pays* in French). This region is home to most of Luxembourg's population. It contains the country's most-fertile soil as well as the capital city.

Luxembourg's population of 401,000 is approximately three-fourths urban and one-fourth rural.

3 ● LANGUAGE

Luxembourg has three official languages: French, German, and Letzebürgesch, a

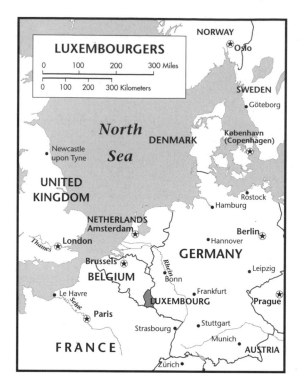

LUXEMBOURGERS

0 100 200 300 Miles

0 100 200 300 Kilometers

NORWAY

Oslo

SWEDEN

Göteborg

North Sea

DENMARK

København (Copenhagen)

Newcastle upon Tyne

Röstock

Hamburg

UNITED KINGDOM

NETHERLANDS
Amsterdam

Berlin

London

Hannover

Thames

GERMANY

Brussels

Leipzig

BELGIUM

Bonn

Rhein

Le Havre

Frankfurt

LUXEMBOURG

Prague

Seine

Paris

Stuttgart

Strasbourg

Munich

FRANCE

AUSTRIA

Zürich

national dialect. Letzebürgesch, which is based on German and French, is the first language of all Luxembourgers. It is learned in childhood and spoken at home. German, which is taught in primary school, is the language of business and the media. French is the language of government. In addition to their native languages, many Luxembourgers also speak English.

4 ● FOLKLORE

According to legend, Count Sigefroid, who founded Luxembourg's capital, married a maiden named Mélusine. What he did not know, however, is that she was really a mermaid. After he found out, she disappeared into the stone walls of the city. It is said that she remains there still. Every seven years she returns, either as a beautiful woman or

as a serpent with a golden key in its mouth. According to tradition, she could be freed if the woman were kissed or the key removed from the serpent's mouth. However, no one has ever accomplished either feat. Mélusine is also said to knit an ever-unfinished garment, completing one stitch every year. It is said that if she completes it before she is freed from the wall, all of Luxembourg will vanish into the rock with her.

5 ● RELIGION

Over 95 percent of Luxembourg's population is Roman Catholic. At least a third of these, however, are nonpracticing Catholics. Luxembourg's constitution guarantees religious freedom to its people.

6 ● MAJOR HOLIDAYS

Luxembourg's legal holidays are New Year's Day (January 1), Easter Monday (late March or early April), Labor Day (May 1), Ascension Day (in May), Whitmonday (in May), National Day (June 23), Assumption Day (August 15), All Saints' Day (November 1), Christmas (December 25), and Boxing Day (December 26).

National Day is a patriotic holiday observed with parades, fireworks, and church services. Luxembourgers also observe local and regional holidays. On St. Bartholemy's Day (August 24), sheep are driven through the streets of the capital. The Broom Parade is held in the city of Wiltz every May when the broom (a bright yellow plant) blossoms.

7 ● RITES OF PASSAGE

Many of the rites of passage that young people undergo are religious rituals, such as baptism, first communion, confirmation, and marriage. In addition, a student's progress through the education system is marked by many families with graduation parties.

8 ● RELATIONSHIPS

A casual handshake is the most common greeting. Close female friends may hug and kiss each other on the cheek three times. Common greetings include *Moien* (Good morning), *Gudden Owend* (Good evening), *Wéi geet et?* (How are you?), and *Bonjour* ("Good day" in French). On parting, the expression *Addi* (Goodbye) and the more formal French *Au revoir* (Until we see each other again) are used (as well as the casual *Salut* and *Ciao,* which are popular with younger Luxembourgians).

9 ● LIVING CONDITIONS

Luxembourg enjoys one of the highest standards of living of any nation in the European Community. The country's traditional rural cottages have thick walls and heavy beams. Many urban dwellers rent modern apartments. Over 60 percent of Luxembourgers own their own homes.

10 ● FAMILY LIFE

The typical Luxembourg household consists of a nuclear family with one or two children. A national law requires adults to take financial responsibility for their aging parents. Parents generally live near the workplace. This allows them additional time to spend with their families enjoying leisure-time pursuits. Women account for roughly one-third of Luxembourg's labor force.

11 ● CLOTHING

The people of Luxembourg wear modern Western-style clothing. Luxembourgers are influenced by fashion trends in neighboring France and Germany, and by Italian fashions as well. Women tend to wear skirts and dresses more often than slacks, and men favor hats. In public, Luxembourgers are always neatly and carefully dressed. Old, worn clothing is reserved for at-home wear and sporting activities.

12 ● FOOD

The cuisine of Luxembourg combines French sophistication and German abundance. Hearty appetites and large portions are the norm. Favorite dishes include Ardennes ham, meat pies with minced-pork filling *(fleeschtaart)*, liver dumplings *(quenelles de foie de veau)*, and rabbit served in a thick sauce *(civet de lièvre)*. Luxembourg is known for its delicious pastries. Plum tarts called *quetsch* are a seasonal treat in September. A type of cake called *les penseés brouillées* is traditionally eaten on Shrove Tuesday (the day before Lent begins, in February).

13 ● EDUCATION

Education is free and required between the ages of six and fifteen. Students begin with six years of primary school, followed by up to seven years of secondary education. Many secondary school graduates attend college in the neighboring countries of France, Belgium, and Germany.

14 ● CULTURAL HERITAGE

In the visual arts, well-known Luxembourgers include seventeenth-century sculptor

Daniel Muller and twentieth-century expressionist painter Joseph Kutter. Luxembourg's literary figures have written in French (Felix Thyes), German (Nikolaus Welter), and Letzebürgesch (Michael Rodange). Paul Palgen is the country's most famous poet. The Grand Orchestra of Radiotelevision Luxembourg is world-famous. Internationally acclaimed photographer Edward Steichen was a native of Luxembourg.

15 ● EMPLOYMENT

About two-thirds of Luxembourg's labor force is employed in such service-related fields as government, trade, and tourism. Close to one-third work in industry, construction, and transportation. The remainder (about 5 percent) are engaged in agriculture. In addition, about 30,000 nonresident laborers commute to work in Luxembourg every day from neighboring countries.

16 ● SPORTS

Popular sports in Luxembourg include jogging, tennis, volleyball, and soccer. Hunting, fishing, cycling, and boating promote enjoyment of Luxembourg's scenic landscape. Favorite winter sports include cross-country skiing and ice skating.

17 ● RECREATION

The people of Luxembourg enjoy socializing in their country's many cafes and pastry shops. One can often find them engaged in informal chess matches in restaurants and cafes. The capital has a folk club, a jazz club, and a society for new music. Almost every household has a television. Movie theaters show foreign films with French or Dutch subtitles. Gardening, camping, and other outdoor activities are also very popular.

18 ● CRAFTS AND HOBBIES

Pottery and other traditional crafts are practiced in Luxembourg. In addition, the Fonderie de Mersch manufactures cast-iron wall plaques that portray local coats-of-arms, scenery, and historic castles. Luxembourg's scenic landscapes are also reproduced on porcelain plates.

19 ● SOCIAL PROBLEMS

Luxembourg is free from many of the social problems that plague other developed nations. There is a high standard of living. Their country enjoys a healthy, stable economy with virtually no unemployment. Employers are legally barred from discrimination based on gender. However, women still earn only fifty-five cents for every dollar earned by men.

20 ● BIBLIOGRAPHY

Clark, Peter. *Luxembourg*. New York: Routledge, 1994.

Delibois, John. *Pattern of Circles: An Ambassador's Story*. Kent, Oh.: Kent State University Press, 1989.

Lepthien, Emilie U. *Luxembourg*. Chicago, Ill.: Children's Press, 1992.

WEBSITES

Luxembourg National Network for Education and Research. [Online] Available http://www.rest-ena.lu/luxembourg/lux_welcome.html, 1998.

World Travel Guide. Luxembourg. [Online] Available http://www.wtgonline.com/country/lu/gen.html, 1998.

Macedonia

The people of Macedonia are called Macedonians. About 65 percent of the population trace their ancestry to Macedonia. Other groups include Albanians, about 21 percent, and Turks, 5 percent. For more information on the Albanians, see the chapter on Albania in Volume 1; and on the Turks, the chapter on Turkey in Volume 9.

Macedonians

PRONUNCIATION: mass-uh-DOE-nee-uhns
LOCATION: Macedonia
POPULATION: 1.95 million (about 70 percent are ethnic Macedonians)
LANGUAGE: Macedonian
RELIGION: Eastern Orthodoxy

1 ● INTRODUCTION

Macedonia, also known as Vardar Macedonia, is named after the river that travels almost the entire length of the country. In the region's early history it was ruled by Philip II (359–336 BC) and his son, Alexander the Great (336–323 BC). After Alexander's death, his territory was divided into four sections. The smallest consisted of Macedonia and Greece. In the following centuries, Macedonia became part of the Roman Empire and, later, the Byzantine Empire. In the sixth and seventh centuries AD, Slavs began to settle in the Balkans.

Eventually, Macedonia came under the control of the Bulgarian crown.

During the latter half of the fourteenth century, the Byzantine Empire was conquered by the Ottoman Turks. Macedonia was plunged into a lengthy struggle for the preservation of its Slavonic heritage and religious identity. With the 1913 Treaty of Bucharest, Macedonia was divided unequally among Greece, Serbia, and Bulgaria. Following World War I (1914–18), the Serbian section of Macedonia became the southernmost part of the newly formed Kingdom of Serbs, Croats, and Slovenes (eventually known as Yugoslavia). At the conclusion of World War II (1939–45), Macedonia became one of the six sovereign republics of communist Yugoslavia.

On September 8, 1991, Macedonians approved a referendum on their country's independence. A new constitution was adopted, that, for the first time ever, turned Macedonia into a parliamentary democracy.

MACEDONIANS

In April 1993, the Republic of Macedonia became a member of the United Nations.

2 ● LOCATION

Macedonia is situated in the south-central area of the Balkan Peninsula in Europe. Despite its landlocked status, its location makes it a crossroads linking Europe, Asia, and Africa. It covers an area of roughly 10,000 square miles (25,900 square kilometers), and its capital city is Skopje (pronounced SKOP-yeh).

The population of the Republic of Macedonia stands at about 1,950,000, with males slightly outnumbering females.

3 ● LANGUAGE

The primary and official language of Macedonia is Macedonian. It is an Indo-European language of the Slavonic family. Like most Slavonic languages, Macedonian is written in the Cyrillic (Russian) alphabet. However, it is derived primarily from Latin and Greek. The Macedonian language has also acquired thousands of Turkish and German words.

There are two customs in naming children. One gives children Christian names, such as Petar (Peter) and Jovan (John), or, for females, Petranka and Jovanka; the other reflects parental wishes, such as Zdravko (Healthy), Stojan (Stay [Alive]), and Spase (Saved).

4 ● FOLKLORE

Most of Macedonia's colorful folklore consists of folktales and aphorisms (witty sayings). The following are typical aphorisms: "Falsehoods have short legs" (lies are soon found out); and "Begin a task, but always have its conclusion in mind" (finish what you start.)

Macedonians like to tell folktales that emphasize a moral or philosophical message, like the following:

In ancient times, a tsar's (emperor's) daughter fell ill, but none of the royal doctors could help her. At last, an old healer took on the problem. He fashioned for the patient a ring on whose band he wrote the saying: "Everything that ever was has passed, and everything that ever will be will pass." One morning he took the ring to the princess and put it on her finger. He said that her illness would go away if she read the saying every night before going to bed, and every morning after waking up. It made her hopeful that her illness also would pass.

Eventually, she did indeed become well again.

5 ● RELIGION

The predominant religion in Macedonia is Eastern Orthodoxy, one of the three principal branches of Christianity.

In every country, the Orthodox Church honors its own regional saints and martyrs in addition to the ones recognized by other Christians. The Macedonian Orthodox Church pays homage to Saints Cyril and Methodius.

6 ● MAJOR HOLIDAYS

On March 8 Macedonians honor the Day of the Woman, which is their counterpart to Mother's Day in the United States. During the communist era (1945–91), Labor Day (May 1) was celebrated with parades, demonstrations, and long political speeches. Today Macedonians regard the same holiday as a day of rest and recreation. The Ilinden (St. Elijah's Day) Uprising, commemorated on August 2, marks the beginning of the Macedonian nationalist movement.

As Orthodox Christians, Macedonians normally celebrate the main Christian holy days several days, or even weeks, later than Catholics and Protestants. For example, Orthodox adherents celebrate Christmas on January 7 rather than on December 25.

7 ● RITES OF PASSAGE

Like people in so many other societies, Macedonians regard the birth of a boy as the most momentous family event. Most babies, male and female, are baptized before their first birthday. A new mother is expected to stay at home and receive no visitors for at least six weeks.

A deceased person's children and siblings are expected to wear dark clothes for about one year following his or her passing. The mother and spouse traditionally continued to do so for the rest of their lives. Memorial services are held on the ninth day, the fortieth day, six months, one year, and three years after the death. On these days, family members go to church and/or to the deceased's graveside. They distribute homemade bread, black olives, feta cheese, and small cups of wine to those attending.

8 ● RELATIONSHIPS

Macedonians usually greet one another with the word *zdravo* (pronounced ZDRAH-vo), meaning "health." They inquire about each other's family members' well-being and their recent activities. Children and teenagers refer to almost all older men as *chichko* or *striko,* meaning "uncle." They address almost all older women as *tetko* or *strino,* meaning "aunt."

In rural areas, there is a special greeting used when passing by people engaged in harvesting or other tasks. One normally exclaims, *Ajrlija rabota!* (pronounced ahr-LI-yah rah-BO-tah), or, loosely translated, "May your work meet with the success you are hoping for!"

9 ● LIVING CONDITIONS

Consumer goods—most of them imported from Germany—are readily available in Macedonia. Automobiles, TVs, VCRs, refrigerators, washers, and dryers may be found in almost every household. Housing is no longer the major problem it was under communism. It is no longer difficult to find an apartment or a condominium. Many families have even built houses in the country or in villages near resort areas.

10 ● FAMILY LIFE

Many Macedonians live in nuclear families, with an average of two children per family. However, intergenerational extended families are also common. Newlyweds often live temporarily with the husband's parents. Also, accepting a widowed in-law from either side into the household is entirely expected. Most older individuals live out their last years in such an arrangement.

Single-parent families are, at least by Western standards, quite rare. Divorce is not unusual, although it is considered acceptable mostly for couples with no children.

Few women ask their husbands to help with any but the simplest household chores. Even younger, professional women insist on keeping the kitchen as their own domain.

11 ● CLOTHING

Macedonians wear modern, Western-style clothing. However, they preserve a certain level of old-fashioned formality in their style of dress. For example, people will generally avoid entering a grocery store, bank, or other public place dressed in work clothes.

Macedonia's traditional, intricately embroidered folk costumes include garments made of coarse, tightly woven wool yarn. Men wear vests, white linen shirts, pants resembling English riding breeches, and a *pojas* (pronounced PO-yahs)—a wide

Cory Langley

Two Macedonian women selling vegetables. The greater part of Macedonia's economy is sustained by small, family-owned businesses such as grocery stores, restaurants, cafes, service garages, and clothing boutiques.

cloth belt. Women wear ankle-length dresses, a wide apron, a white linen shirt, a pojas, and a head scarf. Men's traditional attire is predominantly black, while women's is red and white. For footwear, both genders wear *opinci* (pronounced o-PIN-tsi)—leather slippers with a curved tip.

12 ● FOOD

The principal food on the Macedonian menu is stew, a mixture of meat and vegetables cooked by simmering. Stews are prepared spicy, combined with roux (a thickening agent), and always eaten with bread. Other main staples are feta cheese; roasted banana peppers; and *zelnik,* a flat pastry with cheese, leek, or spinach filling. Supper is the most important meal of the day, often eaten less than an hour before retiring for the night.

Many city-dwellers and probably all villagers make red wine and distill brandy, mostly from grapes or plums. Wine is consumed mainly during the winter months, with fried smoked *kolbasi* (homemade kielbasa, or sausage).

13 ● EDUCATION

Virtually all Macedonians are literate (able to read and write). Because the Macedonian language is spelled phonetically (as it sounds), just about every student is fully literate by the third grade.

Parental and cultural expectations also encourage higher education. Most parents regard it as a family "failure" for any of their children not to have achieved an advanced degree.

14 ● CULTURAL HERITAGE

Despite its small size, Macedonia boasts thirteen active professional theater groups. It also has a philharmonic orchestra and a host of annual folk music festivals held in different cities. There are hundreds of amateur rock-and-roll bands, and professional pop groups, one of which is called Leb i Sol (Bread and Salt). In 1994 the Macedonian film *Before the Rain* received an Academy Award nomination for Best Foreign Language Film from the American Motion Picture Academy.

Traditional music is played by a band composed of a clarinet or a *gajda*—a bagpipe made of lambskin; a bass drum, which hangs from the player's shoulder; an accordion; and a violin. Macedonia also has a great variety of folk dances. These range from the slow *teškoto,* or "heavy" dance, to the exuberant *sitnoto,* or "tiny-stepped dance."

The late-nineteenth-century poetry of the brothers Dimitar and Konstantin Miladinov is still recited by students from primary school through college. A famous twentieth-century work is Kosta Racin's collection of poems entitled *Beli Mugri* (White Dawns).

Every year Macedonia hosts several world-famous cultural events including the Struga Poetry Evenings, the Skopje International Jazz festival, and The World Cartoon Gallery.

15 ● EMPLOYMENT

Most of the jobs currently available in Macedonia—as in the United States—are in the service industry. Much of the nation's economy is sustained by small, family-owned businesses such as grocery stores, restaurants, garages, and clothing stores. Women are well-represented in the work force. They account for at least half of all doctors, teachers, professors, and corporate lawyers.

The great majority of teenagers and college students in Macedonia do not hold summer jobs.

16 ● SPORTS

Soccer and basketball are the two most-watched spectator sports. Soccer is also the most popular sport played by Macedonian children. Young adults also play soccer, though basketball, tennis, table tennis, and chess are equally popular.

17 ● RECREATION

TVs and VCRs may be found in almost every household in Macedonia.

Most Macedonians regard social calls as a sign of respect. It is the custom to attend an open house on a person's name day—traditionally held by males on the feast day of the saint after whom they are named. Whole communities celebrate the name day of their village's patron saint. That day they take off work and freely visit each others' homes, where food and drinks are served.

In the cities, a popular leisure-time activity is the *korzo*. One of the city's main streets is closed to traffic and turned into a promenade (place to stroll) for a few hours every evening.

18 ● CRAFTS AND HOBBIES

Villagers in Macedonia are known for weaving colorful blankets and carpets. In old bazaars (street markets) in the larger cities, one comes across dozens of artisans. These include small goldsmith and silversmith shops selling beautiful, delicate jewelry; *stomnari,* or urn-makers, who still produce glazed terra-cotta utensils such as urns, pitchers, cups, and bowls; and Asian-style carpet shops.

19 ● SOCIAL PROBLEMS

While it was part of Yugoslavia, Macedonia had a poor human and civil rights record. Today, there are dozens of political parties, and no political prisoners. Some long-standing social problems remain, such as alcoholism and spousal abuse. Other problems, such as drug addiction, have developed more recently.

20 ● BIBLIOGRAPHY

Danforth, Loring M. *The Macedonian Conflict: Ethnic Nationalism in a Transnational World.* Princeton, N.J.: Princeton University Press, 1995.

Poulton, Hugh. *Who Are the Macedonians?* Bloomington, Ind.: Indiana University Press, 1995.

Sherman, Laura Beth. *Fires on the Mountain: The Macedonian Revolutionary Movement and the Kidnapping of Ellen Stone.* Boulder, CO: East European Monographs. New York: Distributed by Columbia University Press, 1980.

WEBSITES

Pan-Macedonian Network. [Online] Available http://www.macedonia.com/, 1998.

World Travel Guide. Macedonia. [Online] Available http://www.wtgonline.com/country/mk/gen.html, 1998.

Madagascar

The people of Madagascar are called Malagasy. The original immigrants to Madagascar are believed to have come from East Africa. More recently, immigrants have come from Europe, China, and India. There are about twenty distinct African ethnic groups now recognized on the island. The Merina have been the most powerful group since the late eighteenth century, and resentment of the Merina by the other ethnic groups is a source of social unrest.

Malagasy

PRONUNCIATION: mahl-uh-GAH-see

LOCATION: Madagascar

POPULATION: 12 million

LANGUAGE: Malagasy (Merina); French

RELIGION: Traditional beliefs; Christianity; Islam

1 ● INTRODUCTION

The origins of the Malagasy people remain a mystery. Scholars believe the Malagasy have a combination of Indonesian, Malayo-Polynesian, and African roots.

Supposedly, the Indonesians were the first arrivals. Then came the Arabs, the southern Indians, and merchants from the Persian Gulf. South and East Africans followed, and eventually Europeans. The first Europeans to arrive were the Portuguese, then the Spanish, the British, and finally the French, who conquered the island in 1895.

Today, the Malagasy population of twelve million people is divided into eighteen identifiable ethnic groups in addition to the Comorans, the Karane (Indo-Pakistan), and the Chinese. The white people are classified as either *zanathan* (local-born) or *vazaha* (newcomers).

On June 26, 1960, Madagascar gained independence from France. In 1993, the government changed from a communist dictatorship to a democracy with a free-market economy.

2 ● LOCATION

One billion years ago a piece of land broke away from Africa and moved southeast to become an island continent in the Indian Ocean—Madagascar. Madagascar, located 250 miles (402 kilometers) off the east coast of Africa, is the fourth-largest island in the world. It is approximately 1,000 miles (1,600 kilometers) long and 360 miles (579 kilometers) wide, nearly the size of Califor-

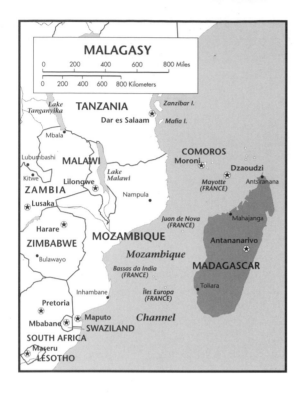

MALAGASY

0	200	400	600	800 Miles
0	200	400	600	800 Kilometers

4 ● FOLKLORE

Malagasy do not consider death to be the absolute end to life. In fact, Malagasy believe that after death, they will continue to be involved in the affairs of their family. Thus, dead family members are honored for their continuing influence on family decisions. Malagasy tombs are usually far more elaborate than the homes of the living.

Many Malagasy believe that spirits are present in nature, in trees, caves, or rock formations, on mountains, or in rivers or streams. Some also fear the *tromba,* when the spirits of the unknown dead put people into a trance and make them dance. The one who is possessed must be treated in a ritual by an *ombiasy* (a divine healer). Quite often, people consult or rely on them to look over the ill or the dying, or to set the dates for important events.

5 ● RELIGION

Roughly half of Malagasy are either Roman Catholic or Protestant, and a small number are Muslim (followers of Islam). Native religions featuring ancestor worship are followed by the rest of the population.

nia, Oregon, and Washington combined. It has a population of about 12 million people.

Many of the species of plants and animals originally found on the island either became extinct or evolved independently. As a result, 90 percent of all species on Madagascar today are unique, found nowhere else in the world.

3 ● LANGUAGE

Malagasy and French are the country's official languages. The Malagasy language belongs to the Malayo-Polynesian family of languages. The Malagasy language includes many dialects. The Merina dialect is the official language of the country and is universally understood.

6 ● MAJOR HOLIDAYS

Madagascar's official holidays include:

January 1	New Year's Day
March 29	Memorial Day
March 31	Easter Monday
May 1	Labor Day
May 8	Ascension Day
May 19	Monday Pentecost Holiday
May 25	Unity African Organization Day
June 26	National Day
August 15	Feast of the Assumption
November 1	All Saints' Day
December 25	Christmas Day

7 ● RITES OF PASSAGE

Malagasy ancestor worship includes a celebration known as the *famadiahana* (turning over the dead). Each year, ancestors' bodies are removed from the family tomb. The corpses are rewrapped in a fresh shroud cloth. Family members make special offerings to the dead ancestors on this occasion. The rites are accompanied by music, singing, and dancing.

8 ● RELATIONSHIPS

On a personal level, the Malagasy people are warm and hospitable. However, in unfamiliar surroundings, they appear to be reserved and somewhat distant. They are not likely to initiate a conversation with strangers, or even to keep a conversation going.

A single handshake and a "hello" is the proper greeting when people are introduced. A handshake is also used when saying goodbye. Among family and close friends, a kiss on both cheeks is exchanged at every meeting. Women, as well as young people of both sexes, initiate greetings when they meet elders.

Refusing anything outright, no matter how politely, is considered rude. It is better to make up excuses than to simply say no to food and drink, or anything else that is offered.

9 ● LIVING CONDITIONS

Overall, Madagascar is ranked as one of the poorest countries in world. Its people suffer from chronic malnutrition and a high (3 percent) annual population growth rate. In addition, health and education facilities are not adequately funded. Basic necessities

Cory Langley

The Malagasy population is divided into eighteen identifiable ethnic groups in addition to the Comorans, the Karane (Indo-Pakistan), and the Chinese.

such as electricity, clean water, adequate housing, and transportation are hard to come by for the average citizen.

There are sharp divisions between the country's upper and lower classes. There is vitually no middle class.

10 ● FAMILY LIFE

Most Malagasy social activities revolve around the family, which usually consists of three generations. Extended family members may live in one household or in a number of households. The head of the family is usually the oldest male or father. Traditionally, he makes major decisions and repre-

Recipe

Akoho sy voanio
(Chicken and Coconut)

Ingredients

6 chicken breasts (any combination of chicken parts may be used)
salt and pepper
2 tomatoes
1 can of unsweetened coconut milk
Oil
2 onions, chopped
2½ teaspoons of ginger
2 cloves of garlic, minced

Directions

1. Sprinkle chicken with salt and pepper.
2. Chop tomatoes and set aside.
3. Heat a small amount of oil in a frying pan. Sauté chicken over medium heat until cooked thoroughly (juice will be clear when the chicken is stabbed with a fork).
4. Add onions to the pan. Cook chicken and onions over medium heat until the onions are golden brown.
5. Add ginger, tomatoes, and garlic to pan. Sauté together for about 3 minutes over medium heat.
6. Reduce heat and add coconut milk. Stir to mix well.
7. Simmer over low heat for 30 minutes. Serve with rice and salad. Serves four.

sents the family in dealings with the outside world. However, this authority is declining among urban dwellers.

Malagasy marriages are preceded by lengthy discussions between the two families. The groom's family will give a sym-

bolic gift, called a *vody ondry,* to pay for the bride. This may be a few thousand Malagasy francs or perhaps one head of cattle. The ancient ideal of having seven boys and seven girls per household is now far from the norm. A more modern expectation today is four children per household.

Women are expected to obey their husbands, but they actually have a great deal of independence and influence. They manage, inherit, and bequeath property and often handle the family finances.

11 ● CLOTHING

The Malagasy wear both Western-style and traditional clothing. The markets are full of poor-quality imported clothes and imitation Western outfits.

Common traditional clothing items include the *lamba,* which is worn somewhat like a toga. Lambas are made in bright, multicolored prints. They usually have a proverb printed at the bottom. In some cases, they are used to carry a child on a woman's back. Older women will wear a white lamba over a dress or a blouse and skirt. It is not common for women to wear pants.

In rural areas, men wear *malabars,* dresslike shirts made of cotton woven fiber. They are usually made in earth tones.

12 ● FOOD

In Madagascar, food means rice. Rice is eaten two or three times a day. It is common to have leftover or fresh rice for breakfast, sometimes served with condensed milk. Lunch and dinner consist of heaping mounds of rice topped with beef, pork, or chicken, with a vegetable relish. Beef is

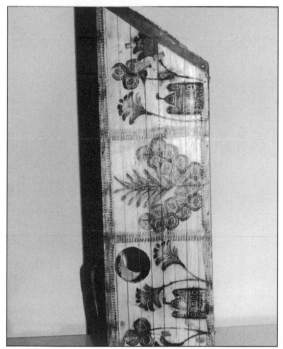

Camille Killens

One of Madagascar's unique musical instruments is the vahila, *a tubular harp.*

usually served only for a celebration or a religious offering. *Koba,* the national snack, is a paté (paste) of rice, banana, and peanut. *Sakay,* a hot red pepper, is usually served on the side with all Malagasy dishes.

Dessert usually consists of fruit, sometimes flavored with vanilla.

13 ● EDUCATION

About 80 percent of Madagascar's population aged fifteen and over can read and write. The level of education varies depending upon geographic area and other factors. Parents commonly send their children to France or elsewhere overseas for higher education.

14 ● CULTURAL HERITAGE

The musical form *Salegy* has become widespread on the island since instruments such as the electric guitar, bass, and drums were introduced. Most Malagasy music and lyrics are about daily life.

Internationally recognized Malagasy musicians include guitarist Earnest Randrianasolo, known as D'Gary; Dama Mahaleo, a Malagasy folk-pop superstar; and Paul Bert Rahasimanana, who is part of Rossy, a group of twelve musicians.

Madagascar's unique melodic instruments include the *vahila,* a tubular harp; the *kabosy,* a cross between a guitar, mandolin, and dulcimer; and *Tahitahi,* tiny flutes, usually of wood, gourd, or bamboo. Percussion instruments include the *Ambio,* a pair of wood sticks that are struck together; and *Kaimbarambo,* a bundle of grasses played many ways.

15 ● EMPLOYMENT

Malagasy men generally do not work full-time throughout the year. Content with satisfying only their families' most basic needs, they may earn wages only three or four months of the year.

Women's role in agricultural work is often more difficult than the men's. It includes carrying water, gathering wood, and pounding rice. Women also have special roles in cultivating crops, marketing the surplus, and preparing food, as well as making domestic crafts.

Business in Madagascar is dominated by non-Malagasy groups, such as Indians, French, and Chinese.

Cory Langley

Madagascar's population is expected to double by the year 2015.

16 ● SPORTS

Typical sports played in Madagascar are soccer, volleyball, and basketball. Other activities include martial arts, boxing, wrestling or *tolona,* swimming, and tennis.

17 ● RECREATION

Most social activities center around the family. Typical recreation includes dining and playing sports together.

Unique Malagasy games include games with stones, board games such as Solitaire and Fanorona, cockfights, singing games, and hide-and-seek.

18 ● CRAFTS AND HOBBIES

Madagascar is known for its basket-weaving and painting on silk.

19 ● SOCIAL PROBLEMS

The primary social problem in Madagascar is poverty. One-fourth of the population has been estimated to be living in or on the verge of absolute poverty. Unemployment is widespread, and the rate of infant mortality is high. *Quatre-amies,* or street children, beg for food or search for it in the garbage.

Poverty is a serious problem in Madagascar. *Quatre-amies,* or street children, beg for food or search for it in the garbage.

Madagascar's population of 12 million is expected to at least double by the year 2015.

20 ● BIBLIOGRAPHY

Bradt, Hilary. *Madagascar.* Santa Barbara, Calif: Clio, 1993.

Mack, John. *Madagascar: Island of the Ancestors.* London: British Museum Publications Ltd., 1986.

Madagascar in Pictures. Minneapolis, Minn.: Lerner Publications Co., 1988.

Preston-Mafham, Ken. *Madagascar: A Natural History.* New York: Facts on File, 1991.

WEBSITES

Embassy of Madagascar, Washington, D.C. [Online] Available http://www.embassy.org/madagascar/, 1998.

World Travel Guide. Madagascar. [Online] Available http://www.wtgonline.com/country/mg/gen.html, 1998.

Malawi

The people of Malawi belong mainly to various groups. About half belong to the Chewa and Nyanja groups, known collectively as Malawi (or Maravi), who arrived in Malawi before the nineteenth century.

Chewa and other Maravi groups

PRONUNCIATION: CHAY-wah
LOCATION: Malawi; Zambia; Mozambique
POPULATION: 5.8 million
LANGUAGE: Chichewa; English
RELIGION: Protestantism; Roman Catholicism; traditional beliefs; Islam

1 ● INTRODUCTION

The Chewa, one of the Bantu peoples, live in central Malawi. They are also found in parts of Zambia and Mozambique. Together, the Chewa and related peoples are known as the Maravi group. In the sixteenth century, the Maravi were the first group of Bantu peoples to move into present-day Malawi. The Maravi first settled at the southern tip of Lake Malawi. They then moved to different parts of the country. The group that migrated westward into central Malawi and eastern parts of Zambia came to be known as the Chewa.

The era of the European and Arab slave trade during the eighteenth and nineteenth centuries nearly destroyed the Chewa. In the second half of the nineteenth century, Malawi was colonized by the British. It became known as Nyasaland. Malawi gained its independence in 1964 under the leadership of Dr. Kamuzu Banda, a Chewa from central Malawi. Dr. Banda ruled Malawi as a dictator for thirty years. In 1994 democracy was finally restored in a dramatic but peaceful transition. Dr. Banda lost the elections to the United Democratic Front led by Bakili Muluzu.

2 ● LOCATION

Malawi is a long, landlocked country in east-central Africa. About the size of North

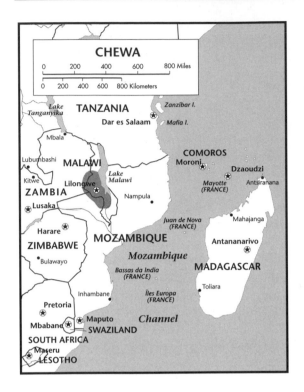

CHEWA

| 0 | 200 | 400 | 600 | 800 Miles |
| 0 | 200 | 400 | 600 | 800 Kilometers |

Carolina, it stretches for about 560 miles (900 kilometers) from north to south. The great variety of terrain, including mountains, plains, valleys, and plateaus, in such a small area results in dramatic variations in climate, soils, rainfall, and plant and animal life. The high Lilongwe Plains are the heartland of the Chewa people and the site of Lilongwe, Malawi's capital.

The Maravi, including the Chewa, account for 58 percent of Malawi's total population of 10 million people (or a total of 5.8 million Maravi).

3 ● LANGUAGE

Nyanja is the main language of the Maravi. It evolved during the colonial era as the standard language of government and education. There are two main dialects of Nyanja. Chichewa is spoken in the central region of Malawi, where most of the Chewa live. Mang'anja is spoken in southern Malawi. Chichewa is understood widely throughout the country. English and Chichewa were made the national languages of Malawi by Dr. Banda's government. English is still the main language of business and government. However, few Malawians speak it. It is taught in schools as a second language.

4 ● FOLKLORE

Chewa storytelling and songs are central to their customs and beliefs. Much of their folklore dwells on drought, fire, famine, and rainmaking.

One of the central figures in Chewa myths is Mbona, a rainmaker among the Mang'anja of Southern Malawi. The story of this mythical hero resembles that of Jesus Christ. He was the only son of his mother, conceived without a man. Like Christ, he performed miracles (in this case, bringing rain in times of persistent drought). Finally, he was killed by his own people. The story of Mbona has developed into a sacred oral text.

5 ● RELIGION

The main religion among the Chewa is Christianity, brought by Catholic and Protestant missionaries in the nineteenth century. Most Chewa follow both Christianity and their own traditional religious beliefs. Their native religion involves a single supreme being. Also important is honoring the departed spirits of ancestors, or *Mizimu*.

Ezekiel Kalipeni

Strip of shops in Lilongwe, the capital.

One key aspect of traditional religion is the all-male *Nyau* secret society, which performs traditional rites of passage.

6 ● MAJOR HOLIDAYS

One of the major holidays in Malawi is Independence Day on July 6. Each year, roads in urban areas are decorated with the Malawian flag. In the daytime, there are political rallies and speeches by politicians. Many women wear the colorful Malawi Congress Party uniform or the current ruling party's yellow colors. The festivities are followed by a night of feasting and dancing. Another significant secular holiday is March 3. This is a day for remembering those who died during the struggle for independence. Prayers are offered in churches throughout Malawi, and somber music is broadcast on the radio.

7 ● RITES OF PASSAGE

Devout Roman Catholics and Protestants mark major life events, such as birth, marriage, and death, within the Christian tradition. However, in much of Chewa society, traditional rites of passage are still an integral part of growing up. Generally, Chewa and Mang'anja boys between the ages of twelve and sixteen are initiated into a

Ezekiel Kalipeni

A man and woman in church on their wedding day.

to sexuality and reproduction. Usually the women of the village accompany the young girls into the bush. There they put them through a course of teasing and instruction. Each evening they return to the village for dancing and feasting.

Even in rural areas, weddings are increasingly being conducted in churches. For those who can afford it, the bridegroom wears a Western-style suit while the bride wears the typical Western white wedding dress with a veil.

8 ● RELATIONSHIPS

To greet each other, men and women of the same age group shake hands vigorously. Hugging is not common in Malawi. When one receives a guest it is customary to prepare food, preferably a chicken. It is considered rude for guests to decline food, even if they have already eaten. A younger person is supposed to bow or look to the side, or even squat on the ground, when being addressed by an elder. Kissing in public is frowned upon. Before initiation, girls and boys are encouraged to play together. After initiation, they are supposed to stay apart until married. However, in urban areas modern dating is quite common.

9 ● LIVING CONDITIONS

The majority of the Chewa live in rural areas with little access to health care facilities, schools, or electricity.

Types of housing are determined largely by location and the availability of building materials. Huts are either circular or oblong with wattle (woven-stick) walls, plastered outside and inside with mud, and roofed with thatch. However, it is not unusual to

semisecret society called *Nyau*, "The Great Dance." This association of masked dancers parades through the villages portraying the spirits of the dead. A Chewa man must belong to the Nyau society to attain full adult male status. During initiation, boys are secluded in the bush for instruction and discipline for about three days.

Girls between age nine and age sixteen undergo a series of puberty and initiation rites known as *chinamwali*. This may be a church-sponsored initiation ceremony that provides religious instruction, or it may be a traditional initiation ceremony, which can last as long as two to three weeks. Young girls are taught traditional customs relating find modern, rectangular houses in rural areas. These are made of bricks and cement, with corrugated iron sheets for the roof, timber doors, and glass windows. In urban areas such as Lilongwe, housing is in short supply. The majority of people are forced to live in shanty towns and other low-income housing.

10 ● FAMILY LIFE

The Chewa have a matrilineal kinship system. This means that inheritances are passed down through the female line. Children are considered to be members of the mother's lineage, and are thus under the guidance of maternal uncles (their mothers' brothers). Young people choose their own marriage partners. However, the marriage cannot be recognized as valid without the approval of the maternal uncles.

Fertility rates are very high. A woman can expect to bear seven children during her reproductive years. Children provide much needed labor in herding livestock and farming. They also serve as a means of social security in old age.

Divorce is quite common and rather simple. Polygyny, the practice of having more than one wife, used to be common. Now only about a third of Malawi males over the age of forty have more than one wife.

11 ● CLOTHING

In urban areas, women usually wear a skirt and a blouse or a colorful modern dress. In rural areas, women commonly wear a loincloth tied around the waist, and a blouse. Men wear pants, shirts, shorts, and occasionally a suit. Middle-income professionals are always dressed in Western-style

Ezekiel Kalipeni

Women in rural areas commonly wear a fabric skirt tied around the waist with a blouse. Most woman have six or seven children.

suits. Under Malawi's former government, women could not wear slacks, shorts, or miniskirts. Men could not have long hair. This dress code was repealed in 1994 under the democratically elected government of Bakili Muluzu.

12 ● FOOD

The Chewa diet consists mainly of *nsima,* a thick porridge made from corn flour. It is eaten with a side dish called *ndiwo,* made from leafy vegetables, beans, and other ingredients. Nsima with ndiwo is usually eaten only at dinnertime. Pregnant women

Recipe

Mtedza (Peanut Puffs)

Ingredients

½ cup butter or margarine
2 Tablespoons sugar
¾ cup finely chopped peanuts
½ teaspoon vanilla
1 cup flour
pinch of salt
1 to 2 cups powdered sugar

Directions

Preheat oven to 325°F.

1. Beat butter (or margarine) and sugar together until fluffy.
2. Add peanuts, vanilla, flour, and salt and mix well to form a soft dough.
3. Roll dough into balls about the size of small walnuts.
4. Arrange balls about 1-inch apart on a well-greased cookie sheet.
5. Bake for 35 minutes.

While the balls are still hot, roll them in powdered sugar. Allow to cool on a rack. Roll cooled balls in powdered sugar again before serving.

caterpillars are collected. The caterpillar's insides are removed, leaving only the skin. The skin is dried in the sun. The dried skins are salted and eaten, like peanuts or pretzels. A recipe for another popular snack, *mtedza* (peanut puffs), is at left.

13 ● EDUCATION

Malawi's education system is patterned after the British model. There are three tiers: primary, secondary, and tertiary. At the end of the four-year secondary school program, students take the Malawi Certificate Examination. Those with the top scores may then attend the University of Malawi. Literacy rates have improved over time. However, they are still very low by world standards. Only about a third of females and a little over half of males aged five years and over are able to read and write.

14 ● CULTURAL HERITAGE

The Chewa have a rich music and dance heritage. Songs are sung at initiation rites, rituals, marriage ceremonies, and during post-harvest celebrations. There are puberty songs, praise songs, funeral songs, work songs, beer-drinking songs, and coronation songs for chiefs.

Several traditional dances are also popular among the Chewa, especially during weddings and other festivals. For example, *mganda* is an all-male dance performed by about fifteen men. They sing and dance in unison following a complex series of steps. The female counterpart of mganda is *chimtali,* usually performed at weddings. There is also the all-male Nyau masquerade dance at initiation and funeral rituals. The

are forbidden to eat eggs for fear of bearing bald-headed babies.

Snacks can include roasted cassava, roasted corn, sweet potatoes, sugarcane, or wild fruits. Even wild insects such as roasted grasshoppers, flying termites, and caterpillar skins are enjoyed as snacks. Every year in late fall (around November) the parks in Malawi are opened for people to go in and collect caterpillars under the supervision of the park rangers. Full-grown

Ezekiel Kalipeni

Women preparing corn flour. A main item in the Chewa diet is a porridge, called nsima, *that is made from corn flour.*

masked dancers are accompanied by several drummers and a women's chorus.

Makhanya is a dance for girls and boys (or women and men) to perform together. It may be performed at weddings, or upon the completion of religious rituals, or in the evenings just for fun. The dancers form two lines, a girls' line and a boys' line. The two lines face each other, while everyone sings and claps their hands. A boy dances forward to a girl opposite him. He tags her, and she then dances back across to tap a boy. He dances back across to the line of girls and the dance continues in this way.

Internationally recognized Malawian literary figures include poet Jack Mapanje,

historian and novelist Paul Zeleza, and others.

15 ● EMPLOYMENT

Approximately 90 percent of the people in Malawi live in rural areas where subsistence farming is the primary economic activity. They grow a variety of crops such as corn (the staple food crop), beans, sorghum, peanuts, rice, pumpkins, cassava, and tobacco (the main cash crop). Only a quarter of the labor force are employed in urban jobs.

16 ● SPORTS

Soccer is the main sport throughout Malawi. The Malawi national team has won a number of regional championships. Every Saturday and Sunday, thousands of people converge on Civo Stadium in Lilongwe to watch various clubs play skillful soccer. Even in rural areas, soccer is the most common sport among school children. Basketball is also a growing sport.

17 ● RECREATION

Traditional dancing provides a source of entertainment in rural areas. In urban areas, young professionals flock to Western-style clubs and bars. Reggae, disco, breakdancing, and rap are popular in bars and beer-and dance-halls.

There are no television programs broadcast in Malawi. However, upper-income families may own a TV and VCR in order to view rental movies.

18 ● CRAFTS AND HOBBIES

The Chewa have a rich tradition of basketry and carved masks. Large, intricate basketry masks known as *Kasiyamaliro* and *Chimkoko* are used in men's initiation rituals.

19 ● SOCIAL PROBLEMS

Malawi's fifteen ethnic groups live in relative peace and harmony with each other. Under the government of Bakili Muluzu, human rights conditions have improved. However, economic conditions, particularly inflation, have gotten worse because of drought in the early 1990s. Other contributing factors are economic mismanagement and corruption.

20 ● BIBLIOGRAPHY

Lane, Martha S. B. *Enchantment of the World: Malawi*. Chicago, Ill.: Children's Press, 1990.

O'Toole, Thomas. *Malawi in Pictures.* Visual Geography Series. Minneapolis, Minn.: Lerner Publications Co., 1987.

Schoffeleers, Matthew J., and Adrian Roscoe. *Land of Fire: Oral Literature from Malawi.* Limbe, Malawi: Popular Publications, 1985.

WEBSITES

Internet Africa Ltd. [Online] Available http://www.africanet.com/africanet/country/malawi/, 1998.

Southern African Dev'ment Community. [Online] Available http://www.sadc-usa.net/members/malawi/, 1998.

World Travel Guide, Malawi. [Online] Available http://www.wtgonline.com/country/mw/gen.html, 1998.

Malaysia

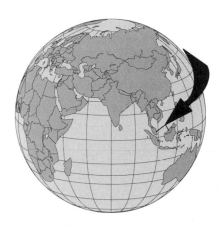

The people of Malaysia are called Malays. The native-born Malays, known as Bumiputras ("sons of the soil") make up about 60 percent of the total population; people of Chinese descent make up about 30 percent; people of Indian, Pakistani, and Bangladeshi descent are about 10 percent. Hostility between the Malays and Chinese has occasionally erupted into violence. Native groups in Malaysia, known as the Orang Asli (aborigines), number about 50,000. For more information on the Chinese, see the chapter on China in Volume 2; on the Indians, the chapter on India in Volume 4; on the Pakistanis, the chapter on Pakistan in Volume 7; and the Bangladeshis, the chapter on Bangladesh in Volume 1.

Malays

PRONUNCIATION: MAY-layz

LOCATION: Malaysia

POPULATION: 11 million

LANGUAGE: Malay; Chinese; Tamil and other Indian languages; tribal languages; English

RELIGION: Islam

1 ● INTRODUCTION

Many Malays believe that their ancestors were originally from the lowlands of Cambodia and the Mekong River Delta of South Vietnam. They moved to the Malay Peninsula and the island of Sumatra because of a shortage of land and natural resources in Cambodia and Vietnam, population overcrowding, and the opportunity to settle new lands in Malaysia.

In the fifteenth century, Malaysia was the site of a popular port, Malacca, where traders from the east (China) and the west (India, Middle East, and Europe) met to trade commodities such as spices. Malacca was conquered by the Portuguese in 1511, taken over by the Dutch in 1641, and handed over to the British in 1811. The British gradually expanded their influence.

The modern country, Federation of Malaysia, formed in 1963. It is made up of thirteen states. Sultans rule nine of the states, and three are ruled by governors. Malaysia practices a constitutional monarchy similar to what is practiced in England. The King is chosen from the nine Sultans once every five years. Elections are also held every five years to elect members of the parliament and the prime minister.

MALAYS

| 0 | 250 | 500 Miles |
| 0 | 250 | 500 Kilometers |

South China Sea

MALAYSIA

BRUNEI

Medan

Natuna
Besar

SINGAPORE

MALAYSIA

Nias

BORNEO

Kepulauan
Mentawai

SUMATRA

Bangka

Kalimantan

Billiton

Kahayan

Palembang

Java Sea

Jakarta

Semarang

Surabaya

Bandung

Madura

Bali Sea

JAVA

Bali

Lombok

INDIAN OCEAN

2 ● LOCATION

Malaysia has a land area of 127,320 square miles (329,760 square kilometers), making it slightly larger than New Mexico. More than half of its land is covered with tropical rain forests. Large areas of these rain forests are being depleted by logging. Malaysia's climate is tropical, with monsoons bringing an average annual rainfall of about 95 inches (240 centimeters). It is warm, sunny and humid throughout the year with temperatures ranging from 73° to 88°F (23° to 31°C).

Malaysia's 19 million people are multiracial. There are three main ethnic groups: the Bumiputera ("sons of the soil") includes 11 million Malays and various ethnic groups in Sabah and Sarawak, and accounts for about 60 percent of the population; the Chinese (30 percent); and the Indians, Pakistanis, and Bangladeshis (10 percent).

3 ● LANGUAGE

Malay is the Malaysian national language. It is taught, with English as a second language, in almost every school in Malaysia.

Although the Malay language is widely spoken in Malaysia, dialects vary between the states. Generally, words are pronounced the way they are spelled, thus it is a very easy language to learn. The Malay language borrows heavily from other languages, including Sanskrit, Portuguese, Persian, Arabic, and English.

Malays typically use Arab names for their children and do not have surnames. A name consists of the person's given name, followed by *bin* (son of) or *binti* (daughter of) and the father's first or full name. For example, Helmy, the son of Ismail Nik Dali, would be Helmy bin Ismail or Helmy bin Ismail Nik Dali. The same principle applies to a woman's name, except that her given name is followed by *binti*. Some common women's names are Fatimah, Lattifah, Zaiton, Aminah, and Zaleha while some common men's names are Ahmad, Sulaiman, Jamalludin, Zakaria, and Ismail.

4 ● FOLKLORE

The Malays regard *Hang Tuah* as their traditional hero. Hang Tuah was noted to be a courageous warrior and a symbol of loyalty to the throne. He proved his loyalty when he killed his best friend, Hang Jebat, who rebelled against his sultan.

Another famous folk tale is about Mahsuri, a princess from the island of Langkawai who was wrongly accused of adultery and was executed. Upon her death, Mahsuri spilled white blood and cursed the whole island for seven generations.

5 ● RELIGION

Malays are devout Muslims (followers of Islam). Islam's influence on the Malays goes back to the late fifteenth century when a sultan was converted to Islam. Malaysia's constitution decrees that all Malays are born Muslim, but there is the freedom to practice other religions such as Buddism, Hinduism, Christianity, and Confucianism.

6 ● MAJOR HOLIDAYS

There are three different New Year's celebrations and holidays: Muslim New Year, Christian (Roman) New Year, and the Chinese New Year. Besides New Year's holidays, the Malaysians celebrate Muslim holidays such as *Hari Raya Aidilfitri* (Eid al-Fitr) and *Aidil Adha* (Eid al-Adha)*;* the Buddhist holiday, *Wesak Day;* the Hindu holiday, *Deepavali;*, and the Christian holiday, Christmas. All offices, both government and private, are closed on these days. Malaysians also celebrate Independence Day (August 31), on which day large-scale parades are held in cities throughout the country.

Hari Raya Aidilfitri is a celebration to mark the end of Ramadan (the month of fasting). It provides an opportunity for Muslims to ask for forgiveness for all wrongs done the previous year. This two-day celebration is a time for joy and happiness. It involves alot of eating and a variety of foods prepared for especially for the occasion.

7 ● RITES OF PASSAGE

There are important rites of passage in traditional Malay society. After birth, a baby and a mother are in a confinement period *(dalam pantang)* of forty-four days. Two common ceremonies during the infant years are *naik buaian*, a ceremony to introduce the baby to his or her cradle, and *potong jambul,* an event when a child's head is shaven to "cleanse" her or him.

The circumcision ceremony for a boy is an elaborate event where relatives and villagers are invited to share the occasion. Circumcisions are performed on boys between the ages of seven and twelve. Traditionally, and still in the villages, the circumcision is performed with a knife on a banana tree trunk by a *mudim,* a person who specializes in performing circumcision ceremonies. Unlike the traditional method, circumcisions in cities are now performed by physicians in hospitals, and the ceremonies are not as elaborate as those of traditional circumcisions. The circumcision of a girl is a private ceremony and is performed on girls in infancy.

Marriage is perhaps the biggest event in a Malay person's life. Although close family friends still arrange marriages, the couple involved must give their full consent. Men are expected to be married by the age of twenty-five to twenty-eight, while women are usually a few years younger.

In the villages, a wedding is usually a two-day affair: the first day of celebration is held at the bride's home, and the following day, at the groom's house. Friends, relatives, and villagers normally help with the preparation. In the *bersanding* ceremony, which is open to the public, the bridal couple sit on a raised dais *(pelamin)*. Parents and relative scatter scented leaves and flower petals *(bunga rampai)* onto the open palms of the bride and groom, signifying blessings. A similar feast and ceremony is repeated at the groom's house on the second day. The affluent in Malay society hold weddings in hotels or large community halls.

Death is a very somber and religious affair in a Malay community. The funeral occurs soon after death, since Islam requires the deceased to be buried as soon as possible. Before burial, the body is placed in the center of the living room to give everyone a chance to offer prayers and pay their last respects. The deceased is then wrapped in white cloth and carried to the graveyard to be buried. The normal mourning period is one hundred days, although special prayers are held only on the first three nights, on the seventh day, the fortieth day, and on the hundredth day.

8 ● RELATIONSHIPS

The traditional Malay greeting when meeting friends in public is, "Where are you going?" The answer is, "For a stroll" or "Nowhere of importance." However, many urban Malays greet each other with "How are you?"

Men and women do not usually shake hands with each other. A Malay woman can only shake hands with a man if she covers her hand with a cloth. A Malay man normally greets another man with a handshake without grasping the hands. He extends both hands to lightly touch the other man's outstretched hands, then brings his hands to his chest, meaning "I greet you from my heart." A Malay woman uses a similar form when greeting another woman.

Pointing with the right forefinger is considered rude, although pointing with the thumb of the right hand with the four fingers folded into the palm is considered polite. It is also considered polite to bend over slightly from the waist, extend the right hand in front of you, touch the right wrist with the fingers of the left hand, then say "May I please pass," when crossing in front of another person.

Upon arrival at a Malay home, shoes must be removed before entering for religious reasons. Shoes are considered "unclean" and may dirty the living room floor, making it unsuitable for prayers. (Muslims pray on a mat laid out on the floor). When visiting relatives or friends, it is appropriate to bring food or fruit as gifts.

9 ● LIVING CONDITIONS

Slightly more than 50 percent of Malaysia's population live in urban areas (cities and towns). Both in the urban and rural areas, the *kampung* (community group) is the center of Malay life. It is a tightly knit community united by ties of family, marriage, or neighborliness, where agreement, compromise, and traditional values reign supreme.

The Malays in the cities own many items such as cars, television sets, VCRs, and refrigerators. Public transportation, such as buses and trains, is reliable and inexpensive. They also have a clean water supply, sanita-

Cory Langley

During the 1990s, the standard of living in Malaysia increased tremendously due to an economic boom.

tion services, and electricity in comparison to those who live in the villages. In the villages, some Malays still rely on kerosene for light, and on wells and rivers for water.

10 ● FAMILY LIFE

The Malays regard marriage and raising a family as the most important aspects of life. A Malay husband plays as much of a role in rearing their children as does his wife. The average family size of Malays in the cities is smaller in than that of Malays in country areas. In the past, it was not unusual for a couple to have more than six children. Today, the average number of children is four.

In Malaysia, there is no welfare system. The extended family is expected to care for each other, particularly those who are poor, sick, and old. Children are expected to look after their parents.

Cats, fish, and sometimes singing birds are reared as pets by Malay families. Dogs are considered "unclean" by Muslims and are not kept as pets in Malaysia.

11 ● CLOTHING

Traditional Malay dress for men and women is based on a simple rectangle of batik cloth. However, the style of wrapping is different for men and women. The women dress in a

Cory Langley

Malay students talk at a bus stop on their way to school

shirt with the batik cloth wrapped and worn as a skirt. The men wear the batik tied as a headcloth.

The women's customary dress covers the whole body, except for their face, hands, and feet. They usually dress in the *baju kurung,* a long-sleeved, loose blouse worn over an ankle-length skirt, and they cover their heads with a scarf as a sign of humility and modesty. A married woman may often wear a *baju kebaya,* a close-fitting lace blouse over an ankle-length skirt. Malay men wear *baju Melayu,* long-sleeved shirts over an ankle-length *sarong* or pants. A Malay man who has made a pilgrimage to Mecca usually wears a white skull-cap, and a woman who has made the pilgrimage wears a white scarf.

Some Malays in the cities dress in Western-style clothing. However, they do not wear shorts, miniskirts, or strapless or sleeveless tops.

12 ● FOOD

Rice is the main food and is eaten at least once a day. Malays eat rice with fish or meat curry and vegetables cooked in various ways. Muslimsm are prohibited from eating any pork, or any other meat that has not been slaughtered by a Muslim.

Malays usually eat with their fingers, so hands are always washed before and after meals. For this, Malays use the *kendi,* a water vessel which is either put on the table or passed around from person to person. While meals are always eaten with the right fingers, the serving spoons provided for all the dishes can only be used with the left hand. The left hand is also used for passing dishes of food and for holding a glass.

One of the Malays' popular breakfasts is *nasi lemak,* rice cooked in coconut milk and served with hot and spicy *sambal* (shrimp or anchovy paste), fish, eggs and vegetables.

13 ● EDUCATION

Malaysia has a literacy (ability to read and write) rate of 92 percent. It is mandatory for all Malays to attend school until the age of fifteen.

14 ● CULTURAL HERITAGE

Traditional Malay music is heard during special occasions. One of their most popular musical ensembles played during such occasions is the *gamelan*, an instrumental ensemble made up of drums, xylophones, metallophones, tuned gongs, and bamboo flutes.

Traditional Malay dances are performed on special occasions, accompanied by the gamelan. These dances are ensemble dances for men only, for women only, and for men and women together. This includes dances such as *Kuda Kepang* (a trance dance), *joget* (a courtship dance), *ghazal* (a dance based on Middle Eastern music that is performed by young women for the enjoyment of sultans and other members of the royal houses), and *mak yong* (a dance-drama performed by actors and actresses in imitation of heroic tales of sultans and princesses of olden times).

15 ● EMPLOYMENT

Traditionally, the Malays in rural areas they are farmers, tending vegetable farms or small holdings of rubber or oil-palm trees. Others are fishers. Malays in cities are often civil servants, laborers, transport workers, or industrial workers. Some have risen to the national elite, holding high-level positions in the government and military.

16 ● SPORTS

A popular Malay games is *sepaktkraw,* or kickball. It is played with a round ball made of rattan which must be kept in the air as it is kicked around or across a net (like volleyball played with the feet) by a group of players standing in a circle. A point is lost whenever the ball touches the ground.

The most popular spectator sport among Malaysians is soccer, known as football in Malaysia. There are soccer leagues even in the smallest towns. It is a common sight everywhere in Malaysia to see youngsters and adults flocking to the soccer fields to play or to watch a soccer game.

Badminton is a national passion in Malaysia, where top Malaysian players are usually among the contenders for world badminton championships. Other Western sports such as volleyball, field hockey, basketball, rugby, squash, and cricket are played in Malaysia.

17 ● RECREATION

Kite-flying is popular among people in coastal villages. Kites are flown mainly as recreation, but sometimes competitions are organized to see who can fly their kites the highest. Spinning tops made of wood is a popular pastime.

In cities, Malays watch Malay, Western (Hollywood), Hindi, and Chinese movies and theater productions. Malaysia has three television channels, which are monitored by the government.

18 ● CRAFTS AND HOBBIES

The Malays have many folk arts and crafts. An exotic folk art is the *wayang kulit,* a traditional shadow-puppet show. The puppets are made of water buffalo hide, stiffened by a piece of buffalo horn, and they have movable arms controlled by a *dalang* (the puppeteer) with thin poles. The puppets are seen only as shadows cast by a light upon a cloth screen. The dalang both recites the narrative of the play, and speaks the parts of each character. The show is usually accompanied by a small *gamelan* (musical ensemble).

Malays are renowned for their refined and delicate woodcarvings. These artistic carvings can be seen on their fishing boats, house panels, and walls. These decorative designs were created both for their elegant appearance and to equip the boats or houses with spiritual power. Traditional Malay houses also have rich decorations and carvings, primarily as decorative pieces on doors, windows, and wall panels.

The weaving of *kain songket* is another fine Malay craft. It is made from silk or cotton yarn and is woven using a wooden loom. The making of kain songket involves a long and complicated process, beginning with preparing the yarn and ending with the actual weaving.

19 ● SOCIAL PROBLEMS

Malaysia's government permits arrest and detention without trial for those considered dangerous to the country. Malaysia has received criticism from human-rights activists for its political actions. The government has arrested individuals who were alleged to threaten the country's racial and religious harmony.

20 ● BIBLIOGRAPHY

American University. *Malaysia: A Country Study.* Washington, D.C.: U.S. Government Printing Office, 1984.

Andaya, Leonard, and Barbara W. *A History of Malaysia.* New York: St. Martin's, 1982.

Craig, JoAnn. *Culture Shock: What Not to Do in Malaysia and Singapore, How and Why Not to Do It.* New York: Times Books International, 1979.

Major, John S. *The Land and People of Malaysia and Brunei.* New York: HarperCollins Publishers, 1991.

Malaysia in Pictures. Minneapolis, Minn.: Lerner Publications Co., 1988.

Wright, D. *Malaysia.* Chicago, Ill.: Children's Press, 1988.

WEBSITES

Interknowledge Corp. Malaysia. [Online] Available www.interknowledge.com/malaysia/, 1998.

World Travel Guide. [Online] Available http://www.wtgonline.com/country/my/gen.html, 1998.

Mali

The people of Mali are called Malians. The main ethnic groups are the Bambara (about 30–35 percent), mostly farmers occupying central Mali; and the Fulani (just over 10 percent) who are of mixed origin. To learn more about the Fulani see the chapter on Guinea in Volume 4.

Malians

PRONUNCIATION: MAHL-ee-uhns

LOCATION: Mali

POPULATION: 9 million

LANGUAGE: French (official), fifteen national languages: Bamana, Bobo, Bozo, Dogon, Juula, Fulfulde, Khassonke, Malinke, Maure, Minianka, Senufo, Soninke (or Sarakolle), Songhai (or Sonrai), Tuareg (or Tamacheq), and Tukulor

RELIGION: Islam; Christianity; indigenous beliefs

1 ● INTRODUCTION

Mali, in west Africa, is among the world's poorest nations. Before European explorers arrived in 1795, the Malinke and Songhai empires developed and flourished in the region. The French conquered the region in the late 1800s. By 1900, the French had consolidated all the land they had con-quered into the colony of *Soudan Français* (French Sudan).

The people of Mali struggled for independence. For a brief period, they joined with Senegal to form the Mali Federation. The combination was not successful, however. The Republic of Mali established its independence on September 22, 1960. At first, Mali was controlled by a socialist government, and then by a military government that lasted until 1991 when militant ruler Moussa Traoré was removed from office by forces hoping to establish democracy in Mali. Within a year, a democratically elected government under the leadership of Alpha Oumar Konaré took over for a five-year term. Konaré was elected to a second term in 1997.

2 ● LOCATION

Located in the interior of west Africa, the Republic of Mali shares borders with seven

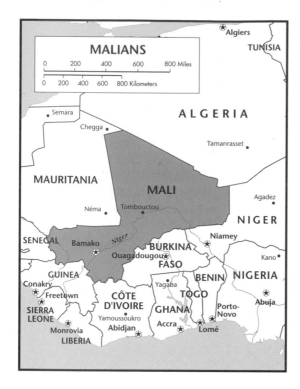

Malians speak Bamana as their mother tongue, and many speak it as a second language. The Juula or Malinke languages are closely related to Bamana. People who speak these three languages can usually understand each other.

Most television programs are in French. The national radio also broadcasts news and other programs in the different national languages.

4 ● FOLKLORE

For many Malians, the ancestors who actively resisted French colonization are folk heroes. Otherwise, heroes and myths vary from one ethnic group to another. As the founder of an ancient empire, Sunjata Keita (c.1200–c.1260) has a special position in the region's folklore. His epic is recited to musical accompaniment in the south and west. Only specially trained *griots* (singers and oral historians) are permitted to perform the epic.

5 ● RELIGION

Between 70 and 80 percent of all Malians consider themselves Muslims (followers of Islam). Except for a small number of Muslims who belong to the Wahhabbiya sect, the majority of Malian women do not wear veils. Offices close at midday on Friday to allow the faithful to participate in Friday prayer at the mosque.

Christians constitute only about 2 percent of the population. The remainder of the population continues to follow native religious practices. These may involve sacrifices to the ancestors, prophecy, and membership in initiation societies.

countries. Its territory extends over 465,000 square miles (1.2 million square kilometers). A large part of Mali is covered by the Sahara Desert and receives less than 12 inches (30 centimeters) of rain a year. As a result, most of the population is concentrated in the southern half of the country. The Niger, one of the major African rivers, crosses Mali, forming a vast interior delta. Mali's population is about 9 million. Well over 1 million people live in the metropolitan area of Bamako, the capital city.

3 ● LANGUAGE

The official language of Mali is French. However, only about one-third of the total population is schooled in French. Local languages remain the preferred mode of communication. Approximately one-third of all

6 ●MAJOR HOLIDAYS

Muslim holidays, as well as Christmas and Easter, are officially recognized. The two most important Islamic holidays are *Eid al-Fitr*, following the holy month of Ramadan, and *Eid al-Adha* (also known as *Tabaski*), celebrated on the tenth day of the last month in the Muslim calendar. Each lasts for three days and is celebrated with public prayers, the slaughter of a ram, and new clothes for family members.

The only secular (nonreligious) holiday is September 22, the Malian day of independence. This holiday commemorates the birth of the independent nation of Mali, ending French colonial rule. The major festivities take place in the capital city and include parades, music, and dancing.

7 ●RITES OF PASSAGE

Special ceremonies mark birth, marriage, and death throughout the country. Details vary among different ethnic groups. In urban areas, women relatives and friends come to the name-giving ceremony for a new baby. They bring gifts of cloth or soap for the mother. In the past, males were circumcised during the teen years. Now, circumcision is commonly done between the ages of eight and ten, or even shortly after birth.

The mother of a bride also receives cloth from her relatives and friends on behalf of her daughter. Men give money to a bridegroom on his wedding day to help him meet expenses. (The husband and his family pay for the wedding festivities.) When someone dies, relatives, neighbors, and friends visit the bereaved family as soon as they can.

Only men accompany the body to the cemetery when the deceased is a Muslim.

8 ●RELATIONSHIPS

Upon entering a household, a visitor gives a short greeting to his or her host. If the visitor is a stranger or someone who visits only irregularly, the host responds with a longer greeting. He inquires about the person's well-being and that of his or her relatives. The visitor then does the same in turn. While these greetings are being exchanged, the host and guest may hold right hands, or they may talk without making any physical contact. Shaking hands is common among coworkers in offices.

Dating often takes place in groups, rather than by a couple alone. Many young people in urban areas now choose their spouses themselves. However, a young man must still send a family representative to the family of the woman he wishes to marry. The woman's family must give their consent and determine the gift exchanges that will take place.

9 ●LIVING CONDITIONS

Life is difficult for the majority of Malians. Wages in many jobs and businesses are low. Those with an income must support extended family members as well as their own nuclear families. All Malians have many obligations toward less fortunate relatives. Households rarely encompass only a nuclear family.

An increasing number of households with access to electricity own television sets and, to a lesser extent, VCRs. The interiors of most rural and urban homes are very modest. Few urban families have such fur-

Cory Langley

A group of Malian women going to the market. Women wear wraparound skirts and tunics or tailored tops.

nishings as a couch, table, chairs, and a china cabinet. Given the climate, much of daily life takes place in the courtyard or in the shade of the veranda.

10 ● FAMILY LIFE

Malian law allows men to have more than one wife. A number of men have two wives. However, only a small percentage have the three or four permitted by Islam. Each wife is entitled to her own house or apartment. When a man has more than one wife, the wives share food preparation responsibilities. Many urban households with a regular income employ live-in domestic servants,

generally young unmarried women from the rural areas.

Women work in all fields. Even women who call themselves "housewives" are likely to earn money through crafts, gardening, or selling home-cooked food.

11 ● CLOTHING

Traditional dress varies for men is the *boubou* (an ample, full-length tunic). Women wear a *pagne* (wraparound skirt) and matching tunic and headdress. Unique colors are often achieved through hand dyeing.

Teenage girls and young women wear wraparound or narrow tailored skirts and matching cotton print tops. A small but growing number of teenage girls in urban areas wear pants.

At work, many men wear Western-style pants and shirts or short tunics. Women wear wraparound skirts and tunics. Imported second-hand clothing from Europe or North America is worn by many when doing manual labor.

12 ● FOOD

Different regions have their own traditional foods. The two staples throughout most of the country are boiled rice and a stiff porridge made of millet. A typical breakfast food is gruel made with millet flour, tamarind, and sugar. Small leavened pancakes made with millet are also eaten. Many people prefer rice to millet, and those who can afford it eat rice daily. Both rice and millet are served with a sauce that may include fresh vegetables, fish, meat, or chicken. In the city, a light meal may consist of boiled rice made creamy with milk and sweetened with sugar. Salad is also gaining in popularity among younger people. Typical snacks include fried plantain or shish kebab (meat on a skewer). A recipe for kyinkyinga (pronounced chin-CHIN-gah), meat kebabs, follows.

13 ● EDUCATION

In the population fifteen years of age or older, general literacy was estimated at 32 percent during the early 1990s. Many students drop out of school during or after elementary school. Many never enter at all or go only to a Koranic school (where teaching is based on the Muslim holy scriptures, the Koran). There are also modernized Muslim schools (*madrasas*) that combine an Islamic education with education in French.

To promote literacy among rural adults, alphabets have been created for the Malinke, Bamana, Fulfulde, Songhai, and Tuareg languages.

14 ● CULTURAL HERITAGE

Groups of musicians frequently tour rural areas during the dry season and perform on demand for a fee. A number of Malian musicians have achieved national and international acclaim. The singer Salif Keita is a national and international star. Since 1970 an arts festival for young people has been held every two years in the capital. Youths who have won local theater, music, and dance competitions compete against those from other regions.

Most of Mali's written literature is in French. Significant writers include Amadou Hampate Ba, Seydou Badian, Nagognime Urbain Dembélé, and Massa Makan Diabaté.

15 ● EMPLOYMENT

The majority of Malians are self-employed, making a living as farmers, herders, fishermen, traders, or artisans. Most of the salaried positions are in the civil service or with international organizations. Many Malians emigrate in search of better work opportunities on a short- or long-term basis.

16 ● SPORTS

Soccer is by far the most popular sport. It is played for fun and in competitions. Basket-

---

Recipe

Kyinkyinga
(West African Kebabs)

Ingredients

2 pounds lean beef stew meat (or liver), cubed

3 green peppers, cut into 1-inch squares

4 medium onions, chopped fine

2 teaspoons fresh ginger, grated

1 Tablespoon flour

1 can of crushed tomatoes (15 ounce size)

1 Tablespoon garlic salt

½ teaspoon Tabasco sauce (Malian cooks use 1 Tablespoon, but this is probably too "hot" for many people)

3 ounces unsalted dry-roasted peanuts, ground to a powder in a food processor

Apple or grape juice (Malian cooks might use sweet wine)

Directions

1. Set cubed meat in a bowl for marinating. Set the squares of green pepper, and about one-third of the peanut powder aside. Combine all other ingredients.

2. Pour about half the seasoning mixture over the meat and allow to marinate for at least one hour.

3. Skewer the meat alternating with the squares of green peppers on metal skewers.

4. Grill the kebabs over hot coals (or under a preheated broiler), turning about every 4 minutes until cooked. Total cooking time will be about 15 minutes.

5. Combine about ½ cup of apple or grape juice with the remaining half of seasoning sauce. Heat to boiling, and boil for a few minutes to thicken the sauce slightly.

6. When kebabs are done, remove them from the grill and sprinkle with remaining peanut powder.

Serve with rice and ladle the sauce over the kebabs.

---

ball has been gaining in popularity and is played by both male and female teams.

17 ● RECREATION

Radios are widely owned throughout the country. People of all ages tune in for their favorite programs. An increasing number of households with access to electricity own television sets, and some even VCRs. People often move their television into the courtyard in the evening to view in the company of neighbors or friends.

Most young people enjoy listening to audio cassettes of folk and popular music, both African and international. Rural youths dance mostly at local festivals. In the city, young people go to discotheques and other dance events on weekends. Movie theaters in the cities attract mainly a young audience with Hollywood, Kung Fu, Indian, and some Malian films. The most popular pastime for young and old is still visiting friends, relatives, and neighbors.

18 ● CRAFTS AND HOBBIES

Different regions and ethnic groups specialize and excel in particular products: Fulbe men in the Mopti region, for example, weave wool blankets. Tuareg women craft dyed leather goods (pillow covers, bags, knife sheaths). Most wool blankets and leather goods are now intended for the tourist market. However, other products are still made primarily for use in the home. These include gold and silver jewelry, pottery, and a variety of mats and basketry. Handwoven cotton cloth is sewn into wraps for women and tunics for men, as well as into blankets.

19 ● SOCIAL PROBLEMS

From 1960 to the overthrow of the Traoré government in 1991, political prisoners were frequently banished to the salt mines of the Sahara Desert. Drug use exists in some youth circles but is discouraged by the government and by Islam.

20 ● BIBLIOGRAPHY

Carpenter, Allan, Thomas O'Toole, and Mark LaPointe. *Mali.* Chicago: Children's Press, 1975.

Imperato, Pascal James. *Historical Dictionary of Mali.* 3rd edition. London: Scarecrow Press, 1996.

O'Toole, Thomas. *Mali in Pictures.* Minneapolis, Minn.: Lerner Publications Co., 1990.

WEBSITES

Interknowledge Corporation. Mali. [Online] Available http://www.geographia.com/mali/, 1998.

World Travel Guide. [Online] Available http://www.wtgonline.com/country/ml/gen.html, 1998.

Songhay

PRONUNCIATION: song-HIGH

LOCATION: Eastern Mali, western Niger, northern Benin

POPULATION: 3 million

LANGUAGE: Dialects of Songhay; French

RELIGION: Islam combined with indigenous beliefs

1 ● INTRODUCTION

The Songhay established one of the three great medieval west African empires in 1463. The first Songhay king, Sonni Ali Ber, extended the boundaries of the Songhay state. His successor, Askia Mohammed Touré, made Songhay a great empire by extending its control throughout much of west Africa. Askia's sons were corrupt, however, and the Songhay empire was weakened during the period that they ruled. By the end of the sixteenth century, Morocco controlled the northern sectors of Songhay. In time, the southern empire splintered into independent territories that were mutually hostile. However, they remained independent until coming under French colonial authority in 1899.

2 ● LOCATION

The Songhay-speaking peoples live near the Niger River in eastern Mali, western Niger, and northern Benin. Songhay country is situated in the semi-arid Sahel region. It consists of flat rocky plains, rocky mesas (land formations) in the south, and sandy dunes in the north. The vast majority of Songhay people live in Mali and Niger.

was a river spirit. Faran grew to be a giant with vast magical powers. As an adult he battled a river spirit, Zinkibaru, for control of the Niger River, and won. But he soon became overconfident. Dongo, the deity of lightning and thunder, demonstrated his anger toward Faran by burning villages and killing people. He summoned Faran and demanded that the giant pay his humble respects by offering music, praise-poems, and animal sacrifices. Dongo told Faran that if he organized festivals, Dongo would descend into the bodies of dancers and help the people along the Niger River.

Modern Songhay stage similar events, called possession ceremonies. The praise-singers, or *sorko,* are said to be direct descendants of Faran Make Bote. In this way, Songhay myths are kept alive through social and religious activities.

3 ● LANGUAGE

Songhay is a language spoken by 3 million people in the Republics of Mali, Niger, and Benin. There are several dialects of Songhay. Because Mali, Niger, and Benin are all French-speaking nations, many Songhay people living in these states speak French.

A typical greeting is: *Manti ni kaani* (How did you sleep?). One usually replies, *Baani sami, walla,* meaning, "I slept well, in health." At bedtime, one says: *Iri me kaani baani,* which means "May we both sleep in health and peace."

4 ● FOLKLORE

The ancestral folk figure Faran Maka Bote is a Songhay culture hero. His father, Nisili Bote, was a fisherman. His mother, Maka,

5 ● RELIGION

Almost all Songhay are practicing Muslims. They pray five times a day; avoid alcohol and pork; observe the one-month fast of Ramadan; and try to the best of their ability to make the *hajj,* the very expensive pilgrimage to Mecca.

However, Islamic practices have not excluded traditional beliefs carried forward from ancient times. Traditional Songhay life is seen as a continuous passage across dangerous crossroads. To help them, the Songhay regularly consult diviners (fortune tellers) and other traditional religious specialists, such as *sohancitarey* (sorcerers), *sorkotarey* (praise-singers to the spirits), and *zimatarey* (spirit-possession priests). These specialists must serve long apprenticeships to master knowledge of history, plants, words, and practices.

6 ● MAJOR HOLIDAYS

Songhay people observe the secular holidays of the countries in which they live. They also celebrate such major Islamic holidays as Muhammad's birthday, the end of the Ramadan fast, and Eid al-Adha (or *tabaski*), which commemorates Abraham's biblical sacrifice of a ram. For tabaski, people slaughter one or two sheep and roast them. They feast on the roasted mutton and offer raw and cooked meat to needier people who come to their door.

7 ● RITES OF PASSAGE

Most Songhay rituals marking major life-cycle events follow Islamic models. However, some practices go back to the days before Islam was introduced to sub-Saharan Africa. Birth, for example, is seen as a time of danger for both mothers and their children. During and immediately following childbirth, men are kept from the mother and child. Mother and child are presented to family and neighbors for the first time at the *bon chebe* (literally, "showing the head"). This is when the child is named. In the past, young boys underwent ritual circumcision at a relatively late age. These days, circumcisions are performed on toddlers by physicians in hospitals.

Once a couple is ready to marry, the groom asks the permission of the bride's father. He is expected to pay his future father-in-law a bride-price, which today is a fixed sum of money. He is also expected to give his future wife and her family many gifts. The expense of marriage makes it difficult for young men to afford to marry. The marriage ceremony is marked by the presentation of gifts. There is also an Islamic contract *(kitubi)* that binds husband to wife.

Divorce is quite common among the Songhay. Men initiate formal divorce by consulting a Muslim cleric and proclaiming, "I divorce thee" three times. Women initiate divorce informally by leaving their husbands, who then proclaim their divorce in the wife's absence.

When Songhay die, they are buried quickly and without fanfare. Mourning lasts for forty days. The family receives regular visits from relatives and friends. During these visits people honor the person who died by talking about his or her life.

8 ● RELATIONSHIPS

Greetings in the morning focus upon work and the health of people in one's compound. The midday greetings ask after one's afternoon. Late afternoon greetings involve questions of health. In the dusk greeting, people exchange wishes for peace and health. The Songhay are known for their generosity. When strangers arrive they are housed, well fed, and treated with great dignity—even if the hosts are poor.

Young men are supposed to be respectful of young women, who in turn are supposed to be shy around young men. This code is expressed in body language. Girls will often look at the ground when talking in public to boys.

9 ● LIVING CONDITIONS

Songhay people in rural areas live within walled or fenced compounds. These usually consist of a main house for the husband, and smaller houses for each of his wives and their children. The houses are usually made of mud bricks and have thatched roofs. More traditional homes are circular huts with thatched roofs. New houses may be made of cement and feature tin roofs. Most social activity is conducted out of doors in the compound, where food is prepared and eaten, and where people visit one another in the evenings.

Songhay in urban areas also live in compounds. The crowded conditions there tend to be less sanitary than those in the countryside.

10 ● FAMILY LIFE

Songhay families tend to be large. In rural areas, brothers live with their father, mothers, wives, and children in large communal compounds. In some cases, more than one hundred people might live in a rural compound. In urban areas, families are a bit more scattered and smaller in size.

Men and women lead fairly separate lives. They do different kinds of work. They eat separately. They often talk only to other people of their own sex. When a marriage occurs, a woman's primary allegiance is still to her own kin, for it is from them that she will inherit wealth. If husbands are abusive, the wife's brothers will often intervene. If a woman earns money, she will keep it for herself or share it with her blood kin.

11 ● CLOTHING

Rural and urban Songhay men today wear a combination of traditional and Western clothing. They generally wear trousers and a loose-fitting shirt that they wear untucked. Younger men might wear used jeans and tee-shirts they buy at the market. Some men, however, prefer to wear the traditional, cotton three-piece outfit. It consists of drawstring trousers, a long-sleeved loose-fitting shirt with an open neck, and a *boubou* (long, full robe).

Most Songhay women rarely, if ever, wear Western clothing. They wear long wrap-around skirts *(pagnes)* and matching tops.

12 ● FOOD

The staple of the Songhay diet is millet. It is consumed in three ways: as a pancake *(haini maasa),* as porridge *(doonu),* or as a paste *(howru).* Millet paste is made by mixing millet flour in a pot of boiling water until the mixture stiffens. This paste is consumed at the evening meal. It is topped by a variety of usually meatless sauces made from okra, baobab leaf, or peanuts. Songhay season their sauces with ginger *(tofunua),* hot pepper *(tonka),* and onion flour with sesame *(gebu).* A recipe for a meatless sauce follows.

13 ● EDUCATION

Education takes two forms among the Songhay: informal and formal. Mothers and fathers informally educate their children in survival skills: farming, fishing, hunting, building huts and houses, cooking, weaving, and sewing. Even though thousands of Songhay children attend elementary school, illiteracy is common. Some Songhay parents see formal schooling as a loss, because educated sons and daughters often move to towns and cities.

Recipe

Peanut and Greens Stew

Ingredients

4 Tablepoons oil
1 onion, chopped
½ cup chopped peanuts
2 Tablespoons creamy peanut butter
1 tomato, chopped
¼ cup tomato paste
3 cups finely chopped spinach or Swiss chard (wash first and trim coarse stems and fibers)
¼ teaspoon red pepper
Pinch of salt
Pinch of pepper

Directions

1. Heat 2 tablespoons oil in large skillet over medium heat. Add onion and peanuts. Cook for about 3 minutes, stirring constantly, until onion is soft.
2. Add 2 more tablespoons of oil and heat.
3. Stir in peanut butter, tomato, tomato paste, spinach, red pepper, salt, and pepper. Reduce heat.
4. Cover and simmer for about 30 minutes, stirring occasionally.
5. Serve over millet or rice.

Adapted from Carole Lisa Albyn and Lois Sinaiko Webb. *The Multicultural Cookbook for Students.* Phoenix, Ariz.: Oryx, 1993.

For their formal education, the majority of Songhay go through the educational systems of Niger or Mali.

14 ● CULTURAL HERITAGE

The Songhay are proud of their heroic past and celebrate it in song, dance, and epic poetry. Singing, dancing, and praise-songs, performed by *griots* (both male and female), are central to the celebration of births, marriages, and holidays. Epic poetry is also performed on secular and religious holidays. Poetry performances are frequently broadcast on national radio.

15 ● EMPLOYMENT

The principal activity of most Songhay men has been millet and rice farming. Since farming is seasonal, many Songhay men have developed secondary occupations: trading, transport, or tailoring. Many spend the nonplanting season working for wages in distant cities. Most Songhay women remain wedded to domestic activities. In some cases, divorced women sell cooked foods or trade in cloth to support themselves.

16 ● SPORTS

Soccer is the major sport among Songhay boys and young men. Boys and men also race horses, in competitions and for fun. During secular holidays, villages sponsor horse races and present the winners with prizes.

Wrestling is the other major sport. The idea is not to pin one's opponent but merely to throw him to the ground. Songhay girls are not encouraged to participate in sports.

17 ● RECREATION

Religious rituals such as spirit-possession ceremonies are also occasions for entertainment. In many Songhay towns, young people stage plays at the local theater. Towns also sponsor gatherings for young people where they can dance and socialize.

Television has become an important medium of entertainment in many of the larger Songhay towns. Neighborhood chiefs, who own televisions, will invite their neighbors into their compound for evenings of television viewing.

18 ● CRAFTS AND HOBBIES

Songhay are well known for weaving blankets and mats. The elaborate cotton blankets (*terabeba*) woven by men in the town of Tera are highly prized throughout the Sahel. Women living along the Niger River weave palm frond mats that feature geometric designs.

19 ● SOCIAL PROBLEMS

There are two great social problems facing the Songhay. The first is the ever-present prospect of drought and famine. Many devastating droughts and famines have prompted the widespread migration of rural Songhay to towns and cities.

The second principal social problem involves political instability in the Republic of Niger, home to many of the Songhay.

20 ● BIBLIOGRAPHY

Charlick, Robert. *Niger: Personal Rule and Survival in the Sahel.* Boulder, Colo.: Westview Press, 1991.

Stoller, Paul. *Fusion of the Worlds: An Ethnography of Possession Among the Songhay.* Chicago: University of Chicago Press, 1989; paperback edition, 1997.

Stoller, Paul, and Cheryl Olkes. *In Sorcery's Shadow: A Memoir of Apprenticeship Among the Songhay of Niger.* Chicago: University of Chicago Press, 1987.

WEBSITES

Interknowledge Corporation. Mali. [Online] Available http://www.geographia.com/mali/, 1998.

World Travel Guide. [Online] Available http://www.wtgonline.com/country/ml/gen.html, 1998.

Glossary

aboriginal: The first known inhabitants of a country.

adobe: A brick made from sun-dried heavy clay mixed with straw, used in building houses.

Altaic language family: A family of languages spoken in portions of northern and eastern Europe, and nearly the whole of northern and central Asia, together with some other regions.

Amerindian: A contraction of the two words, American Indian. It describes native peoples of North, South, or Central America.

Anglican: Pertaining to or connected with the Church of England.

animism: The belief that natural objects and phenomena have souls or innate spiritual powers.

apartheid: The past governmental policy in the Republic of South Africa of separating the races in society.

arable land: Land that can be cultivated by plowing and used for growing crops.

archipelago: Any body of water abounding with islands, or the islands themselves collectively.

Austronesian language: A family of languages which includes practically all the languages of the Pacific Islands—Indonesian, Melanesian, Polynesian, and Micronesian sub-families.

average life expectancy: In any given society, the average age attained by persons at the time of death.

Baha'i: The follower of a religious sect founded by Mirza Husayn Ali in Iran in 1863.

Baltic states: The three formerly communist countries of Estonia, Latvia, and Lithuania that border on the Baltic Sea.

Bantu language group: A name applied to the languages spoken in central and south Africa.

Baptist: A member of a Protestant denomination that practices adult baptism by complete immersion in water.

barren land: Unproductive land, partly or entirely treeless.

barter: Trade practice where merchandise is exchanged directly for other merchandise or services without use of money.

Berber: a member of one of the Afroasiatic peoples of northern Africa.

Brahman: A member (by heredity) of the highest caste among the Hindus, usually assigned to the priesthood.

bride wealth (bride price): Fee, in money or goods, paid by a prospective groom (and his family) to the bride's family.

Buddhism: A religious system common in India and eastern Asia. Founded by Siddhartha Gautama (c.563–c.483 BC), Buddhism asserts that suffering is an inescapable part of life. Deliverance can only be achieved through the practice of charity, temperance, justice, honesty, and truth.

Byzantine Empire: An empire centered in the city of Byzantium, now Istanbul in present-day Turkey.

cassava: The name of several species of stout herbs, extensively cultivated for food.

caste system: Heriditary social classes into which the Hindus are rigidly separated according to the religious law of Brahmanism. Privileges and limitations of each caste are passed down from parents to children.

Caucasian: The white race of human beings, as determined by genealogy and physical features.

census: An official counting of the inhabitants of a state or country with details of sex and age, family, occupation, possessions, etc.

Christianity: The religion founded by Jesus Christ, based on the Bible as holy scripture.

Church of England: The national and established church in England.

civil rights: The privileges of all individuals to be treated as equals under the laws of their country; specifically, the rights given by certain amendments to the U.S. Constitution.

coastal plain: A fairly level area of land along the coast of a land mass.

coca: A shrub native to South America, the leaves of which produce organic compounds that are used in the production of cocaine.

colonial period: The period of time when a country forms colonies in and extends control over a foreign area.

colonist: Any member of a colony or one who helps settle a new colony.

colony: A group of people who settle in a new area far from their original country, but still under the jurisdiction of that country. Also refers to the newly settled area itself.

commonwealth: A free association of sovereign independent states that has no charter, treaty, or constitution. The association promotes cooperation, consultation, and mutual assistance among members.

communism: A form of government whose system requires common ownership of property for the use of all citizens. Prices on goods and services are usually set by the government, and all profits are shared equally by everyone. Also, communism refers directly to the official doctrine of the former Soviet Union.

compulsory education: The mandatory requirement for children to attend school until they have reached a certain age or grade level.

Confucianism: The system of ethics and politics taught by the Chinese philosopher Confucius.

constitution: The written laws and basic rights of citizens of a country or members of an organized group.

copra: The dried meat of the coconut.

cordillera: A continuous ridge, range, or chain of mountains.

coup d'ètat (coup): A sudden, violent overthrow of a government or its leader.

cuisine: A particular style of preparing food, especially when referring to the cooking of a particular country or ethnic group.

Cushitic language group: A group of languages that are spoken in Ethiopia and other areas of eastern Africa.

Cyrillic alphabet: An alphabet invented by Cyril and Methodius in the ninth century as an alphabet that was easier for the copyist to write. The Russian alphabet is a slight modification of it.

deity: A being with the attributes, nature, and essence of a god; a divinity.

desegregation: The act of removing restrictions on people of a particular race that keep them socially, economically, and, sometimes, physically, separate from other groups.

desertification: The process of becoming a desert as a result of climatic changes, land mismanagement, or both.

Dewali (Deepavali, Divali): The Hindu Festival of Lights, when Lakshmi, goddess of good fortune, is said to visit the homes of humans. The four- or five-day festival occurs in October or November.

dialect: One of a number of regional or related modes of speech regarded as descending from a common origin.

dowry: The sum of the property or money that a bride brings to her groom at their marriage.

Druze: A member of a Muslim sect based in Syria, living chiefly in the mountain regions of Lebanon.

dynasty: A family line of sovereigns who rule in succession, and the time during which they reign.

Eastern Orthodox: The outgrowth of the original Eastern Church of the Eastern Roman Empire, consisting of eastern Europe, western Asia, and Egypt.

Eid al-Adha: The Muslim holiday that celebrates the end of the special pilgrimage season (hajj) to the city of Mecca in Saudi Arabia.

Eid al-Fitr: The Muslim holiday that begins just after the end of the month of Ramadan and is celebrated with three or four days of feasting.

emigration: Moving from one country or region to another for the purpose of residence.

empire: A group of territories ruled by one sovereign or supreme ruler. Also, the period of time under that rule.

Episcopal: Belonging to or vested in bishops or prelates; characteristic of or pertaining to a bishop or bishops.

exports: Goods sold to foreign buyers.

Finno-Ugric language group: A subfamily of languages spoken in northeastern Europe, including Finnish, Hungarian, Estonian, and Lapp.

fjord: A deep indentation of the land forming a comparatively narrow arm of the sea with more or less steep slopes or cliffs on each side.

folk religion: A religion with origins and traditions among the common people of a nation or region that is relevant to their particular life-style.

Former Soviet Union: Refers to the republics that were once part of a large nation called the Union of Soviet Socialists Republics (USSR). The USSR was commonly called the Soviet Union. It included the 12 republics: Russia, Ukraine, Belarus, Moldova, Armenia, Azerbaijan, Uzbekistan, Turkmenistan, Tajikistan, Kazakhstan, Kyrgizstan, and Georgia. Sometimes the Baltic republics of Estonia, Latvia, and Lithuania are also included.

fundamentalist: A person who holds religious beliefs based on the complete acceptance of the words of holy scriptures as the truth.

Germanic language group: A large branch of the Indo-European family of languages including German itself, the Scandinavian languages, Dutch, Yiddish, Modern English, Modern Scottish, Afrikaans, and others. The group also includes extinct languages such as Gothic, Old High German, Old Saxon, Old English, Middle English, and the like.

Greek Orthodox: The official church of Greece, a self-governing branch of the Orthodox Eastern Church.

guerrilla: A member of a small radical military organization that uses unconventional tactics to take their enemies by surprise.

hajj: A religious journey made by Muslims to the holy city of Mecca in Saudi Arabia.

Holi: A Hindu festival of processions and merriment lasting three to ten days that marks the end of the lunar year in February or March.

Holocaust: The mass slaughter of European civilians, the vast majority of whom were Jews, by the Nazis during World War II.

Holy Roman Empire: A kingdom consisting of a loose union of German and Italian territories that existed from around the ninth century until 1806.

homeland: A region or area set aside to be a state for a people of a particular national, cultural, or racial origin.

homogeneous: Of the same kind or nature, often used in reference to a whole.

Horn of Africa: The Horn of Africa comprises Djibouti, Eritrea, Ethiopia, Somalia, and Sudan.

human rights issues: Any matters involving people's basic rights which are in question or thought to be abused.

immigration: The act or process of passing or entering into another country for the purpose of permanent residence.

imports: Goods purchased from foreign suppliers.

indigenous: Born or originating in a particular place or country; native to a particular region or area.

Indo-Aryan language group: The group that includes the languages of India; also called Indo-European language group.

Indo-European language family: The group that includes the languages of India and much of Europe and southwestern Asia.

Islam: The religious system of Muhammad, practiced by Muslims and based on a belief in Allah as the supreme being and Muhammed as his prophet. Islam also refers to those nations in which it is the primary religion. There are two major sects: Sunni and Shia (or Shiite). The main difference between the two sects is in their belief in who follows Muhammad, founder of Islam, as the religious leader.

Judaism: The religious system of the Jews, based on the Old Testament as revealed to Moses and characterized by a belief in one God and adherence to the laws of scripture and rabbinic traditions.

khan: A sovereign, or ruler, in central Asia.

khanate: A kingdom ruled by a khan, or man of rank.

literacy: The ability to read and write.

Maghreb states: Refers to Algeria, Morocco, and Tunisia; sometimes includes Libya and Mauritania.

maize: Another name (Spanish or British) for corn or the color of ripe corn.

manioc: The cassava plant or its product. Manioc is a very important food-staple in tropical America.

matrilineal (descent): Descending from, or tracing descent through, the maternal, or mother's, family line.

Mayan language family: The languages of the Central American Indians, further divided into two subgroups: the Maya and the Huastek.

mean temperature: The air temperature unit measured by the National Weather Service by adding the maximum and minimum daily temperatures together and diving the sum by 2.

Mecca: A city in Saudi Arabia; a destination of Muslims in the Islamic world.

mestizo: The offspring of a person of mixed blood; especially, a person of mixed Spanish and American Indian parentage.

millet: A cereal grass whose small grain is used for food in Europe and Asia.

monarchy: Government by a sovereign, such as a king or queen.

Mongol: One of an Asiatic race chiefly resident in Mongolia, a region north of China proper and south of Siberia.

Moors: One of the Arab tribes that conquered Spain in the eighth century.

Moslem *see* **Muslim.**

mosque: An Islam place of worship and the organization with which it is connected.

Muhammad (or Muhammed or Mahomet): An Arabian prophet (AD 570–632), known as the "Prophet of Allah" who founded the religion of Islam in 622, and wrote the Koran, (also spelled Quran) the scripture of Islam.

mulatto: One who is the offspring of parents one of whom is white and the other is black.

Muslim: A follower of Muhammad in the religion of Islam.

Muslim New Year: A Muslim holiday also called Nawruz. In some countries Muharram 1, which is the first month of the Islamic year, is observed as a holiday, in other places the new year is observed on Sha'ban, the eighth month of the year. This practice apparently stems from pagan Arab times. Shab-i-Bharat, a national holiday in Bangladesh on this day, is held by many to be the occasion when God ordains all actions in the coming year.

mystic: Person who believes he or she can gain spiritual knowledge through processes like meditation that are not easily explained by reasoning or rational thinking.

nationalism: National spirit or aspirations; desire for national unity, independence, or prosperity.

oasis: Fertile spot in the midst of a desert or wasteland.

official language: The language in which the business of a country and its government is conducted.

Ottoman Empire: A Turkish empire that existed from about 1603 until 1918, and included lands around the Mediterranean, Black, and Caspian seas.

patriarchal system: A social system in which the head of the family or tribe is the father or oldest male. Ancestry is determined and traced through the male members of the tribe.

patrilineal (descent): Descending from, or tracing descent through, the paternal, or father's, family line.

pilgrimage: religious journey, usually to a holy place.

plantain: Tropical plant with fruit that looks like bananas, but that must be cooked before eating.

Protestant: A member of one of the Christian bodies that descended from the Reformation of the sixteenth century.

pulses: Beans, peas, or lentils.

Ramadan: The ninth month of the Muslim calender. The entire month commemorates the period in which the Prophet Muhammad is said to have recieved divine revelation and is observed by a strict fast from sunrise to sundown.

Rastafarian: A member of a Jamaican cult begun in 1930 that is partly religious and partly political.

refugee: Person who, in times of persecution or political commotion, flees to a foreign country for safety.

revolution: A complete change in a government or society, such as in an overthrow of the government by the people.

Roman alphabet: Alphabet of the ancient Romans from which alphabets of most modern European languages, including English, are derived.

Roman Catholic Church: Christian church headed by the pope or Bishop of Rome.

Russian Orthodox: The arm of the Eastern Orthodox Church that was the official church of Russia under the tsars.

Sahelian zone: Eight countries make up this dry desert zone in Africa: Burkina Faso, Chad, Gambia, Mali, Mauritania, Niger, Senegal, and the Cape Verde Islands.

savanna: A treeless or near treeless grassland or plain.

segregation: The enforced separation of a racial or religious group from other groups, compelling them to live and go to school separately from the rest of society.

Seventh-day Adventist: One who believes in the second coming of Christ to establish a personal reign upon the earth.

shamanism: A religion in which shamans (priests or medicine men) are believed to influence spirits.

shantytown: An urban settlement of people in inadequate houses.

Shia Muslim *see* Islam.

Shiites *see* Islam.

Shintoism: The system of nature- and hero-worship that forms the native religion of Japan.

sierra: A chain of hills or mountains.

Sikh: A member of a community of India, founded around 1500 and based on the principles of monotheism (belief in one god) and human brotherhood.

Sino-Tibetan language family: The family of languages spoken in eastern Asia, including China, Thailand, Tibet, and Myanmar.

slash-and-burn agriculture: A hasty and sometimes temporary way of clearing land to make it available for agriculture by cutting down trees and burning them; also known as swidden agriculture.

slave trade: The transportation of black Africans beginning in the 1700s to other countries to be sold as slaves—people owned as property and compelled to work for their owners at no pay.

Slavic languages: A major subgroup of the Indo-European language family. It is further subdivided into West Slavic (including Polish, Czech, Slovak and Serbian), South Slavic (including Bulgarian, Serbo-Croatian, Slovene, and Old Church Slavonic), and East Slavic (including Russian Ukrainian and Byelorussian).

sorghum: Plant grown for its valuable uses, such as for grain, syrup, or fodder.

Southeast Asia: The region in Asia that consists of the Malay Archipelago, the Malay Peninsula, and Indochina.

Soviet Union *see* **Former Soviet Union.**

subcontinent: A large subdivision of a continent.

subsistence farming: Farming that provides only the minimum food goods necessary for the continuation of the farm family.

Sudanic language group: A related group of languages spoken in various areas of northern Africa, including Yoruba, Mandingo, and Tshi.

Sufi: A Muslim mystic who believes that God alone exists, there can be no real difference between good and evil, that the soul exists within the body as in a cage, so death should be the chief object of desire.

sultan: A king of a Muslim state.

Sunni Muslim *see* Islam.

Taoism: The doctrine of Lao-Tzu, an ancient Chinese philosopher (c.500 BC) as laid down by him in the *Tao-te-ching*.

Third World: A term used to describe less developed countries; as of the mid-1990s, it is being replaced by the United Nations designation Less Developed Countries, or LDC.

treaty: A negotiated agreement between two governments.

tribal system: A social community in which people are organized into groups or clans descended from common ancestors and sharing customs and languages.

tundra: A nearly level treeless area whose climate and vegetation are characteristically arctic due to its northern position; the subsoil is permanently frozen.

untouchables: In India, members of the lowest caste in the caste system, a hereditary social class system. They were considered unworthy to touch members of higher castes.

Union of the Soviet Socialist Republics *see* Former Soviet Union.

veldt: A grassland in South Africa.

Western nations: General term used to describe democratic, capitalist countries, including the United States, Canada, and western European countries.

Zoroastrianism: The system of religious doctrine taught by Zoroaster and his followers in the Avesta; the religion prevalent in Persia until its overthrow by the Muslims in the seventh century.

Index

All culture groups and countries included in this encyclopedia are included in this index. Selected regions, alternate groups names, and historical country names are cross-referenced. Country chapter titles are in boldface; volume numbers appear in brackets, with page number following.